Pearls of Jewish Wisdom on Living with Kindness

Pearls of Jewish Wisdom on Living with Kindness

SHMULY YANKLOWITZ

RESOURCE *Publications* • Eugene, Oregon

PEARLS OF JEWISH WISDOM ON LIVING WITH KINDNESS

Resource Publications
An Imprint of Wipf and Stock Publishers
199 W. 8th Ave., Suite 3
Eugene, OR 97401

www.wipfandstock.com

PAPERBACK ISBN: 978-1-6667-7979-0
HARDCOVER ISBN: 978-1-6667-7980-6
EBOOK ISBN: 978-1-6667-7981-3

06/21/23

This book is dedicated to the countless, nameless, humble servants who dedicate every day to kindness endeavors, supporting the sick, homeless, dying, mentally ill, animals, and anyone in need of love and care. May they all continue to thrive and continue to inspire all of us to do our part.

Contents

Introduction

IT WOULD BE DIFFICULT to imagine a model of a well lived life that did not include kindness at its heart and from which all else emanates. The most noble of people throughout time have suggested that the goal of life is to make a difference, to be of service, and to give back. Certainly, one can make the case that kindness is central to the Jewish project. In fact, Rabbi Joseph B. Soloveitchik writes[1] that the central *mitzvah* of the 613 *mitzvot* is that of following the ways of God (imitatio Dei).

The Rav's[2] brother, Rabbi Ahron Soloveichik, taught[3] that *mitzvot* such as "love your neighbor" and "walk in His ways" are in the realm of *hovot halevavot* (duties of the heart); the obligation is to internalize love of one's neighbor and develop character traits modeled for us by God's actions, such as mercy and compassion.

The Talmud teaches[4] that it is better to jump into a burning hot furnace than shame another. Tosafot here teaches[5] that shaming another is one of the three cardinal sins for which one must be ready to give up their life, as it is in a sense akin to murder.[6] Living with kindness, then, means avoiding behaviors that hurt others whenever possible.

Even more so, it means proactively supporting others. Consider the value of sharing. Some rabbis came to consider a lack of sharing to be "*middat Sedom*" (a trait of the most wicked types of people, such as those of Sodom). The rabbis were even willing to dismiss property rights and use force

1. Polsky, "Reflections of the Amidah,"
2. The Rav is an honorific used exclusively for Rabbi Soloveitchik.
3. Soloveichik, Aharon *Od Yosef Yisrael Beni Hai*, 4
4. Babylonian Talmud, Sotah 10b
5. Tosafot's (the Tosafists') commentary on Babylonian Talmud, Sotah 10b
6. Others do not read the Talmud literally and do not believe that one must die before shaming another, since it is not listed (in Babylonian Talmud, Pesachim 25a) as one of the cardinal sins for which one must die. See Rabbi Binyamin Tabory, *The Weekly Mitzva*, p. 15.

to ensure that people shared with one another. According to the Rosh,[7] "We force them to distance themselves from evil traits and to act with generosity towards their fellow when they would not lose anything by doing so."[8] Rabbi David Polsky writes:

> Commentary by Rabbi Jacob Joshua Falk (18th century Poland/ Germany) illustrates that these compulsions against sodomy limit property rights. He explains that, really, whether or not an owner loses is much less significant than another person gaining from them. The very fact that the squatter benefits from the owner's property would be enough to generate an obligation to pay, whether or not the owner suffers a loss because of it. However, he explains, not wanting to help others even when we don't lose anything from it is a Sodomite tendency. We therefore constrain the owner's typical legal rights so as not to reinforce their sodomy.[9] In stark contrast to the Sodomite view of property rights as sacrosanct, the rabbinic principle of *kofin al middat Sedom* [dispensing with property rights, as opposed to the Sodomite view] suggests that *halakhah* views property rights as merely contingent.[10]

Rabbi Aharon Lichtenstein writes:[11]

> *Kofin al middat Sedom* absolutely contradicts the prevailing notion that a person is the supreme ruler over [their] property. . .and that as long as [they do] not cause others direct damage, [they] can do with [their] property as [they please]. . . Property rights are "liable to be set aside in the face of other moral factors—including the welfare of others.

Indeed, sometimes, governments and societies need to compel goodness. But this is, of course, not the ideal. The ideal society is one in which people live their lives eager, almost begging, to do good.

In this book, we will share 40 lessons, each with its own unique theme. The common thread to the series is living with deeper kindness. How can the Jewish tradition inspire us to live with deeper love and compassion? How can Jewish pearls of wisdom inform how we care for one another?

---

7. Rosh is an acronym for Rabbeinu Asher, 13th century France/Spain
8. Ben Yechiel, *Teshuvot HaRosh*, 97:2
9. Falk, *Penei Yehoshua*, Bava Kama 20a
10. Rabbi David Polsky in his commentary on Parshat Vayera
11. Lichtenstein, "Alei Etzion 16: Kofin Al Middat Sedom: Compulsory Altruism?"

The book contains five sections: Kindness Toward Specific Individuals; Kindness Toward All Individuals; Kindness Through Restraint; Care for Our Environment; and Self-Improvement as a Catalyst for Kindness to Others. The first two sections address proactive kindness towards our fellow humans; the third addresses kindness by avoiding hurting others; the fourth, kindness towards all of God's creations, including animals and nature, as kindness cannot be only people-directed; the fifth serves as a starting point and catalyst for all of the above, for without first being kind to ourselves and improving our general character we cannot be truly kind towards others.

Our argument is not only that God wants us to live with kindness and that Torah necessitates it, but that kindness has the greatest chance of bringing happiness and meaning to our lives. When I was privileged to donate a kidney, many people told me they thought that it was a selfless thing to do. But while that's true, in all honesty, it brough me enormous joy and meaning. I didn't donate for myself, but I must admit that I feel I gained more than I gave.

Serving the dead (e.g., providing for a dignified burial) is considered to be the ultimate *chesed shel emet*,[12] the highest level of kindness, since the deceased cannot repay the giver of kindness.[13] But, perhaps, this very fact also makes such an act even more rewarding. A truly virtuous person will indeed find meaning in it. A well-balanced individual is one whose sense of joy is aligned with their moments of living virtuously.

We will each need to find new and creative ways to give and to trust that this will in turn add meaning to our lives. The challenge is to figure out what to do and when. We also must ponder what specific traits of kindness we want to imbue in our children. For example, is empathy the highest manifestation of being kind? While we may wish that every person be empathetic, it may not be the most important measure of kindness. Some may be deeply empathetic but not channel that compassion and care into behaviors that help others. Others may not be as empathetic but hold other ethical principles that lead them to being really kind to others.

In Judaism, what matters most is that we actually help. Imagine a doctor or nurse who is a bit emotionally cold but goes above and beyond in service. Now imagine another doctor or nurse who is very warm and friendly and emotionally present but doesn't go above and beyond in care.

Brian Goldman writes:

> If lack of empathy is the problem, what is the solution? In his
> 2017 book, *Against Empathy: The Case for Rational Compassion*,

---

12. *Chesed shel emet* literally means "kindness of truth" or "true kindness."

13. Rashi on Genesis, 47:29

Yale professor Paul Bloom argues that empathy based on emotion motivates people to help in ways that are counterproductive. He writes that our brains are programmed to enable us to empathize with one person at a time, which dooms us to ignore the needs of many. Bloom says that whom we empathize with is biased in favour of those who look and act like us. . . Instead of empathy, Bloom advocates for what he calls rational compassion, dispensing with emotional involvement in favor of helping others based on an objective calculation of costs, benefits, and risks.[14]

Do we want to raise our children to make moral decisions emotionally or cognitively? And what tools will they use to navigate complex moral dilemmas? To whom will they feel most obligated to show kindness, and how will they navigate the boundaries of their responsibility?

We will learn through experience, and as addressed in this book, that the complexity of living with kindness consistently and thoughtfully sometimes requires stepping back. Batya Gallant writes:

The Torah advocates wholeness, not perfection, and trains us in *middas hachesed*, an inclusive attitude toward each element of God's creation. In creating myself as a *ba'al chesed*, this dual action requires extending myself to other people (expansion), and then retreating (contraction) to self-nurture when necessary.[15]

Our project is central to the Torah.

In the Five Books of Moses, the word *chesed* (kindness) appears 248 times. Generosity, compassion, grace, patience, and love are all held up as divine qualities we are meant to embody in our own lives.[16]

Abraham used his own kindness to teach people around him about God's kindness.[17] And in return, God's kindness informs and strengthens our own commitment to kindness. One fascinating *midrash* describes how humans show preference to some people over others, while God is egalitarian:[18]

---

14. Goldman, *A Question of Kindness*, 7
15. Gallant, *Stages of Spiritual Growth*, 63
16. Morinis, *With Heart in Mind*, 4–5
17. *Babylonian Talmud*, Sotah 10a--0b
18. *Midrash Sifri*, Bemidbar #133

And Tzelofhad's daughters drew near:[19] When Tzelofhad's daughters heard that the land would be divided according to the tribes—to males and not to females—they all gathered with each other for advice. They said, "The goodness of God is not like the goodness of flesh and blood. Flesh and blood show greater goodness to males than to females, but the One-Who-Spoke-the-World-into-Being is not so, but is good to all, as it is said. . . 'The Lord is good to all and shows kindness to all creatures.' "[20]

We are not God and never will be. But we can spend our lives seeking to emulate the most noble model imaginable. It is my deep hope and prayer that this book will reinforce each of our commitments to be just, kind individuals, to do what we can, wherever we are, whoever we are, to bring light to darkness, to bring hope where there is despair, and to bring repair where this brokenness.

19. Numbers 27:1
20. Psalms 145:9

#1

Bikkur Cholim, Visiting the Sick

THE FIRST CASE THAT we learn of in the Torah of the mitzvah of *bikkur cholim*[1] (visiting the sick) occurs in Genesis 18:1.

> God appeared to [Avraham] in the plains of Mamre; he was sitting in the doorway of his tent at the heat of the day. He raised his eyes and saw that there were three men standing by him. . .

Rashi teaches[2] that God was visiting Avraham at the opening of his tent in the plains of Mamre because Avraham was healing from his circumcision.[3]

Rabbi Hama ben Rabbi Hanina, in the Talmud, also uses this event as the example for why we should, indeed why we must, visit the sick.[4] He connects this story in the Torah to another Torah mandate: "You shall walk after the Lord, your God."[5] Similarly, Rav Yosef taught[6] that another verse, "You shall show them the path that they should take,"[7] means that we must engage in acts of lovingkindness, specifically including visiting the sick.[8]

So, for most Torah commentators, *bikkur cholim* is not one of the specific 613 biblical mitzvot,[9] but is included in the general mitzvah of *chessed*

1. The term *bikkur* literally means "inspecting" or "checking in." Regarding *bikkur cholim*, then, it implies checking in on the sick to see how they are faring.

2. Rashi on Genesis 18:1

3. *Babylonian Talmud*, Bava Metzia 76b

4. *Babylonian Talmud*, Sotah 14a

5. Deuteronomy 13:5

6. *Babylonian Talmud*, Bava Metzia 30b. Also see BT Bava Kama 99b–100a

7. Exodus 18:20

8. *Babylonian Talmud*, Bava Metzia 30b.

9. See Rambam, who argues that general acts of kindness that are not explicitly

(kindness) as well as that of emulating the Divine. Sefer Mitzvot Katan,[10] however, as well as Behag,[11] specifically included *bikkur cholim* as one of the 613.[12]

There is a powerful story in the Talmud[13] about a student who became sick and no one visited him. Then his teacher Rabbi Akiva visited the student and helped him with some of his needs. As Rabbi Akiva was leaving, his student in recovery screamed out to Rabbi Akiva: "You have saved my life." Shook from this pronouncement, Rabbi Akiva taught: "Anyone who does not visit the sick is akin to a murderer."

Rambam (Maimonides) seems to be influenced by this story, in that he teaches not only the positive mitzvah to care for the sick but also issues a harsh warning against those who ignore their needs.

> Bikkur cholim is a mitzvah that is obligatory upon all. Even people of higher stature are required to visit people of lower stature. Numerous visits daily should be made as long as this does not inconvenience the patient. Whoever visits the sick is considered to have taken away part of the illness, and whoever does not visit is akin to a murderer.[14]

We live in a world of complex human relationships and power dynamics. One might have mistakenly thought that a poor person should visit a rich person who is sick but not vice versa, or that an adult should visit their elderly parent who is sick but not vice versa, or that a student should visit their teacher who is sick but not vice versa. Rambam, based on Rabbi Akiva's story, reminds us that there is no power status when caring for the sick. We are all frail flesh and bones and need care, no matter who we are. It is for this reason that in the Mi Shebeirach prayer for the sick, honorifics and titles are customarily omitted when inserting the patient's name. We are all on the same playing field when we fall ill.

The rabbis taught:

> Rabbi Judah ben Shila said in Rav Assi's name [who in turn said it] in R. Yohanan's name: There are six things, the fruit of which

---

included in the 613 mitzvot are not biblical commandments but rabbinic commandments (Mishneh Torah, Sefer Hamitzvot, principle 1). They are based not only on the principle of emulating God (Deuteronomy 28:9), but also "You shall love your neighbor as yourself" (Leviticus 19:18).

10. Sefer Mitzvot Katan, perhaps better known by its acronym Semak, was authored by Rabbi Yitzchak of Korbeil, a French Tosafist.

11. Behag is the acronym for Ba'al Halachot Gedolot, authorship unknown.

12. Tabory, *The Weekly Mitzvah*, 14.

13. *Babylonian Talmud*, Nedarim 40a

14. *Mishneh Torah*, Hilchot Avelut 14:4

a person eats in this world, while the principal remains for them for the world to come. They are: hospitality to wayfarers, visiting the sick, meditation in prayer, early attendance at the Beit Hamidrash (study hall), rearing one's children to the study of the Torah, and judging one's neighbor in the scale of merit.[15]

The rabbis further taught that there is no measure for this mitzvah, given its importance:

There is no measure for visiting the sick. What is meant by, 'there is no measure for visiting the sick?' R. Joseph thought to explain it: its reward is unlimited. Said Abaye to him: Is there a definite measure of reward for any precept? For we learnt: Be as heedful of a light precept as of a serious one, for you know not the grant of reward for precepts! But Abaye explained it: Even a great person must visit a humble one. Raba said: [One must visit] even a hundred times a day.[16]

It is easy when one is healthy to forget the pain and isolation involved with sickness. The Talmudic rabbis, in their statements and stories, are doing all they can to never let us forget.

Rabbi Harold Kushner wrote: "Is good health a person's normal condition and sickness an aberration, or is health a deceptive interlude while we wait for something else to go wrong?"[17] In this simple reformulating of what it means to be sick, Rabbi Kushner reminds us that we all can become ill at any time.

The rabbis even attempt to quantify the impact of our visits to the sick. "R. Abba son of R. Hanina said: 'One who visits a sick person takes away a sixtieth of his pain.'"[18]

Perhaps this attempt to quantify the impact of *bikkur cholim* was intended to serve as a catalyst for each of us to engage in this mitzvah and not leave it to someone else. Another implication may be that one individual's visit has a different nature than that of another, and that the patient can thereby benefit from all such visits.

The rabbis taught that we should sit on the floor when visiting the sick.

One who visits the sick must not sit upon the bed, or on a stool or a chair, but must [reverently] robe themselves and sit upon the ground, because the Divine Presence rests above an invalid's

---

15. *Babylonian Talmud*, Shabbat 127a

16. *Babylonian Talmud*, Nedarim 39b–41a

17. Kushner, *Who Needs God*, 26

18. Kushner, *Who Needs God*, 26

bed, as it is written, The Lord sets the Divine self upon the bed of languishing.

This, however, only applies when the ill person is lying on the ground so that a visitor who sits will be higher than them. But if the sick individual is lying on a bed, it is correct to sit on a chair.[19]

What a profound lesson! Where is God to be found? Among the sick! So we are to sit on the floor in awe of the Divine presence. It can be reasoned further that standing above the sick can be intimidating, and we want to embrace a most humble stance at such a sensitive time.

We should not just "check the box" after showing up for a brief visit. Rather, we should also try to proactively assist the sick. The Aruch HaShulchan writes:

> The essential part of the commandment to visit the sick is to investigate the needs of the patient and to do whatever they require, as is stated in the Talmud[20] regarding the student of Rabbi Akiva who became ill. . . And how beautiful it is that in many cities, groups of people—called "sleep groups" stay with sick people all night long and look after their needs. During the day, in general, most of the patient's needs are met by relatives, but at night, as much as they wish to stay awake, the relatives are exhausted from working all day and caring for the patient. . .[21]

The rabbis taught that in addition to visiting the sick and healing the sick that we should pray for the sick.

> Rav Shisha the son of Rav Idi said: one should not visit a sick person, not in the first three hours of the day nor in the last three hours of the day, so that the visitor should not give up on praying for God's mercy. The first three hours, a sick person's mind is at ease, the last three hours, illness becomes more intense.[22]

Some of us may hold a theology where we believe praying for the sick may be a way to call upon the omnipotent Divine to engage in healing. But for other, praying for the sick is less a call to God and is more a call to community to support. We mention the names of the sick in our community to remind us of our responsibility and collective role to do our part.

---

19. *Shulchan Aruch*, Yoreh De'ah 335:3
20. *Babylonian Talmud*, Nedarim 40a
21. *Aruch HaShulchan*, Yoreh De'ah 335:3
22. *Babylonian Talmud*, Nedarim 40a. Also see *Shulchan Aruch*, Yoreh De'ah 335:4

Rav Avraham Yitzchak Kook offers a unique commentary on an important Talmudic passage which he specifically relates to the mitzvah of visiting the sick.

> Rabbi Avraham Yitzhak Kook offers yet another model for understanding the absence of formal commandments dealing with certain ethical issues.[23] Rav Kook notes that, although in general, Jewish law maintains that "greater is one who is commanded than one who acts from the spirit of volunteerism,"[24] this principle applies only to ritual laws. With regard to the ethical realm, it is preferable that ethical behavior be a natural outgrowth of an awareness of right and wrong, rather than based on a divine command. Imagine if someone visits the sick, helps the needs, or comforts mourners simply because God commanded him to do so. . . Ironically, it is when we act ethically, based on a profound respect for our fellow man—and not based on a divine command—that we actually experience an authentic interaction with God and His ideals.[25]

Yes, there is a mitzvah to visit the sick. Yes, we want to cultivate our spiritual orientation toward striving to be Godly. But at the end of the day, the real spiritual revolution is about cultivating empathy and to truly love others and care for them simply because we care for them. Our intentions matter.

The story is told about Rabbi Aryeh Levin, known as the Tzaddik of Jerusalem, who once accompanied his wife to the doctor. When the doctor asked about the nature of the visit, Rav Levin responded, "Our toe hurts."

Rav Levin so strongly identified with the pain of his wife that he referred to it as *our* foot. This is an example of true, empathetic *bikkur cholim*.

On the other hand, the rabbis were far more concerned that the right things happened and that people are taken care of than about the purity of our motives. For example, they taught:

> If a person says, 'I am giving this coin to charity so that my [sick] child will live,' or 'so that I will make it into the World-to-Come,' he is completely righteous.[26]

Humans can strive to be like angels but we are not angels and our motives can never be totally selfless. Doing good for good, albeit imperfect reasons is to be expected.

23. Kook, Iggerot HaRe'aya 1:89
24. *Babylonian* Talmud, Bava Kama 87a
25. Silverstein, *Jewish Law as a Journey*, 209–210
26. *Babylonian Talmud*, Pesachim 8a–b

Because of how large a demand one's sickness places upon the community and on society, and because of the sanctity of life, we must do all we can to preserve our own health. This is so important that Rambam goes so far as to suggest that our sleep is itself a mitzvah.

> If a person sleeps in order to allow his mind to rest and to give rest to his body so that he should not become sick and unable to serve God because of illness, in this case his very sleep is service of God.[27]

A colleague of mine shared the following story. Every Friday, while serving as a hospital chaplain intern, he would visit an elderly woman who had a prolonged hospital stay. Each week, at the conclusion of the visit, the woman would say, "It was nice seeing you, Rabbi." And each week the rabbi followed with "I'll see you next week." One week, though, she ended the visit by saying, "It has been nice seeing you, Rabbi." The difference in expression is so nuanced that the rabbi didn't notice it. When he responded with the usual "I'll see you next week," she in turn stated: "Rabbi, you didn't hear what I said. I didn't say 'It was nice seeing you' as I always do; I said 'It's been nice seeing you.' I won't be seeing you anymore."

When my colleague asked her if she wished to explain, he was taken a bit aback when she added that she was going to die that afternoon. She explained that until then she wasn't ready to die yet, but now she was ready. At that point, the rabbi leaned over, gave her a kiss on the forehead, and told her that it had been nice seeing her too and that he wished her well on her journey to the next world. The woman passed away later that afternoon.

On a personal note, I recall my time in a hospital after a major surgery and how strengthening the visits were for my spirits and for my healing. In particular, one stranger (a chassidic rabbi who had undergone the same procedure that I had) offered to sleep the night on the couch next to my bed. Waking up and seeing him there helped me to feel less alone. Not only was he physically with me but he was with me in understanding what I was feeling based upon his own experiences. I'll never forget him.

Life is short, but life is equally sacred. We must do all we can to save life and to preserve life. Visiting the sick is so important not only because of the abstract value of life, but also because of the specific dignity of the one who is suffering. One cannot measure the healing benefit that *bikkur cholim* brings to the sick. May we be united together in sickness of body, mind, or spirit, as well as in health.

---

27. *Mishneh Torah*, Hilchot De'ot 3:3

#2

Kibbud Av Va'Eim, Honoring One's Parents

WE OFTEN THINK, AS children, that the goalis independence but a touching story reminds us of the role our parents can play for us.

> A little boy was struggling to lift a heavy stone but could not budge it. The boy's father, who happened to be watching, said to his son, "Are you using all your strength?"
> "Yes, I am," the boy said with irritation.
> No, you're not," the father answered. "You have not asked me to help you."[1]

I recall hearing Jane Goodall speak and she told the group about her mother. She said she was once asked if she was scared to move, as a very young woman, into a tent in the jungle and sleep with leopards, gorillas, centipedes, and snakes unaware of how to study the animal kingdom, let alone survive within it. She said the only reason she wasn't terrified was because her mother came with her to protect her. Because her mother entered the wilderness with her, she said, she was able to ultimately dedicate her life to the work of conservation. Indeed, how many mothers, and fathers, have changed the world by supporting the dreams of their children, at all costs?

For those of us who were fortunate, our parents, even with all of their inevitable human faults, were there to help us carry heavy loads in our lives. It is something we can never forget.

---

1. See Joseph Telushkin, *A Code of Jewish Ethics, Volume 2: Love Your Neighbor as Yourself*, 39–40

The Torah commands us to both honor our father and mother[2] and revere them.[3]

While at first glance the two verses cited above seem to be identical, there are several significant differences between them. In the first, the one we are most familiar with as it is found in the Ten Commandments, we are told: *Kabeid et avicha v'et imecha* (Honor your father and mother). In the second we find: *Ish imo v'aviv tira'u* (A person should revere their mother and father). Notice the switch in the order here. Regarding honor, the father is written first; regarding reverence, it is the mother who is mentioned first.

The Talmud explains that a child (perhaps an adult child as well) would be more inclined to show honor, displaying acts of love, to one's mother, the more loving parent. Therefore, the father is placed first, to indicate that he is of equal, not lesser, importance when it comes to honor. The converse is true regarding reverence: One would be more inclined to revere one's father, and therefore the mother is placed first.

As the two different verses essentially convey the same command, the Talmud further focuses on the differences between the two actions describing how one must treat their parents. *Kibbud* (honor) refers to what one must proactively do for one's parents, i.e., serve them and take care of them. *Yirah* (reverence) refers to what one must refrain from doing or saying to one's parents, i.e., not sitting in a parent's chair. Another example recorded in the Talmud is for a child to simply not respond if a parent goes so far as to throw his wallet into the river. While very difficult for a child to not react in such a situation, this example of the Talmud does make it clear to us the value we must all strive to place on reverence for our parents.

Regarding not sitting in a parent's chair, a beautiful thought is shared in the name of Rabbi Joseph B. Soloveitchik[4]. Upon taking leave of a house of mourning, one traditionally recites: *HaMakom yenacheim etchem b'toch she'ar aveilei Tziyon viYerushalayim* (May the Omnipresent One comfort you among all mourners of Zion and Jerusalem). Rabbi Soloveitchik suggests that the reference to God as *HaMakom* at this juncture (the word *hamakom* literally meaning "the place") calls to mind the command to not sit in one's parents *makom*. He explains that this is true while a parent is alive. As long as a parent is living, it is forbidden to sit in their seat. But once the parent passes away, a role reversal takes place, and the child is now obligated to, metaphorically, sit in that very place. In other words, what we

---

2. Exodus 20:12

3. Leviticus 19:3

4. This interpretation of HaMakom was related in an address by Rabbi Yosef Adler of Teaneck, NJ, who heard it directly from Rav Soloveitchik.

are conveying to the mourner is that you now have an opportunity to take your parent's place, to continue their holy work, as they are no longer able to do so. As one leaves the mourner's home, s/he expresses to the mourner that hopefully this opportunity and charge, thereby ensuring that the parent lives on, will bring the mourner some comfort.

The Talmud[5] extends honoring one's parents to step parents and older siblings.[6] The Rambam (Maimonides) explains[7] that honoring these three individuals is not an end in itself, but rather a means toward honoring one's father and mother. Putting it another way, honoring one's sibling leads to honoring one's parents. Another idea behind this may be that one's older sibling may have more commonly carried the heavier weight as a caregiver for the parents and so by honoring them as a caregiver, we're supporting our parents as well. Honoring a step-parent could have the same effect. So it seems that if one's mother was no longer living, for example, one would no longer be commanded to honor her husband.[8]

What are we trying to achieve by honoring our parents? According to the Rambam[9], it is a *mitzvah bein adam lachavero* (a command between man and his fellow man). It is about ethics, proper moral conduct. According to the Ramban (Nahmanides) and Rabbeinu Bahya, however, it is a *mitzvah bein adam laMakom* (between man and God). Parents partner with God in creating a child, and we honor God by honoring our other partners in creation. It is perhaps for this reason that while the first five of the ten commandments deal with *mitzvot bein adam laMakom* and the last five with mitzvot *bein adam lachaveiro*, honoring one's parents is #5, listed as the last of the first category while at the same time eliding into the second category. *Kibbud Av va'eim*, then, is perhaps to be viewed as both man-to-man and man-to-God.

A different argument for why honoring parents is a *mitzvah bein adam laMakom*, offered by Rabbi Meir Simha HaKohen of Dvinsk,[10] is based on the *halachah* that if a parent asks their child to violate a command of the Torah, the child should obey the Torah and not their parents. He argues that

---

5. *Babylonian Talmud*, Ketubot 103a

6. Or perhaps only the oldest sibling, not all older siblings.

7. Maimonides, *Sefer Hamitzvot*, principle 2

8. This is by no means meant to suggest that one should not honor a step-parent in this situation. The opposite is true, as one is required to treat all humans with respect. What is referred to here is simply a technical application of the verse regarding *kibbud av va'eim*.

9. Maimonides, *Rambam on Mishnah*. Peah 1:1

10. Dvinsk, *Meschech Hochmah*, Leviticus 19:3

since honoring parents is about honoring God, it certainly cannot contradict or override honoring God.

A convert is considered as a "newborn child," with a fresh start. So, must a convert honor their non-Jewish biological parents? The Shulhan Aruch[11] teaches that a convert is not permitted to shame or curse their parents, lest one say that conversion leads to a lowering of moral standards. This ought to be obvious in of itself, even absent the reasoning of the Shulhan Aruch, since religious transformation should increase our moral responsibility rather than let us off the hook. And little should change about our gratitude toward our parents and for all they have given us.[12]

It is well known that millions of elderly Americans are neglected at their most vulnerable time. Jewish law, however, requires multiple times and in multiple ways that we honor our parents.[13]

How does the United States, which has traditionally been reluctant in implementing social welfare policies taken for granted in Europe, compare with the rest of the industrial world? Currently, nearly ten million adults ages fifty and older[14] care for elderly parents in America, with little governmental assistance. This number has tripled in fifteen years, so now about one in four adult children provide personal or financial care for their parents. A study conducted by a group of insurance, caregiving, and policy think tanks concluded that, taking into account wages, Social Security and pension money, the average adult who becomes a caregiver for an aging parent spends nearly $304,000.[15] In addition, caregivers undergo tremendous stress, and suffer higher rates of cardiovascular disease and alcohol abuse, among other illnesses. On top of this, Social Security benefits in America do not increase when personal care costs rise, as they do in some European nations.

One bright spot is that many adults can now take up to twelve weeks off from work to care for an ill parent (or any other family member) without losing their job under the Family and Medical Leave Act of 1993.[16] Unfortunately, this does not go far enough, because this leave is without pay and therefore an unaffordable option for nearly all working Americans.

11. Karo, *Shulhan Aruch*, Yoreh Dei'ah 241:9

12. There is a wealth of responsa regarding sitting *shiva* for a non-Jewish biological convert as well as reciting the *kaddish* prayer. Common practice is for one to sit shiva, or part of shiva, if they choose to do so (either out of respect for the deceased parent or as an expression of their own mourning), but at the same time not an *halachic* obligation.

13. Exodus 20:11, Exodus 21:15, Exodus 21:17, Leviticus 19:3, Deuteronomy 27:16

14. Braunstein, Glenn D. "Caring for Aging Parents Is Labor of Love—With a Cost"

15. Ibid.

16. Ibid.

Medicare may help pay for some short-term care, and Medicaid can cover expenses for those with inadequate resources,[17] although these are dependent on individual state requirements, which are constantly under attack today. Currently, as the Medicare website notes, private funds are used for eldercare: "About half of all nursing home residents pay nursing home costs out of their own savings. After these savings and other resources are spent, many people who stay in nursing homes for long periods eventually become eligible for Medicaid." In other words, if you want nursing care as an elderly person, be prepared to lose all your resources. Other programs, such as Meals on Wheels, are also dependent on state funding (with some federal aid that is also under attack), and we cannot assume that it will continue as is in the current atmosphere of austerity. Other options usually rely on independent insurance or health plans that require additional payments.

While the United States remains a wealthy nation, and many can afford their own care, we should heed Jewish law and truly honor our parents. The rabbis tell a story which is codified as *halachah*:[18]

> They inquired of Rav Ula: "How far does honoring/dignifying parents extend?"
> He said to them: "Go out and see what one [non-Jew] did in Ashkelon. His name was Dama ben Netinah. Once the Sages sought merchandise for a price of sixty myriads, but the key was resting under his father's head, and he did not disturb him. . ..
> When Rav Dimi came, he said: Once he was wearing a gold diadem and sitting among the greats of Rome, when his mother came and tore it off him, and hit him over the head and spit in his face, but he did not humiliate her."[19]

Even when mistreated and shamed by a parent, many demands to honor parents still remain. To be sure, there are limits too!

> One whose mother or father breaks down mentally—
> He must make the effort to behave with them in accordance with their condition until [God] has mercy on them;
> but if it is not possible for him to stand it, because they have become greatly insane –
> he may go and leave them behind, so long as he commands others to treat them properly.[20]

17. http://www.medicare.gov/Nursing/Payment.asp
18. Karo, *Shulhan Aruch*, YD 240:3
19. *Babylonian Talmud*, Kiddushin 31a
20. Karo, *Shulchan Aruch*, Yoreh Dei'ah 240:10

Jewish law wisely and prophetically notes the mental and physical strain that an elderly parent with Alzheimer's or dementia can have on a family. However, the law also mandates that we provide some degree of proper care for them. We should not force families to go into bankruptcy in order to avoid placing their parents in virtual warehouses where their parents will be neglected and mistreated.

This is not always easy. Of course, sometimes one may have a conflict between one's spouse and one's parent and one has to navigate difficult relational tensions. On the one hand, one has the mitzvah of honoring parents and on the other hand, the mitzvah of *shalom bayit*, peace in one's own home.

There is a subjectivity and relativity to how we honor others. We cannot impose set rules. One might ask: how does my parent need, or want, to be honored? In addition to honoring them by serving them and engaging with them, we honor our parents by being our best in the world. When one is a mensch, living with virtue, one gives one's parent *nachas* (parental pride).

Further in seeking to honor our parent, we can at times come to honor someone else's parent, beyond the letter of the law. Consider this touching story:

> Although Chastity's father died, she continued to text him every morning & night to update him on her life. She longed for his support and loving presence in her life. Then on the 4th anniversary of his death, she texted him one last time recapping everything he'd missed—how she had overcome cancer and graduated college.

But to her shock, she received a text reply!

> "Hi sweetheart, I am not your father, but I have been getting all your messages for the past 4 years. I look forward to your morning messages and nightly updates. My name is Brad and I lost my daughter in a car wreck August 2014 and your messages have kept me alive. When you text me, I know it's a message from God."

Sometimes when we don't give up on trying to connect and honor our parents, we can come to bring joy and honor to others as well. Our children will learn how to honor us by how they saw us honor our parents. We honor our parents and others because its right but also because its important role modeling for the next generation.

The thing is that this is not only an ossified, unrealistic demand based on an idealized or no longer extant religious society. We see models for contemporary implementation around the world today. Our parents sacrificed so much for our well-being throughout their lives, when we were not able to fend for ourselves. As a society, we must recognize this and provide for them when they, too, are no longer physically independent themselves.

#3

Ezrah L'Dalim, Supporting the Poor and Lifting Up the Downtrodden

THE TORAH TEACHES US of the importance of giving *tzedakah* (charity).[1] "If there will be a poor person among you. . . do not harden your heart or close your hand from your poor brother. Rather, open your hand to him. . ."[2]

The Talmudic sage Rabbi Assi taught that "The commandment of giving *tzedakah* is equal to all the other commandments combined."[3]

The Rambam (Maimonides) writes that we are to be particularly careful with our *tzedakah* giving because it is the defining characteristic of the first Jew, Avraham.[4] The Rambam's count of the 613 biblical *mitzvot* lists both a *mitzvat aseh* (positive commandment)[5] to give *tzedakah* and a *mitzvat lo taaseh* (negative commandment)[6] to refrain from giving.[7] Some actually count the negative commandment as two separate *mitzvot*: to not harden our hearts and also not close our hands,[8] as quoted in the verse above. Although people should perform *mitzvot* volitionally and joyfully,

1. It is instructive to note that the word *tzedakah* literally means an act of righteousness. Giving charity is thus but one means of fulfilling the *mitzvah* of *tzedakah*.

2. Deuteronomy 15:7–11

3. *Babylonian Talmud*, Bava Batra 9a.

4. Maimonides, *Mishneh Torah*, Laws of Mattnot Aniyim 10:1

5. Maimonides, *Sefer Hamitzvot* no. 195

6. Maimonides, *Sefer Hamitzvot* no. 232

7. While all agree on the significance of the total number 613 regarding the commandments of the Torah, no two lists are identical. Rambam (Maimonides), for example, includes several *mitzvot* not included by Ramban (Nachmanides) and vice versa.

8. Behag (Behag is an acronym for Ba'al Halachot Gedolot, authorship unknown).

this *mitzvah* was deemed so important that the rabbis even allowed for some coercion regarding those who would not give to the needy.[9]

But, wait, we each only have so much to give! The Talmud[10] therefore teaches that one who convinces another to give is actually greater than one who gives themself. Some are shy to ask others to support causes, but it is an important part of being committed to kindness. When we raise money by asking others to support our organizations and the vulnerable in our midst, we are not taking, of course, but giving.

The monumental work *Orchot Tzadikim* goes even further, saying that monetary hand-outs alone are not enough:

> And when you give charity, you should accompany it with loving-kindness, such as buying with money something that the poor need in order to spare them the bother of buying it themselves.[11]

A modern-day example of the above concept has become commonplace in preparation for Passover. While there is a rabbinic *mitzvah* (in addition to the regular, everyday one) of providing *ma'ot chitim*[12] funds to the needy in order to have the necessary provisions for the *seder*, many community soup kitchens prepare food packages including all the items for the *seder* plate as well as a full meal. Some go even beyond that and include chocolates and/or other delicacies.

Further, the giving itself is not enough but also our interpersonal engagement.

> Rabbi Isaac said:[13] "Whoever gives a small coin to a poor man has six blessings bestowed on them, but the one who speaks a kind word to them obtains eleven blessings."[14]

The rabbis teach that we dare not shame the poor by blaming them for being lazy.

> If the rich man says to this same poor person: 'Why do you not go and work and get food? Look at those hips! Look at those

---

9. *Babylonian Talmud*, Bava Batra 8b. Also see BT, Rosh Hashanah 6a. Also see the Ritva's commentary on Ketubot 49b. See the Rambam's *Mishneh Torah*, Laws of Mattnot Aniyim 7:10. See *Shulchan Aruch*, Yoreh Dei'ah 249:2.

10. *Babylonian Talmud*, Bava Batra 9a

11. *Orchot Tzadikim*, 313.

12. *Ma'ot Chitim* literally means money for wheat (which in turn is used to bake matzah).

13. *Babylonian Talmud*, Bava Batra 9b

14. citing Isaiah 58:10–12

legs! Look at that fat body! Look at those lumps of flesh! The Holy one, be blessed, says to them: 'it is not enough that you have not given them anything of yours, but you must set an evil eye upon what I have given them, must you?' Consequently, if they have begotten a son, there is nothing in their hand. Of all that they possessed they will not leave for their child, nor take unto themself, anything![15]

We should not only open our hearts and our hands, but our homes, too, when possible. Rabbi Dr. Daniel Sperber records an amazing kabbalistic *minhag* (Jewish custom) mentioned by Rabbeinu Bechaye that those who were particularly generous hosting the poor and strangers in their home were buried in coffins made out of their dining room tables![16]

I am aware of a rabbi and rebbetzin[17] who, during their forty years of service to their community literally had an open-door policy. They did not lock their door until 2:00 AM daily, always making themselves available to all needing assistance. They also took in anyone who, for any reason, needed a temporary home, no questions asked.

Our obligation is not only to the individual but to the community. Rambam teaches:

> One who settles in a community for thirty days becomes obligated to contribute to the charity fund together with the other members of the community. One who settles there for three months becomes obligated to contribute to the soup kitchen. One who settles there for six months becomes obligated to contribute clothing with which the poor of the community can cover themselves. One who settles there for nine months becomes obligated to contribute to the burial fund for burying the community's poor and providing for all of their needs of burial.[18]

So to whom specifically are we obligated? According to one Talmudic passage, it is quite clear.

> Yosef learned regarding the verse "When you lend money to my people" (Exodus 22:24): (If the choices before you are) a Jew and a non-Jew, a Jew has preference; the poor or the rich, the poor takes precedence; your poor (your relatives) and the (general) poor of your town, your poor come first; the poor of your city

---

15. *Vayikra Rabba*, Parshat Behar 34:4
16. Sperber, *Minhagei Yisrael vol. III*, 184
17. This rabbi and rebbetzin prefer anonymity for the purpose of this publication.
18. Maimonides, *Mishneh Torah*, Laws of Gifts to the Poor, 9:12

and the poor of another town, the poor of you own town have priority.[19]

But this assumes all factors are equal, which they rarely or never are. What if one's parent has a minor illness but one's neighbor's need is greater? What if a fellow Jew in one's town has a minor financial challenge but a stranger on the other side of the world is about to starve to death? Obviously, then, these and other variables must be taken into consideration in deciding who takes precedence.

The rabbis teach that we are obligated to Jews and gentiles alike!

> Our Rabbis taught: We sustain the non-Jewish poor with the Jewish poor, visit the non-Jewish sick with the Jewish sick, and bury the non-Jewish dead with the Jewish dead, for the sake of peace.[20]

According to many, "*darchei shalom*" (ways of peace) is about Jewish survival. Historically, it was not rare for gentiles to conclude that Jews cared more about Jews than gentiles and thus kill them over that fact. So to survive, we should pay attention to all. The Rambam, on the other hand, says "*shalom*" is an attribute, indeed a Name of God, and thus we follow the path of peace as a religious end in itself.

The preeminent 20th-century *poseik* (halachic decisor) Rabbi Moshe Feinstein picked up on this point about all factors not being equal and the difficulty of having clear answers in cases of triage.

> Let us say that there is a poor man who needs to eat today, but it is not a case of saving a life, and there is a relative who isn't wanting today, but he needs something for tomorrow. The relative has also [been] judged as being a poor person who is entitled to two hundred zuz.[21] Even if the law weren't that you give to your relatives first, we don't need to be precise in our rulings that put relatives first. Instead, that rule only applies when the need is the same between the two of them, both in terms of time and in terms of degree of need. We only learn that if the two of them are entitled to the same *tzedakah*, then you must give to your relative first. However, when the need of the non-relative is more urgent and greater in itself, you must give to him... And even for the poor, when they are both relatives, or both non-relatives, we learn that you should give to whomever you wish.[22]

19. *Babylonian Talmud*, Bava Metzia 71a
20. *Babylonian Talmud*, Gittin 61a
21. Zuz is an ancient monetary coin.
22. Feinstein, *Iggrot Moshe*, Yoreh Deah, Part 1, Section 144

When must I give immediately, and when must I delay and verify? Part of this question is addressed by the Shulchan Aruch:

> If someone comes and says, "feed me," you don't check him to see if he is an imposter, but you feed him right away. If there is a naked person who comes and says, "give me clothing," you check him to see if he is an imposter. And if you know him, you give him clothing right away.[23]

The Ramban (Nachmanides) writes:

> We are commanded to save the life of a non-Jew and to save them from harm, that if they were drowning in a river or a stone fell upon them, we must use all of our strength and be burdened with saving them; and if they were sick, we engage to heal them.[24]

One midrash[25] raises a fascinating point about why we pray in the plural grammatical form.[26]

> Everyone is equal before the Holy One, blessed is He. . . Know that concerning Moshe, the greatest of all the prophets, the same is said of a poor man. Of Moshe it is written 'A prayer of Moshe the man of G-d' (Tehillim 90:1), and of a poor man it says 'A prayer of the afflicted, when he faints and pours out his complaint before the Lord' (ibid. 102:1). In both cases, the word 'prayer' is used to teach you that before G-d all are equal in prayer.[27]

Sadly, it is easy to dehumanize the poor. One may rationalize that perhaps poverty is not painful for them since they're used to it. A recent psychology study[28] found that people in poverty are perceived as being less susceptible to pain.

> National health statistics indicate that wealthy people receive more substantial pain treatment than poor people. In this work,

---

23. Karo, *Shulchan Aruch*, Yoreh Deah, Laws of Tzedakah, Section 251 Part 10. Also see *Mishneh Torah*, Laws of Matnot Aniyim, 7:6

24. Maimonides, commentary on *Sefer HaMitzvot*, Mitzvah 16

25. *Shemot Rabbah* 21:4

26. The requests in the *Shemoneh Esreh* prayer, for example, are written in the plural: "Return us; Forgive us; Heal us, etc.

27. Hilsenrath, *Torah Ethics of Interpersonal Relationships*, 337

28. Dolan, "New psychology research finds that poor people are perceived as being less susceptible to pain." lines

we aimed to better understand how stereotypes might contribute
to such socioeconomic (SES) based disparities in healthcare. . .
Much of the previous work seeking to better understand factors
that may underlie these pain disparities had focused on struc-
tural-level (e.g., lack of access to quality care or insurance) and
patient-level (e.g., adherence to treatment regimens, exercise,
smoking and alcohol use) factors. Yet, little work had focused
on potential perceiver-level biases (e.g., providers' stereotypes
or biases) that might aid in explaining treatment disparities.

We might have thought that to be a Jewish leader what matters most is
one's resume or one's leadership skills. Rabbi Soloveitchik, however, makes
the priority clear. Here he describes the religious person (what he terms
"halakhic man"):

He takes up his stand in the midst of the concrete world, his feet
planted firmly on the ground of reality, and he looks about and
sees, listens and hears, and publicly protests against the oppression of the helpless, the defrauding of the poor, the plight of the
orphan. The rich are deemed as naught in his view. He is the
father of orphans, the judge of widows. My uncle, R. Meir Berlin
[Bar-Ilan], told me that once R. Hayyim of Brisk was asked what
the function of a rabbi is. R. Hayyim replied: 'To redress the
grievances of those who are abandoned and alone, to protect the
dignity of the poor, and to save the oppressed from the hands of
his oppressor.' Neither the ritual decisions nor political leadership constitutes the main tasks of halakhic man. Far from it. The
actualization of the ideals of justice and righteousness is the pil-
lar of fire which halakhic man follows, when he, as a rabbi and
teacher in Israel, serves his community.[29]

It is very easy in wealthy nations to favor "the system" or "the economy" over individual suffering. Consider this famous rabbinic critique of
Roman society.

Rabbi Yehoshua ben Levi reports, "When I went to Rome, I saw
pillars of marble that were covered with blankets so that they
would not crack from the heat or freeze from the cold. I also saw
a poor person with only a thin reed mat below him and a thin
reed mat on top of him."[30]

29. Soloveitchik, *Halakhic Man*, 91
30. *Vayikra Rabbah* 27:1

We must make it our priority to favor the individual's needs and suf-fering over "the system." We, as "halakhic man," and as human beings, must provide the poor with more than "a thin reed mat" before we "cover our marble pillars with blankets."

We recite blessings on *mitzvot bein adam laMakom* (between people and God) and not on *mitzvot bein adam lachaveiro* (between man and man). Reb Simcha Bunim of Peshischa taught specifically in regard to *tzedakah*:

> Why don't we recite a blessing over the *mitzvah* to give charity? Because if one had to make a blessing [on giving *tzedakah*] like any other positive *mitzvah*, it would require preparation, im-mersion in the *mikvah* with the proper mystical intentions or something similar, and in the meantime the poor would starve to death.[31]

For this reason, we don't wait for others to ask us to give but rather we run toward them! "The way of those who do acts of loving-kindness is to run after the poor."[32] The story is told of Moses Montefiore that the king asked him how much he was worth. Montefiore wrote down a number but the king didn't believe it. "I've seen all your businesses and your property. You are worth much more!" "Oh," Montefiore replied, "you want to know how much I own? The number I gave you is what I am worth: it is how much I have given away in the last year!" Indeed, our success in life should be measured not by what we accumulate but by what we have given.

The Ishbizher Rebbe asks[33]: "Why were the Jews chosen?" His answer is: "Avadim hayyinu (we were slaves)!" And he explains that God loves the weak and is aligned with the downtrodden. And if we are to emulate God then we too are to choose those who need us most! May we always run toward providing life to others, in turn providing them with dignity and spiritual healing.

31. *Siach Sarfei Kodesh* 1:13
32. *Babylonian Talmud*, Shabbat 104a
33. Yaakov Leiner of Izhbitz, *Beit Yaakov on Torah*, Parshat Va'etchanan #14, 360

#4

De'agah L'Yeladim, Caring for Children

WHILE THE TORAH OBLIGATES us to honor and revere[1] our parents, it does not explicitly command us regarding the reverse, caring for our children.

Nevertheless, the Talmud teaches[2] that one has an obligation to support their young children. This Talmudic passage does not indicate whether or not this obligation is biblical or rabbinic in nature. The Rambam,[3] however, seemingly implies that the mitzvah of supporting our children is a biblical command. He writes:

> Just as one is required to provide food for his wife, so too is he required to provide food for his minor sons and daughters. . . If he does not wish to do so, he is less than an impure bird which feeds its young.[4]

It takes so much to care for our children. First, there are all of the most basic necessities: a safe home, food, clothes, schooling, and medical and dental care, to name a few. Then there are the greater human needs one needs for actualization: nurturing, hugging, inspiring, listening, respecting, and setting aside time for connecting to who they are as individuals.

In addition to wanting to meet the basic needs and the deeper needs of our children, we also want to influence them toward nourishing the best

---

1. As discussed in a previous chapter, *kibbud av va'eim,* honoring one's parents, includes caring for and providing for them.

2. *Babylonian Talmud,* Ketubot 65b

3. Maimonides, *Mishneh Torah,* Hilkhot Ishut (Laws of Marriage) 12:14

4. Providing for the needs (food and otherwise) of one's wife is a biblical *mitzvah.* By Rambam's equating this command with providing for one's children, one can infer from his words that the latter is biblical as well.

moral and spiritual paths. This is actually more complicated than we may think. We can preach and teach to our children all day long, but if we do not live by those values ourselves, there will be no power of influence. Children are sponges of behavior and thought. They watch us when we think they are not, and we cannot take off our role model "hat." Our children learn from, and mimic, our behavior, for good and for bad. Becoming a parent requires that we are as vigilant about our own behavior and the origins of our actions and thoughts just as much as we consider our children's.

Transformative education happens through mentorship and a life of modeled virtue. A Talmudic tale:

> Rabbi Yohanan stood and kissed Rabbi Elazar on the head. Rabbi Yohanan said, "Blessed is God, the Lord of Israel, who gave such a son to Abraham our father; for he knows how to understand, and investigate, and expound upon the works of the Chariot (a particular mystical revelation). There are those who preach well, yet they do not practice. There are those who practice well, but they cannot preach. You practice what you preach! Happy are you, Abraham our father, that Elazar ben Arakh is your offspring!"[5]

The study of Judaism cannot remain academic. By its very design and essence, Torah is meant to be lived, practiced in every aspect of life, some of which we may not even be aware of ourselves. It is the guide to the depths of human nature, both the good, the bad, and the ugly. The rabbis taught the danger of merely studying Torah from the outside but missing the soul of the tradition:

> Rabbi Yishmael bar Rabbi Yossi said: One who studies Torah in order to teach, is given the means to study and to teach; and one who studies in order to practice, is given the means to study and to teach, to observe and to practice.[6]

One cannot be a true "teacher" without observing and practicing what they study and teach. "Practice what you preach" is not merely advice and admonishment, it is axiomatic to being an effective parent or teacher.

This is not so easy, however, when one is an idealistic dreamer who teaches many profound values. Here is an example of one who succeeded in this manner:

Prime Minister David Ben-Gurion did not just preach the values of equality when he read the Proclamation of Independence. He frequently

5. *Babylonian Talmud*, Hagigah 14b

6. *Pirkei Avot*, 4:6

modeled them in humble ways. One example: Ben-Gurion actually used to receive hundreds of letters (too many for him to answer on his own). He saw that one was from three out-of-work Arabs. He spent most of that afternoon calling people in the government to find them jobs.[7] This was not easy or typical in the 1950s amidst continued conflict.

I can recall as a child watching my father speak to the homeless with such respect, and my mother teaching children with such patience; and observing as an adult my mentor Rabbi Avi Weiss hugging every maintenance custodian he met, my dear wife modestly showing care for others when it seems no one is watching, and my high school teacher spending her free time to challenge me in my thinking and direction. These role models, among many others, shaped my character more than any words they spoke because behind their actions was genuine and active care.

A child watches their parents very closely. It is not in the set moments of our lives, such as the proverbial dinner table lesson that a value will be inculcated. It is typically in watching how a child's parents talk to one another, how one's father speaks with the cashier, and how one's mother converses with a frustrating telemarketer. To teach virtue one must model virtue. To parent with values, one must live with those values consistently even when one thinks that no one is watching.

Rav Avraham Yitzchak HaCohen Kook, the first Ashkenazic Chief Rabbi of Israel, taught:

> The pure righteous do not complain of the dark, but increase the light; they do not complain of evil, but increase justice; they do not complain of heresy, but increase faith; they do not complain of ignorance, but increase wisdom.

In short, it is incumbent upon each of us to lead by example!!

Rav Kook lived up to this teaching as a tremendous force of proactive good. Our role is to be a source of light and to walk with light. It is all too easy to profess virtue, but to live with virtue is the real challenge. It is all too easy to enter polemics complaining about the system, but we must work to change the system each day of our lives to further a more just and holy society. How we treat our fellow human beings, both those who live in our household and in the outside world, echoes a greater distance than we could ever imagine. Actions have a rippling effect.

While education at home is primary, of course we must be deeply concerned with the broader curriculum our children are provided as well. One of the most potent indicators of a sustained, Jewish life is an upbringing that

---

7. St. John, *Ben-Gurion: Builder of Israel*, 105

nourishes the intellectual dynamism of Jewish thought and lived experience. That being said, consider the typical Jewish educational experience. Whether through day school or supplemental programs, the vast majority of curricula tend to focus on Jewish identity development, (varying levels of) Hebrew linguistics, Jewish texts, Israel engagement, Jewish history, comfort with Jewish culture, socialization, and the like. These individual elements are important, of course, but I believe the number one priority in nurturing a child's faculty is missing from the aforementioned list.

That pedagogical priority is character development.

And by character development, I don't mean a vague, general awareness of *middot* (character traits) that help guide people through their daily lives. Rather, when I think about character development, I specifically mean the cultivation of *mussar* (character refinement) principles. One of the best ways to instill character refinement and development in children is by encouraging them to ask questions. The questions we ask are reflections of our individuality, our way to relate to any material we are being taught. Refining one's spiritual practices through the practice of inquiry not only allows for the internalization of deep truths, it prepares the mind and soul to venture out beyond normative comfort zones and into the recesses of the unknown. If we are to raise the next generation of dreamers, then this is an essential lesson we must impart to, and inculcate in, our children.

Indeed, we can only address the messiness of our children's outer world to the extent that we have the ability to address the messiness of their inner worlds. We bring light to others *only* if *we* model leadership and good deeds from a place of inner light and balance. While there are countless ethical virtues that we need our children to cultivate, these capabilities can only be displayed if they're represented in everyday situations. When students are taught humility, courage, patience, and gratitude, among the multitude of other positive traits, they're getting an education that goes beyond the page. To be sure, facts will come and go. Texts will be studied and forgotten. But our inner lives—the lens with which we encounter ourselves, other people, and God—become part of a permanent epistemology of spiritual discovery.

When we approach life from the virtue of *hitlamdut* (seeking to learn and grow from every encounter), Jewish commitments are sustained and refreshed. At the same time, ethical and spiritual lives grow and flourish. Because of this view, I'm not calling for minor, superficial adjustment: say, adding a small *mussar* curriculum to the school. I'm calling for radical change: making *mussar* the central element of Jewish education. I am not indicating that the remainder of what comprises Jewish education should be tossed out the window. However, through this style of *mussar* based teaching, students will be adding another deeper layer in learning Hebrew, history, Jewish culture, cultivating their identities, and developing friend-ships, all through the lens of *mussar* sensibilities and character refinement. But most of all, they will become part of a continuous tradition that goes beyond the basic standard, where the end goal is developing our children to be righteous and holy. They become more self-aware, more other-aware, and more God-aware. We enrich their souls through emotional intelligence while simultaneously instilling a deep-rooted vivacity of Jewish wisdom.

We need our students to learn spiritual truths: awe, wonder, trust, and faith. But we cannot do it without providing a platform for them to flour-ish. Often, Jewish education becomes stuck in a pattern of box-checking: Alef-Bet, *check*; Five Books of Moses, *check*; Crusades and expulsions, *check*; the miracle of Israel, *check*. Where is the fire? Where is the questioning? Where is the zest for learning what is beautiful, remarkable, and unique about Jewish teachings? When everything becomes rote, intellectual stasis prevails; stagnation follows. There can be no growth without exploration via the individual's lens.

This is precisely the implicit message of a dictum in Pirkei Avot re-garding *tefillah* (prayer):[8]

> Do not allow your prayer to become rote. Rather, it must be [an experience] of seeking mercy and petition before God.

What's true of *tefillah* is equally true with regard to Jewish education. And just as one whose prayer becomes rote may lead to his/her abandoning prayer altogether, educators and parents who teach by rote place their chil-dren and students in greater risk of abandoning Jewish practice altogether. Where is the personal? That sense of our children understanding that they are part of an assembly of continuation, questioning, and evolution.

But exploring new avenues of engagement is difficult as well. I have seen this personally. When at VBM we launched our Teen *Mussar* Fellow-ship, I was skeptical. After all, isn't *mussar* for adults? Do teens have the maturity to look at their inner lives and articulate it in a reasonable manner with peers? My fears were allayed almost instantly. I learned that the capac-ity is most certainly there and, in fact, I know from parenting my young children that it is there from their formative years. Children are sometimes the wisest people in the room, able to absorb, understand, and contemplate past the capacity of an adult mind, which if not consciously opened up, has the tendency to harden over time.

Teaching Judaism to the next generation, with character development and refinement as a starting point around which all the rest is centered, is

---

8. *Pirkei Avot*, 2:13

an imperative not only because we are commanded to do so, but because we have the opportunity to shape the lives of countless souls in a positive manner. We should—*indeed we need!* —to commit to passing this wisdom down. By doing so, we demonstrate that Jewish wisdom is forever relevant; it will allow students to thrive as they go through life. This wisdom, this model of education, helps impressionable minds to be successful at school and work, to develop meaningful relationships, and, most importantly, to have a rich and rewarding spiritual life in which to cultivate happiness; this happiness will—with God's help—pass down to the next generation. And the next.

And the next.

#5

Ahavat HaGeir, Loving the Stranger

WE ARE CALLED UPON to love our fellow Jew, but a more difficult task for many is the other charge to love the *geir* (the stranger). We naturally may feel closer to the former through the shared cultural, historical, or religious ties that bind us together as a nation. The latter is more alien to our consciousness because we share less direct connections. However, we must keep in mind that all things that divide us come secondary to the one and most important thing that unites us with the stranger. That we are all human beings, and we share the same human experiences.

There are two types of strangers: the convert and the foreigner. On a biblical level, we are talking about a *geir* who is a foreigner in our midst. This definition of *geir*, while not explicitly stated in the Torah, is borne out in the verse instructing us to love the *geir*: *"Va'ahavtem et hageir, ki geirim heyitem b'Eretz Mitzrayim"* (*"You must love the stranger, for you were strangers in the land of Egypt*).[1] We are to love the *geir* because we ourselves were in that same situation. Clearly, this refers to our having been strangers, or foreigners, in Egypt, not converts. This type of *geir* is akin to an immigrant, asylee, or refugee. It is a status most think they will never find fit, until they find themselves in the position.

On a Talmudic level, we are talking about a convert, a gentile who has entered our community not as one fleeing *from* but fleeing *to* (i.e., to convert into the Jewish religion and culture). Let's start with our exploration of the convert.

The path of the Jewish convert can be strenuous and taxing on the soul. The processes that have been established over centuries have acted as

1. Deuteronomy 10:19

both bulwark and entry way to a life of keeping the commandments and devoted to Torah learning. But how are we doing, as a collective Jewish community, in taking care of our brothers and sisters who seek to become part of the ways of the Torah and *mitzvot* and intertwine themselves with our fate and destiny?

Based upon some of the recent events emerging from the office of the Chief Rabbinate in Jerusalem, one would think that the Torah's attitude towards converts would be something along the lines of: "Exercise extreme caution with those who want to convert" or "Act with spite toward all those who want to join the Jewish People." After all, when rabbis create lists[2] to arbitrarily invalidate conversions performed by other rabbis, and in some cases even invalidate the converting rabbis themselves, all the while making the standards of what makes a Jewish convert "legitimate" more stringent and opaque, they bring needless suffering and unwarranted shame to those who have dedicated months, sometimes even years, to accepting the covenants of Judaism. It is an offense to a person's soul.

Sadly, shame might be the standard feeling based on the events of the current moment. What other conclusion might one come to? One may think the guiding text for the seemingly obstinate members of the Chief Rabbinate is the unusual one that states:[3] "Proselytes are hurtful to Israel as a sore on the skin."[4]

In fact, however, in addition to the verse quoted above, the Torah, time and time again, vigorously commands us to love and protect converts. Maimonides taught:

> Loving a convert who has come to rest under the wings of the Almighty [fulfills] two positive commandments: one for the convert who is [also] included among the "fellows" [whom we are commanded to love] and one *because* they are a convert, and the Torah states: "and you shall love the convert."
> God has commanded us concerning the love of a convert just as God commanded us concerning loving God, as it states: "and you shall love God, your Lord." God loves converts, as the Torah notes: "and God loves converts."[5]

Admittedly, there will be certain individuals who become angry or jealous that "outsiders" who enter the covenant of the Jewish people are actually

---

2. Maltz, "The Israeli Chief Rabbinate's Blacklist: A Guide for the Perplexed" lines

3. *Babylonian Talmud*, Yevamot 109b

4. While this source is meant to be understood in a certain context, when taken out of context it can be, and often is, abused and applied as if it is a legal, halachic ruling.

5. Maimonides, *Mishneh Torah*, Hilkhot Deot 6, 4

to be given more honor and protection, but also that overcoming these nega-tive emotions is the spiritual work of those more secure and privileged in our communities. Consider how the midrash explains this phenomenon:

> A king has many flocks of sheep, and one day a stag appears and joins the sheep. The stag grazes with the sheep and returns with them at night, as if he were a sheep. When the shepherds tell the king of the stag, the king takes great pride and interest in it and ensures that the shepherds treat the stag with special care. The shepherds question the king, asking, "You have thousands of animals over which you take no personal interest, so why do you care so much about one animal?" The king answers them, "My sheep have only one flock to join, and cannot leave, but this stag has the whole world to choose from, yet he chose my flock. He surely deserves my special attention and cares."[6]
>
> Elsewhere in Jewish thought, we find other sources that demonstrate that there is a moral imperative to love and protect converts. This is partially due to the fact that they are far more vulnerable and susceptible to exploitation and discrimination either by the Jewish flock or the one they came from. But con-comitantly, this can also be due to the fact that converts are to be viewed as courageous, spiritual journeyers who have come to contribute and overcome great obstacles to do so. Sources point to the figure of Yitro (Jethro), Moses' father-in-law, as a para-gon for Jewish conversion. Having spent most of his life as an idol-worshiping shepherd in Midian, Yitro later became drawn to the miracles of Torah and the God of the Israelites. Indeed, expanding on this point, there is an explication in the Talmud that God seeks out individuals with unique spiritual attributes to join the Jewish people.[7]

Through this lens, every convert is especially chosen by the Divine to actualize their potential at a point later in life. The kabbalists explain that converts already had the sparks of a Jewish soul within them. The holy sparks were just waiting for discovery and elevation.

The Ba'alei Ha'Tosafot (Tosafists) explain the burden put upon those born Jewish. Firstly, they must do all they can to be accepting of converts and prevent any suffering, and secondly, since converts tend to be particularly careful in their observance,[8] those born Jewish may feel implicated since

---

6. *Bamidbar Rabba* 8:2

7. *Babylonian Talmud*, Gittin 56a

8. This concern that converts may be more diligent in their observance is indeed one explanation of the quote from the Talmud above, that converts are hurtful to Israel.

they do not reach the same level.[9] To be sure, Rav Saadia Gaon[10] teaches that this *mitzvah* does not begin once one has converted to Judaism but once one begins that conversion journey.[11] Even before one begins the delicate process, support has to be present and gentle. We don't distress those in the process only to embrace them once they've rigorously jumped through all the hoops. The wounds of a trauma may heal, but the scars remain. Rather, the Torah commands for love and justice to begin at the beginning.

The Sefer HaChinuch reminds us that the *mitzvah* is not merely to love, but also to prevent gratuitous anguish and suffering:

> We are commanded to love the convert. In particular, we are di-
> rected not to cause converts to suffer in any way, but rather to do
> them good and act as charitably as they deserve. The converts
> are all those who have abandoned their religion and joined ours.
> About this group, the Torah says,[12] "Love the stranger [convert]
> since you were strangers.[13]

So, again, how are we doing? There is undoubtedly much room where we can improve on both the individual, communal, and national levels. For starters, the monopoly of who is and who can be a Jew must be decentralized. Afterall, people's dignity and lives are at stake.

Being the leaders of a new and compassionate vanguard that welcomes converts and greets them with open arms, rather than suspicion, has to be the path forward for Judaism to thrive. It is a spiritual call to arms. Converts should never be used as pawns in internecine temporal battles within their transformative moments of spiritual import. Ensuring that all those who seek the beauty of *mitzvot* become full-fledged members of the community with love and care is a holy task we can, and must, accomplish.

While loving the convert, as we have explored, remains quite challeng-ing, it can be even more challenging to love the immigrant. This individual arrives at our border or at our doorstep not as someone who wishes to be-come like us but wishes to maintain their full uniqueness yet still have full

---

9. *Babylonian Talmud*, Yevamot 47b; Kiddushin 70b-71a

10. Rav (Rabbi) Sa'adia Gaon was a 9th-century Iraqi Jewish philosopher, exegete and grammarian.

11. *Sefer HaMizvot of Rav Saadia Gaon*, Mitzvah 10. In his commentary, Rabbi Perlow quotes the 12-th century Spanish rabbi Ri Barcelona as explicating this point.

12. Deuteronomy 10:19

13. *Sefer HaChinuch*, Mitzva 431

acceptance. We are reminded: "There shall be one law for the native and the immigrant who lives among you."[14]

On Passover, Jews celebrate not only the liberation of the Hebrew slaves from oppression and cruelty, but also the blessings that free movement ordain to a nation seeking to form an identity. One could argue that the Passover story is primarily about embracing an ethical consciousness of the stranger. Yet an even more pertinent and contemporary read is that Passover is about cultivating the crucial emotion of empathy, especially when it comes to seeing life through the eyes of the immigrant, the asylum seeker, and the refugee.

As a people who have suffered oppression—not only in biblical times but throughout our history — we are consistently instructed not to attack immigrants with hateful rhetoric, precisely because we have felt this pain. Our forefather Abraham was commanded to become an immigrant.[15] Elsewhere in the Torah, there are positive commandments to love the foreigner in our midst[16] and negative commandments against oppressing or perverting justice for them in any way.[17]

Elaborating on that prohibition, the midrash teaches regarding the verse we quoted earlier: "'You shall not wrong or oppress the stranger, for you were strangers in the land of Egypt.' You shall not wrong with words, and you shall not oppress financially."[18] Adding onto this our sages taught that "one who embarrasses another in public is as if they are committing murder."[19] We cannot single out and oppress an individual with words or actions based on who they are or where they come from. To do so would cause untold physical and emotional harm.

The sages of the Talmud supported the right to immigrate and move around freely: "One who has not made good in one place and fails to move and try their luck in some other place has only oneself to complain about."[20] One cannot remain stuck in an underprivileged region, the rabbis tell us, if it is a clear dead end for oneself and one's family.

We not only owe immigrants their inherent and basic human rights, we also have specific religious obligations to go above and beyond to protect them from harm, as proven by the disproportionate number of times

14. Exodus 12:49

15. Genesis 12:1

16. Deuteronomy 10:18

17. Exodus 22:20; Deuteronomy 24:17

18. *Mekhilta d'Rabbi Yishmael*, Parshat Mishpatim

19. *Babylonian Talmud*, Bava Metzia, 58a

20. *Babylonian Talmud*, Bava Metzia 75b

and number of ways the Torah instructs us to be ethically mindful toward this population. Our responsibility to the immigrant — or perhaps, more aptly, the heroic journeyer — requires that we honor the image of God in all people.

Jewish tradition reminds us not to become like the land of Sodom, the paradigmatic evil society described in the Book of Genesis, which is said to have been cruel to strangers in its midst. "They issued a proclamation in Sodom saying, 'Everyone who strengthens the hand of the poor and the needy and the stranger with a loaf of bread shall be burnt by fire.'"[21] The foremost crime of Sodom was that they did not sustain the needs of the stranger passing through their lands.

Further, we are instructed: "Do not despise the Edomite, for he is your brother; do not despise the Egyptian, for you were sojourners in his land."[22] This verse goes even one step further than the general *mitzvah* to love the *geir*, as here we are instructed not to hate even those who oppressed and maltreated us. It seems almost irrational for the Torah to mandate that a Jew may not hate an Egyptian (particularly considering that the Torah was given to the very generation that had been enslaved in Egypt). Nevertheless, the Torah mandate does indeed go that far. How much more so, then, must we be sure not to mistreat, and to even welcome, immigrants and asylum seekers who neither they nor their people have done us any harm.

Time and again, Jewish tradition tells us that God is the owner of all the land. From this teaching, we come to understand that Jewish ethics apply to all people, not simply those born in a given place. Rabbi Samson Raphael Hirsch, elaborating on the meaning of never turning another person away from comfort or refuge, explained that there are no preconditions for receiving basic rights other than being human: "The absolute equality in the eyes of the law between the native and the foreigner forms the very basic foundation of Jewish jurisdiction."

Rabbi Joseph B. Soloveitchik, who wrote and spoke so eloquently on the intersection between traditional Jewish thought and contemporary attitudes, commented on the notion that those who journey to foreign lands to seek freedom often become the most ardent and patriotic: "When the need arises, the nomad stands up and fights for his freedom, and many a time proves superior in battle to the settled king." The history and contributions of diaspora Jewry to the societies in which they call home are a living testament of that principle. We should regard the history of all immigrants to be as such.

21. *Pirkei D'Rebbe Eliezer* 25
22. Deuteronomy 23:8

But perhaps it was Emmanuel Levinas, the French Talmudist and arguably the foremost philosopher of Jewish ethics of the 20th century, who said it best: "The respect for the stranger and the sanctification of the name of the Eternal are strangely equivalent."

As Jews, our ancestors have been eternal immigrants, from Abraham to Ellis Island. They were my heroes, as are the modern immigrants striving to survive and thrive in a challenging world.

The prophetic day will come when our society sees the immigrants among us not as scoundrels but as heroes who were willing to make dangerous and uncertain treks from home, learn new languages, and cultural lexicons, all to support themselves and their families. We can, indeed we must, do all in our power to hasten the realization of that day.

#6

Kevurat HaMeitim, Burying the Dead

JUDAISM IS A LIFE-AFFIRMING religion, embracing the sanctity of life. The Torah teaches: "You shall observe my statutes and my laws, which man must do, and live by them."[1] As the words "and live by them" are at the same time obvious and ambiguous, the Talmud comments:

> How do we know that saving a life overrides the laws of Shabbat? For the verse states, "And live by them," [i.e., the *mitzvot*] and not die by them.[2]

The Talmud goes on to explain that one may not perform a positive *mitzvah* if it will result, or perhaps even if it only *may* result, in death.

Of course, there are times that our tradition asks us to be willing to die before violating certain *mitzvot*,[3] but the general rule is "live by them!" The Rambam makes clear how serious this mandate is by directly connecting it to Shabbat observance:

> It is forbidden to delay in a matter of transgressing the Shabbat for the sake of one whose life is endangered, as it is written, "That a person will do them, and live by them"—and not die by them. Thus you see that the laws of the Torah do not bring vengeance upon the world, but rather compassion, kindness and peace in the world.[4]

1. Leviticus 18:5

2. *Babylonian Talmud*, Yoma 85a-85b

3. One must give their life rather than transgress the three "cardinal sins": idolatry, adultery, and murder.

4. Maimonides, *Mishneh Torah*, Hilchot Shabbat 2:3

Another prime example of this dictum is that it is forbidden for one to fast on Yom Kippur if it entails risking one's life.[5] This is equally true regarding a pregnant woman fasting if her fetus' life is at risk.

A pregnant woman, who had previously suffered a stillbirth, was told by her doctor that she may eat on Yom Kippur. Even so, the woman was unsure and nervous about the effect that fasting may have on her unborn child. She consulted a highly regarded *poseik* (halachic authority), who instructed her to eat despite the doctor's assurance. The rabbi later explained to the woman's husband that he understood from her dilemma that, given her history, her worrying alone could endanger the life of the fetus, and he therefore concluded that she must eat.[6]

So should we conclude that we should not think much about death, since, after all, Judaism is so life-affirming? The Talmudic rabbis teach us that we should, in fact, hold a daily death-consciousness moment even while being life-affirming:

> Akavyah the son of Mehalalel said: Contemplate three things and you will not come to transgression: Know from where you have come, to where you are going, and in front of Whom you will have to give an accounting.[7]

By focusing on our death, we can remember how much work we have to do in this world and how short our time is. By recalling the origin of death, the eating of the fruit of the tree of knowledge of good and evil,[8] we recall the birth of human moral consciousness.

Adam and Eve, and perhaps most of us, if once again posed with the dilemma of choosing blind immortality or morally charged mortality, would probably choose the latter. The rabbis taught:

> Rav Abba Bar Kahana said: When Adam confessed to God that he had eaten from the tree, he said, "And I *eat* from the tree."[9] The Torah does not write that "Adam *ate* from the Tree." This

---

5. It is orally reported that Rav Chaim Soloveitchik, the grandfather of Rabbi Joseph B. Soloveitchik and Rabbi Aaron Soloveichik, would often instruct those who sought his counsel regarding fasting on Yom Kippur to eat. He was once asked why he was so lenient with regard to fasting on Yom Kippur. He responded that he was not lenient regarding fasting on Yom Kippur; rather, he was strict regarding *pikuach nefesh* (sanctity of life).

6. Both the rabbi and woman in this case prefer to remain anonymous.

7. *Pirkei Avot* 3:1

8. Genesis 2:17

9. Genesis 3:13

comes to teach that Adam ate from the tree and (if faced with the choice in the future), he would do so again.[10]

While there are several explanations offered for this strange midrash, it is quite reasonable that Adam was affirming precisely what we mentioned above, that he would rather be a morally charged mortal than immortal with no moral consequences or conscience.

Yet if we are too death-conscious, we might find life to be futile and not invest in this world. It's for this reason that every human may hold a deeply seated fantasy of immortality. And it is for this reason that God hides our time of death from our hearts. The rabbis taught:

> Had God not hidden the concept of death from the heart of man, man would not construct nor plant, for he would say, "To-morrow I will die, so why should I toil for the sake of others?" Therefore, God hid death from the hearts of men, so that they will build and plant. . .[11]

We are charged with striking a balance, not an easy task in the least. We must affirm life and engage in creating a better world for ourselves and all human beings and creations, and at the same time be constantly aware that our time in this world is limited.

We may also conclude that we are to care about the body in this world and the soul in the next world. Afterall, it says in Ecclesiastes: "The dust re-turns to the land, as it was; and the spirit returns to God, Who gave it."[12] But a formulation with such a binary approach would be too simplistic, since it is clear that we care about the soul in this world in addition to the body and that we care about the body after one's life in addition to the soul.

The Sfat Emet[13] teaches how the body and soul are interconnected.

> This is the wonder of the human being, in which a Divine soul is present in a physical body, as the Rema writes[14] in explaining the words "who performs wonders"—God binds the spiritual soul with the physical body.[15]

---

10. *Bereishit Rabba* 19:22

11. *Midrash Tanchuma*, Kedoshim 8

12. Ecclesiastes 12:7

13. The *Sfat Emet* was authored by Rabbi Yehudah Aryeh Leib Alter, a Polish *Hasidic* master. He himself is often referred to by the name of his work.

14. Karo, *Orach Chaim*, 6

15. *Sfat Emet*, Parshat Tazria, 5640

If we were only concerned about the soul and not the body, we would not care about what happens with the body after life. But humans are created *b'tzelem Elokim* (in God's image)[16] and on the simple read of the verse, that has a physical dimension to it in addition to a spiritual dimension. For this reason, we learn in the Torah that not honoring a corpse is an insult to God.

> When a person is legally sentenced to death and executed, you must then hang them on the gallows. However, you may not allow their body to remain on the gallows overnight, but you must bury it on the same day. Since a person who has been hanged is a curse to God, you must not [let the hanging body] defile the land that God your Lord is giving you as a heritage.[17]

As we see here, it is not just the righteous person who represents God, but even the corpse of one killed for doing something as atrocious as deserving capital punishment.[18] Every human being has a piece of God's image.

Jewish practice is to bury a body quickly to help comfort and liberate the soul. The Talmud teaches that not only is one's family mourning the death of their departed, but also one's own soul is in mourning!

> "Rabbi Chisda said: A person's soul mourns for him all seven days of shiva (the seven-day mourning period)."[19]
> Rabbi Abahu said: Everything said in front of the deceased is known, until the grave is sealed. Rabbi Chiya and Rabbi Shimon bar Rebbe had a disagreement. One maintained (that the deceased is aware) until the grave is sealed, and one said until the flesh decomposes.[20]

Further, the rabbis teach that the person is present[21] at their own eulogies.[22] We don't start to officially comfort the mourners right at death but first prioritize the burial laws. Rabbi Maurice Lamm wrote:

---

16. Genesis 1:27

17. Deuteronomy 21:22:23

18. While capital punishment is, and must be, a subject for debate in our time, it is beyond the scope of this essay. For our purposes, it suffices to say that even the Talmudic sages frowned upon a *beit din* (Jewish court) imposing the death penalty.

19. *Babyloonian Talmud*, Shabbat 152a

20. *Babyloonian Talmud*, Shabbat 152b

21. This is obviously a reference to the soul.

22. *Babyloonian Talmud*, Shabbat 153b

Judaism regards burial procedures, for the most part, [as devoted to] *yekara d'shichva*, the respect, honor, and endearment
of the deceased. . .

The Sages wisely noted that one cannot and should not comfort
the mourners while their dead lie before them. Comfort and relief come later, after funeral and burial arrangements have been
completed and the dead have been interred. Until that time, the
deceased remains the center of concern. His honor and his integrity are of primary importance.[23]

We want to move on to comforting mourners and engaging in our
own mourning process, but first we must make sure the dignity of the deceased is maintained and that the burial needs are met.

There are people who struggle financially to attend to the burial needs
and who could use our help. It is our responsibility to assist those in this
time of need. There are unfortunately also those who spend very extrava-
gantly, thus raising the communal norms for how much others think they
should spend.

I was recently meeting with a family to make the funeral arrangements
and prepare the eulogy. I informed the mourning children that they might
consider wearing an old garment at the funeral so that we could tear *keriah*
(the rending of a garment) before the ceremony as is traditionally done. The
response I received was the first I had ever heard of its kind. The son told
me that he would not do it. He said that for his father, he would only tear his
nicest new garment. His father deserved it. I was very inspired by his unique
commitment and how much this ritual meant to him.

There are many meaningful ways to mourn for loved ones; excessive
spending on caskets and tombstones, however, is likely not the optimal Jewish choice.

The Chafetz Chaim taught that more important than saying kaddish
for a deceased parent or buying a nice memorial tombstone is doing *chesed*
(acts of kindness) in their honor.[24] He suggests that using funds to donate
books to a synagogue or establish a loan fund for the poor is more important and useful than purchasing a grand deluxe monument for a cemetery.

While perhaps forty percent of Americans opt for cremation,[25] most
still choose burial, which usually involves a tombstone or some other grave
marker. And while scant data are available for the cost involved, the "average"

23. Lamm, *The Jewish Way in Death and Mourning*, 28

24. Kagan, *Ahavat Chesed* 2:15

25. http://voices.yahoo.com/why-many-people-choosing-cremation-over-tradi-
tional-4222431.html?cat=7

cost of a headstone or tombstone is often estimated at $1,500–2,000.[26] A simple grave marker can cost as little as $200.[27] Single or double granite monuments in a Jewish cemetery cost anywhere from just under $1,000 to $4,000,[28] while more elaborate inscribed grave markers cost $7,000 or more,[29] and upright headstones reach $10,000 or more.[30] In mid-2022, I was told that these numbers have rapidly increased and that even modest Jewish funeral expenses would be over 20k (compared to cremation costing only around 2k).

Jewish funerals and burials in the West, while usually less than the costs incurred by Christians (who often require embalming, rental of a funeral home for several days, etc.), can still be very expensive. The cost can be divided into three price ranges:[31] relatively low ($500-$4,000), medium ($4,000-$6,000, as offered by the Jewish Burial Society or similar groups), or high ($10,000-$15,000), mostly depending on the casket chosen. The purchase of a plot (and additional liner or vault) and the fee for opening and closing the grave adds several hundred to several thousand dollars to the cost.

It should be noted that in Israel, the deceased are buried directly in the ground with no casket. And rather than ornate, large funeral homes, at most there are small, rather plain, one-room halls. Both of these differences between Israel and America help to keep the cost down.[32]

Around the world, there are differing attitudes toward grave markers. In Asia, Hindus and Buddhists customarily cremate their dead, and there are no tombstones. In the West, many cemeteries have become tourist attractions, where people visit the burial places of famous artists, sculptors, composers, performers, and political figures. Paris's Père Lachaise Cemetery and Vienna's Zentralfriedhof Central Cemetery are two that draw many thousands of tourists annually. The Old Jewish Cemetery in Prague, in which notable Czech Jews like the Maharal are buried,[33] draws a steady

26. http://www.iscga.org/how-much-does-a-gravestone-cost.html

27. http://www.fletchermemorial.org/how-much-does-a-memorial-headstone-cost/

28. http://www.brightonmemorialchapel.com/MonumentsCaskets/JewishMonuments/

29. http://www.fletchermemorial.org/how-much-does-a-memorial-headstone-cost/

30. http://www.iscga.org/how-much-does-a-gravestone-cost.html

31. "Jewish Funeral Cost."

32. *Halachah* demands that the dead are buried directly in the ground. As a casket is mandated in (most areas of) America, *halachah* views a wooden casket as acceptable, since wood is biodegradable. Alternatively, some caskets have a few small holes on the bottom, thereby creating a more direct connection with the ground.

33. http://www.tripadvisor.com/LocationPhotoDirectLink-g274707-d275221

stream of tourists who tread the narrow passageways. Some object to the commercialism, as you must pay a fee for a ticket to a number of Jewish historical sites and then join with tourists whose attitudes may not be appropriate. Others defend the practice[34] on the grounds that the money raised helps preserve the old Jewish section of Prague. In the United States, people visit Forest Hills to see the graves of Hollywood actors or Woodlawn cemetery in New York City, among others, to see the elaborately sculpted graves and mausoleums of famous historical figures.

Does an elaborate tombstone, or a cemetery that is a tourist attraction, advance the ideals that our ancestors stood for? Would it not be better for us to use our funds to honor the dead by helping the vulnerable in society or devoting time to bring justice to the world? After all, the Shelah HaKadosh[35] taught that one's acts of *chesed* and *tzedakah* (charity) can not only salvage a parent from a harsh judgment in the world to come, but can move them straight through the gates of the Garden of Eden.

Jewish law forbids speeding up the return of the human body to the earth (through cremation) or slowing it down (through mummification). Rather, we respectfully dress the body in modest shrouds and return it to the Creator through the earth. For many, the grief of the mourning experience is compounded by the stress of the accompanying financial burden. We should be sure to change the precedent from being so prohibitively expensive.

Can one follow one's own wishes after one's loved one passes rather than what was requested? According to a deontologist, the answer would be no. As a duty, one should honor what was committed. According to a secular consequentialist, however, one can do as they deem best now since there is no longer a duty to someone not alive. So if one is religious, they can override a secular request for cremation. Or, perhaps, on the opposite end, one who can't afford the religious request of burial might choose the secular request of cremation. Jewish texts sort through the competing tensions of the value of burial vs. the value of honoring one's requests if there is a clash. It is not a simple legal, or emotional, matter.

The Mishnah teaches that in addition to the behavioral aspects of mourning, there is a significant emotional component arguing that "grief is only of the heart."[36] To properly fulfill the *mitzvah* of *nichum aveilim*

-i59955931-Old_Jewish_Cemetery_Stary_zidovsky_hrbitov-Prague_Bohemia.html

34. Ibid.

35. The Shelah HaKadosh, Rabbi Yeshayahu Horowitz, was a 17th-century Czech rabbi and kabbalist. He spent his later years in Safed, Israel.

36. *Babylonian Talmud*, Sanhedrin 6:8

(comforting the mourning), we should be sure to model modest mourning which focuses more on healing, growth, and kindness, and less on grandiose conspicuous consumption to honor the deceased.

The Talmud teaches:

> Rabbi Simlai expounded: The Torah begins and ends with kindness. At its beginning, we learn of God's kindness for Adam and his wife when God made clothing for them. And at its end we are told of God's kindness when God buried Moshe (Moses).[37]

We are asked to emulate the Divine. Serving on a *chevra kaddisha* to wash a body can be an inspiring cat of service. To care for a corpse is a *chesed shel emet* (a true act of kindness since there can be reciprocity, nothing received in return). Managing a loved one's funeral and burial does not have to mean spending a lot of money. Rather, a proper Jewish burial means making it a priority for the sake and honor of the deceased, for the sake and honor of the living, and for the sake and honor of the Divine image.

---

37. *Babylonian Talmud*, Sotah 14a

#7

De'agah L'Yetomim, Caring for Vulnerable Children

THE TORAH CHARGES US to care for the *yatom* (vulnerable child). We are commanded, "Do not oppress the widow and orphan."[1] Elsewhere we are told that we must leave the tithe[2] and forgotten wheat[3] in the field for the *yatom* and widow, as they do not necessarily have anyone to provide for them. While the term *yatom* at its core refers to a child who has lost both parents or even one parent, it also refers to a child who has living parents but who must live outside of their care due to abuse, neglect, or hardship. In short, the *yatom* is the child that is particularly vulnerable because they are lacking full parental support.[4]

The number of foster children in America continues to rise as we fail to contain child abuse and child neglect. And with each passing year, even with countless potential parents ready to open their homes to vulnerable children, the process to foster or adopt remains incredibly difficult. Beyond our American borders, around the world, there are millions of children whose only wish is to be loved, to have a stable family structure, and to escape the fleeting conditions of a life in the foster-care system or raised in institutions. Along with everything else happening in the world today, the fact that countless children don't have a permanent loving family or a safe home

1. Exodus 21:22

2. Deuteronomy 14:29

3. Deuteronomy 24:19

4. We will translate "*yatom*" as "vulnerable child" throughout to avoid any possible confusion or misunderstanding that foster children are orphans, which they are usually not.

47

to call their own is one of the disgraceful truths of modern times. Where there is great suffering, the Jewish people must emerge to bring healing.

The plight of foster children is not an abstract concept for me, and I don't write about this topic from a distance. For many years, my wife and I have gone through the tribulations of providing a loving environment to foster children to the best of our ability. We've gone through the counseling, the certification, the frantic late-night calls from agencies looking to place a child at a moment's notice, and the pain of seeing the foster child whom we've loved and cared for taken away in the blink of an eye. We always support reunification with family, even when it feels misguided; we learned to give up control.

During times of greatest challenge, I turn to the wisdom of the Torah, which speaks so powerfully about the obligations that we all have to vulnerable populations. A community needs to take responsibility for those who don't have living parents or don't have parents equipped at the moment to care for them. Yet, this biblical precept seems to be overlooked in the present-day, where the barriers for adoption are so high and the prospect to extend a loving home to a child in need is so difficult, demanding, and arduous, that too many feel they are not up to the task. But if we know that the Torah is sensitive to the plight of the *yatom*, to the point that it reminds us on three occasions that we must care for them, why isn't our Jewish community doing more to prioritize the ability to protect these children?

The need for our collective participation is so urgent. According to statistics[5] from Administration for Children and Families, a part of the Department of Health and Human Services, it was estimated that Child Protective Service units across the nation received 3.6 million referrals, which involved approximately 6.6 million children. Of these children, only about 150,000 of them will be placed in foster homes and only 50,000[6] will end up being adopted. Nearly a quarter of them will develop long-term Post-Traumatic Stress Disorder, a fifth will be homeless by adulthood, seventy-one percent of the young women will be pregnant before age twenty-one, and over half will be unemployed by age twenty-four. So much needless suffering. So much wasted potential. The stomach-dropping bumps of such an unsteady track are all too palpable.

The consequences of being raised in a broken home are real for so many children—too many—and the effects not only stunt the development of these innocent souls, but they also affect the economic and social bonds

---

5. http://www.acf.hhs.gov/sites/default/files/cb/cm2014.pdf

6. http://www.acf.hhs.gov/sites/default/files/cb/trends_fostercare_adoption2014.pdf

that bring our nation together. If you don't grow up in a home with a loving family, then your chances at success in life are so much dimmer. We want to help give children their best start in life, the ability to shoot for the stars! I believe we owe them and ourselves the emotional discomfort bringing these unfamiliar children into our care. As hard as that is, the alternative of children having no loving home in the interim is *never* a good option. We don't, or at least shouldn't, have children in order to gain in some way or with some expectation that it'll be easy. Rather, we take care of vulnerable children—those we gave birth to and those we've brought in to our homes to foster or adopt—because ensuring that every child is loved is the greatest moral obligation and spiritual privilege we are charged to fulfill!

Although there are many challenges, we know it's an important *mitzvah* to participate. The rabbis taught:

> One who rescues and raises a vulnerable child in one's home fulfills a tremendous *mitzvah*, since there is a community responsibility to support impoverished vulnerable children.[7] We must allocate our communal funds to support vulnerable children.[8]

The Rambam (Maimonides) explains how we must show the highest sensitivity toward vulnerable children:

> Whoever irritates them, provokes them to anger, pains them, tyrannizes them, or causes them loss of money, is guilty of a transgression.[9]

And the great prophet Isaiah teaches us to "Defend the cause of vulnerable children."[10]

If we had infinite time, resources, and energy, more people would foster and adopt children needing homes, but so many of us do not have, or feel that we do not have, that luxury. And we always know that taking on one more demanding all-embracing *mitzvah* means that something else is likely to lose out. Consider this story about the Skulener Rebbe, who taught that one should even show more care to a vulnerable child than to one's own children.

> The Rebbe stayed in Europe after World War II, defying the Soviets, to look after refugees and keep vulnerable children in his home. On one cold night, he found a vulnerable child on his

7. *Babylonian Talmud*, Ketubot 50a

8 *Babylonian Talmud*, Ketubot 67b

9. Maimonides, *Mishneh Torah*, Dei'ot 6:10

10. Isaiah 1:17

> floor crying without a blanket. He went and took the blanket off
> of his old[er] child and gave it to the vulnerable child. His son
> understood, but nonetheless the Skulener Rebbe said, "My dear
> son, please understand. You have a father. You can at least warm
> yourself with that. That child has no one in the world; let him at
> least have a blanket."

Indeed, a vulnerable child will often have much greater needs than one's own non-vulnerable (or less-vulnerable) biological child. From personal experience, I know there are times one would need to be prepared to choose the needs of the non-biological child over the biological child. We might not do it or phrase it like the Skulener Rebbe has, but such a dilemma is very real.

The *yatom* is not only vulnerable, but is also potentially heroic. Consider some of the great leaders in our history who grew up outside the home of their biological families.

> When the child grew up, she brought him to Pharaoh's daughter
> to be her son. She named him Moses, for she said, "I drew him
> out of the water."[11]

The greatest prophet in Jewish tradition, Moshe, was adopted. From this story, the rabbis teach that one who raises a child is considered to have given birth to them:

> "When the child grew up, she brought him to Pharaoh's daugh-
> ter, to be her son," to teach you that one who raises his friend's
> son is as if he birthed the child. And so, it is written regarding
> Naomi, "And the women neighbors gave him a name, saying, 'A
> son is born to Naomi!'" (Ruth 4:17). And this is what is also said
> in Chronicles, "And his Hayehudiya (Jewish) wife bore him. . ."
> (ibid. 4:18). Hayehudiya is Batya, the daughter of Pharaoh, who
> converted and became Jewish.[12]

Then consider one of the greatest heroes in Jewish tradition: Esther!

> He was foster father to Hadassah—that is, Esther—his uncle's
> daughter, for she had neither father nor mother. The maiden
> was graceful and beautiful; and when her father and mother
> died, Mordechai adopted her as his own daughter.[13]

---

11. Exodus 2:10
The name Moses, or Hebrew Moshe, is a play on the verb meaning to "draw forth."
12. Ben Eliezer, Tobiah, *Midrash Lekach Tov*, on Exodus 2:10
13. Esther 2:7

Consider further how future redemption will have emerged from a foster mother!

> Naomi took the child and held it to her bosom. She became its foster mother, and the women neighbors gave him a name, saying, "A son is born to Naomi!" They named him Obed; he was the father of Jesse, father of David.

The 19th-century Ukrainian biblical commentator Malbim teaches here:

> Naomi took the child. . . accordingly, she was his foster parent, and she carried him as a foster mother would her son, and the neighbors said that "A son is born to Naomi," for that is the truth: He is her son through Levirate marriage. . . His name was Oved (worker, worshipper) as he was destined to worship Hashem, and he was the father of Yishai (Jesse), from whom the Kingdom of David will come forth. . .[14]

Beyond the Torah, consider also how some of our greatest sages in the Talmud were foster children:

> When Rav Yosef heard his mother's footsteps, he would say, "I will stand before the arriving Divine Presence." Rabbi Yoḥanan said, "Fortunate is one who never saw his father and mother, as it is so difficult to honor them appropriately." Rabbi Yoḥanan himself never saw his parents. When his mother was pregnant with him, his father died; and when she gave birth to him, she died. And the same is true of Abaye.[15]

These are very sensitive matters, and we can all be as sensitive as possible in caring not only for these children but for the families supporting them. Perhaps the hardest part of fostering is letting go of the child once the child is ready to transition out of your home.

Thirty years in the future, I imagine myself walking down a busy street. All my children are now grown, perhaps with children of their own, and my wife and I are alone at home.

In this vision, I see myself on a business trip halfway across the country. As I make my way out of my hotel towards my destination, I lock eyes on

---

14. *Malbim on Ruth* 4:16–17

15. *Babylonian Talmud*, Kiddushin 31b

The Gemara asks: Is that so, that Abaye never saw his mother? But didn't Abaye say on many occasions, 'My mother told me?' The Gemara answers: That mother was actually his foster mother, not his birth mother.

a stranger—but something about him looks familiar. We exchange glances, but proceed with our busy lives. Yet I know I've seen those eyes before.

Being a foster parent means journeying on a challenging path. Besides all the normal tribulations of taking care of a child are the added burdens that each foster child carries with them. Given that most foster children are emerging from traumatic experiences of neglect and/or abuse during their early lives, it's a delicate task to simply offer unconditional love and support.

But besides these known challenges lie the challenges of the unknown: the unenviable task of learning how to detach after you've worked so hard to attach.

If you feel called, as I do, to provide care to a foster child, you treat that child like he or she is your biological child. You pour out all or your love, all your patience, all your care. But then, at a moment's notice, this child—a defenseless being—can be compelled by outside institutional forces to leave, hopefully to reunite with a biological family member. This is the goal, but also a foster parent's agony: We feel bonded and connected with a child whom we may hope to love forever.

And, in the passing of a moment, the child is gone.

Of course, the intended goal of fostering is usually reuniting biological family members with their children. Foster parents should, of course, be rooting for the success of the biological parents and hoping that they can fulfill the court's requirements to have their child return home. Nevertheless, there is a further level of pain if you feel the court's decision to return the child to its family was a premature decision, or worse.

In my family's experience, one of our foster children moved into a drug rehab facility. As wonderful as it was that the mother had become clean, it was hard to imagine the child living in that institution. I still grasp for answers, though they never seem to appear.

In my own experiences, I have not mastered the full spiritual art of learning to attach and detach from the children I have been fortunate to foster. But I have certainly grown.

The wisdom from Thích Nhất Hạnh, a Buddhist Zen master and peace activist, has been helpful. Looking at a pile of photographs of vulnerable children, he meditates until "I no longer see an 'I' who translates the sheets to help each child, I no longer see a child who received love and help. The child and I are one: no one pities; no one asks for help; no one helps. There is no task, no social work to be done, no compassion, no special wisdom."

Big questions reside in the practice of fostering a child: Am I the child's savior, or simply her caregiver? Am I this child's salvation, or only his temporary steward? Not seeing myself as the savior of this child is vital. Rather, in personal terms, these children always remain a part of my soul, whether they remain with me and my family or whether they return.

From my own Jewish tradition, there is a lot of wisdom around the two concepts of *emunah* (faith) and *bitachon* (trust). It is not a blind faith when we let the child go, nor is it a complete trust in the case plan. Instead, it is a cautious faith, a tentative trust. We never know for sure what is best for the child, but we try our hardest to place infinite trust in the process. We learn to let go. The love stays in our heart even though the child is no longer in our home. Rather than let go of such love, the task is to channel it toward our other children or a new foster child that arrives.

The truth is that in life, we will always have to let go. Whether it is dropping off a child at nursery school for the first time, or later at college, or moving far away from a sibling, or sitting at a loved one's death bed, there are valuable and difficult moments during our lives where we have to let our hearts be open even when we don't see someone as often as we'd like. It is a struggle to make yourself vulnerable. But "to love is to be vulnerable," as C.S. Lewis wrote. "Love anything and your heart will be wrung and possibly broken."

Indeed, we see our foster child and we let him see us. Should anyone of us be blessed to welcome a foster child into our home, may he or she come to love us and we come to love them. As Alfred Lord Tennyson once famously wrote, "'Tis better to have loved and lost than never to have loved at all."

Indeed, when the moments call for us to lay down our spiritual armor, all we can do is open our hearts and keep on serving.

And perhaps one day, I will pass a man in the street. Giving each other gentle smiles that one gives a stranger, neither of us will recognize the other. For that brief moment, our eyes lock. And I know I've seen these eyes before. And then, through a process that is not understood by the mundane mind, our souls will connect. Our souls will know that we once laid on the floor singing the alphabet together. That we enjoyed cuddling and exploring the vastness of the backyard. That we shared tears and laughter. That we shared happy times with kisses and hugs. This "soul truth" will be enough. And I pray every day that it will continue to be enough. In this passing moment, this stranger and I will be one. We will have lived different lives, but we will have a shared past. We may have forgotten each other's faces, but never each other's spirit. This love shall always endure.

#8

Temichut Kallah v'Chatan, Supporting the Bride and Groom

THERE IS A GREAT mitzvah of *simchat chatan v'kallah* (bringing joy to a groom and bride)[1]. There are many different ways to achieve this goal, of course. Some may support them financially or support indirectly through supporting a *gemach* (charitable institution where one might get a free wedding dress or suit or the like). Some give gifts.[2] Others will sing, dance, or say uplifting words at the wedding. One sage in the Talmud, Rav Shmuel ben Rav Yitzhak, would juggle myrtle twigs before the bride.[3]

A story is told of a modern *mussar* teacher:

> At weddings, R' Itzele was the life of the party. He danced on tabletops, sang, and composed rhymes in order to fulfill the *mitzvah* of making the bride and groom happy. Even at the Jerusalem *chupah* (the traditional Jewish canopy ceremony) of R' Naftali Amsterdam and his second wife, who were both in their seventies, R' Itzele did the same. When asked whether so much rejoicing was called for on this occasion, he answered, "In the *halachah* of rejoicing with a bride and groom, there is no difference whether the couple are twenty of seventy."[4]

1. *Babylonian Talmud*, Brachot 6b

2. In this manner, *simchat chatan v'kallah* is being fulfilled either leading up to the wedding or following it. Financial support and gifts can also be viewed as adding to the *simchah* of the wedding itself, as the couple can rejoice knowing that they are assisted in establishing their new home.

3. *Babylonian Talmnud*, Ketubot 17a

4. Zaitchik, *Sparks of Mussar*, p. 96

Based on the Talmud, our morning liturgy includes *hachnasat kallah* (providing for a bride) as one of the acts one will benefit from in this world and in the world to come.[5]

The rabbis suggest that one is being God-like when they attend a wedding and strive to bring joy to the couple. Why is this God-like? The rabbis explain that at the first wedding, between Adam and Eve, there was no one else there but God to celebrate. So too, we should emulate the Divine and rejoice with the couple. Afterall the religious goal of a wedding is not being overly lavish and spending a fortune but rather for the couple to feel the deepest joy at this lifecycle milestone and at this communal celebration of their love.

It might seem like this is only a positive *mitzvah*: one should support brides and grooms at their time of celebration, but the Chafetz Chayim teaches a powerful lesson about how there may be a negative *mitzvah* here as well.

> Rejoicing in your neighbor's joy.[6] Jewish sources cite helping a bride and groom as an example of how to fulfill this commandment. So seriously does Jewish law take this responsibility that the Chafetz Chayim's son recorded that his father told him that someone who attends a wedding and makes no effort to bring joy to the newly married couple—for example, through singing, dancing, and speaking warm words to them—is guilty of a form of stealing. The family making the wedding celebration spends a great deal of money and expects the guests to do what they can to make the bride and groom happy. Therefore, to attend a wedding feast and not try to bring joy is a transgression.[7]

Beit Hillel even thinks that pleasing a bride and groom is so important that we can even lie to do so.

> The Rabbis taught in a *baraita*:[8] How do we dance before the bride? [How do we praise the bride to the groom?] Beit Shammai says, "[We praise and describe] the bride as she is." But Beit Hillel says, "[In all cases we give praise and say] that the bride

5. *Babylonian Talmnud*, Shabbat 127a

6. This is a general *mitzvah*, not specific to a *chatan* and *kallah*.

7. Telushkin, *A Code of Jewish Ethics, Volume 2*, 27–28. In his book, Rabbi Telushkin cites: Cites Harvey, "Love," in Cohen and Mendes-Flohr, eds., *Contemporary Jewish Religious Thought*, 559

8. A *baraita* is similar to a *Mishnah*, although, for any number of reasons, is not included in the corpus of Mishnah. More often than not, this is due to the *baraita* expressing an idea already mentioned in a *Mishnah*, and would thus be redundant.

is pleasant and kind." Beit Shammai said to Beit Hillel, "Now, if she were lame or blind do we say about her that she is a beautiful and charming bride? But the Torah has said: 'Distance yourself from falsehood!'" Beit Hillel said to Beit Shammai, "According to your view, if someone made a bad purchase in the market [and he asked your opinion on the purchase, and he had no way of returning the item], should one praise it in the purchaser's eyes or denigrate it? Of course, you would say that one should praise it in his eyes. [We should therefore praise even a homely bride]."[9]

Another story is told of a great 20th-century rabbi who lied for the sake of honoring a bride and groom:

Reb Shlomo Zalman Auerbach[10] assumed the responsibility for rearing an orphan who lived in his neighborhood. . . .. When the boy was dating, he spoke to Reb Shlomo Zalman about the dilemma with which he was grappling. The relationship was getting serious and. . .the boy was short quite a bit from what her family held to be his share of the wedding expenses. He was reluctant to reveal the astronomical sum they were demanding. Reb Shlomo Zalman interrupted the troubled young man to apprise him of some good news. "If you are already speaking about money," he said, improvising, "you should know that I have been overseeing a fund all these years on your behalf. This fund now totals $5,500."

The boy could not believe his ears. Not only was this fund a windfall, but the amount of money in the account was precisely the sum he was missing. This young man had never divulged to anyone, including his benevolent 'foster father,' the figure that he was expected to provide. And the benevolent foster father never divulged the fact that until the day of that conversation, the 'fund' was nonexistent.[11]

So, why is this all so important? For the Torah, the family is the center of the world. More than a shul or school, the home is the center. The family is the foundation of our lives. To strengthen the Jewish people and strengthen the world, we need to strengthen the family unit. We want couples to get off on the right start. We want them to emerge with so much support and joy that they are elevated so high. Inevitably, relationships will have moments

9. *Babylonian Talmud*, Ketubot 16b-17a

10. Rabbi Shlomo Zalman Auerbach was considered one of the leading *halachic* authorities of his day.

11. Telushkin, *You Shall Be Holy*, 445

of decline, but the higher the couple's starting point, their decline will hopefully not go so low, due to such joyful formative experiences surrounding the wedding day, among many others to come afterward.

Furthermore, it is more important to help a couple prepare for a marriage than merely for the wedding. For this one reason, one might consider not only supporting a *chatan* and *kallah* for their wedding but also for the *shanah rishonah* (first year of marriage). This is yet another reason why gift giving, whether in the form of money or household items, is of great significance. Individual gifts, taken as a whole, will certainly go a long way towards accomplishing this goal.

The Torah drives this point home in instructing us that the groom is exempt in the first year of marriage from going to war.

> When a man has taken a bride, he shall not go out with the army or be assigned to it for any purpose; he shall be exempt one year for the sake of his household, to give happiness to the woman he has married.[12]

Similarly, many a *rosh yeshiva* (rabbinical head of a *yeshiva*) will instruct his newly married students that they should remain at home with their wives in the evening hours rather than spending that time in the *beit midrash* (study hall).

We also celebrate a couple so fully because we know how hard it is for a successful match to be made. One Talmudic source explains, perhaps hyperbolically:

> Rabbah bar Bar Chana said in the name of R' Yochanan: And it is (as) difficult (for G-d) to match up (a man and a woman for marriage) as it is to split the sea (to create a national relationship), as it is stated: 'G-d gathers individuals to a house. G-d releases prisoners at suitable moments.'[13]

Today it can often be even harder to find someone since the dating apps provide so many choices but also condition many toward hyper-particularity and a transactional sense of dispensability from the norms of the dating marketplace.

Now, the discussion up to this point as been heteronormative, but it seems clear to me, given how central the home and how central families are to Torah life, that we must also affirm homes and families for gay families. It seems equally clear to me that one hiding their sexual orientation and marrying someone they're not attracted to is forbidden, as it will ultimately lead

12. Deuteronomy 24:5
13. *Babylonian Talmud*, Sotah 2a

to suffering for both partners. It also seems clear to me that no one should be condemned to isolation, as that prevents their actualizing and establishing a family life they so desire and puts them at risk. So the only option left is that everyone who wishes should find a loving partner to build a home with and to try to build a family with.

In fact, the Talmudic sage Rav Nachman teaches that marriage is only secondarily about procreation and primarily about love and partnership.[14]

> Rav Nachman said in the name of Shmuel that even though a man has many children, he may not remain without a wife, as it says, 'It is not good that man be alone.' But others say that if he does have children then he may abstain from procreation and he may even abstain from taking a wife altogether.[15]

One Talmudic teaching shares that one is not missing only a little, but practically everything, when they cannot find a partner.

> R' Tanhum said in the name of R' Chanilai: Any man who does not have a wife lives without happiness, without blessing, and without goodness. . . In the west (Israel), without Torah and without a protective wall. . . .. Rava bar Ulla said, without peace.[16]

Marriage is considered a pathway to the Divine. For this reason, a marriage is also a *brit* (covenant). Rabbi Joseph Soloveitchik explains:

> The Bible equated the great historical covenant binding the charismatic community to G-d with the limited private covenant that unites two individuals in matrimony. On the one hand, the great covenant has been compared by the prophets time and again to the betrothal of Israel to G-d; on the other hand, the ordinary betrothal of woman to man has been raised to the level of covenantal commitment. Marriage as such is called *brit*, a covenant. Apparently, the Bible thinks that the redeeming power of marriage consists in personalizing the sexual experience, in having two strangers, both endowed with equal dignity and worth, meet. And the objective medium of attaining that meeting is the assumption of covenantal obligations which are based upon the principle of equality. Hence, we have a clue to the understanding of the nature of matrimony. All we have to

---

14. To be clear, Rav Nachman is referring to a hetero relationship. Nevertheless, the principle remains the same.

15. *Babylonian Talmud*, Yevamot 61b

16. *Babylonian Talmud*, Yevamot 62b

do is analyze the unique aspects of covenantal commitment and apply them to the matrimonial commitment.[17]

On the opposite end, we also talk about ourselves as marrying God. The following verse is recited upon wrapping the tefillin around one's finger in the morning, similar to how one might put on a wedding ring:

I will betroth you to Me forever, and I will betroth you to Me with righteousness, justice, kindness, and mercy. I will betroth you to Me with fidelity, and you shall know God.[18]

And so, we bring joy to those getting married for several reasons:

1. They matter! We want them to be happy and taken care of at this formative moment in their lives.

2. We want to emulate the Divine and be Godlike by bringing joy to those getting married just as God did with Adam and Eve.

3. We want to strengthen our community and the world, and by strengthening families, we can help to achieve that goal.

4. Lastly, we understand that the *brit* between those in love resembles the *brit* between humanity and God and the Jewish people and God. Strengthening commitment is itself a religious enterprise.

Mazal Tov to all who enter the covenant of marriage!

17. Soloveitchik, *Family Redeemed*, 41–42
18. Hoshea 2:21–22

#9

De'agah L'Almanot, Caring for Widows

TODAY, PEOPLE WITH MEANS have savings and often times life insurance policies too. Unless a family is in poverty, an *almanah* (widow) should not necessarily be completely broken financially. But in the ancient world, prior to retirement savings and life insurance policies, if only the man had the ability to work outside the home, a widow would often be left without a means to protect herself. For this reason, the Torah continues to emphasize and remind us of how much attention we must place on protecting the widow.

The Torah teaches, for example:

> You shall not ill-treat any widow or orphan. If you do mistreat them, I will heed their outcry as soon as they cry out to Me, and My anger shall blaze forth and I will put you to the sword; your own wives shall become widows and your children orphans.[1]

The *almanah* is commonly linked up with the other two most vulnerable categories of people in the Biblical ethos: the *geir* and the *yatom* (the stranger and the orphan). In the Midrash, Rabbi Yossi taught:

> Why does God love orphans and widows? It is because they have nobody to turn to except God, as it says, "A Father of orphans and a Judge of widows is God in God's holy dwelling."[2] Therefore, one who steals from them is considered to have

1. Exodus 22: 21–23
2. Psalms 68:6

stolen from God, because God is their Father in heaven and will get angry."[3]

But, interesting enough, the *mitzvah*, according to the Rambam (Maimonides), applies not only to the financially vulnerable, but to all *almanot*.[4]

> A person is obligated to show great care for orphans and widows because their spirits are very low and their feelings are depressed. This applies even if they are wealthy. We are commanded to [show this attention] even to a king's widow and his orphans, [as it is written,] "Do not mistreat any[5] widow or orphan."[6] How should one deal with them? One should only speak to them gently and treat them only with honor. One should not cause pain to their persons with [overbearing] work or aggravate their feelings with harsh words and [one should] show more consideration for their financial interests than for one's own. Anyone who vexes or angers them, hurts their feelings, oppresses them, or causes them financial loss, transgresses this prohibition. Surely this applies if one beats them or curses them. Even though [a person who violates] this prohibition is not [liable for] lashes, the retribution one suffers for its [violation] is explicitly stated in the Torah:[7] "I will display My anger and slay you with the sword."
>
> There is a covenant between them and the One who spoke and created the world that whenever they cry out because they have been wronged, they will be answered, as [the Torah] states:[8] "When they cry out to Me, I will surely hear their cry."[9]

It is interesting and instructive to note that Rabbi Samson Raphael Hirsch[10] suggests that the word *almanah* shares the same root as the word

---

3. *Shemot Rabba* 30:5

4. *Almanot* is the plural form of *almanah*.

5. Rambam deduces this from the seemingly extra word "any" in the original Hebrew verse. The verse reads: "*Kol almanah v'yatom lo te'anun*" (Any widow or orphan do not oppress.) The verse could have simply omitted the word "*kol*" and would thus translate as "A widow and orphan do not oppress." Furthermore, the word "*kol*" can also be translated as "every" (rather than "any"), indicating that every *almanah* is included regardless of her status.

6. Exodus 22:21

7. Exodus 22:23

8. Exodus 22: 22

9. Maimonides, *Mishneh Torah*, Hilchot De'ot, chapter 10

10. Rabbi Samson Raphael Hirsch was a 19th-century German philosopher, commentator, and grammarian.

ilem (a mute),[11] as a widow may feel she is not in a position to speak up or has no one to speak up on her behalf.

Perhaps the most well-known story of the proper treatment of an *almanah* in the Tanach[12] is the book of Ruth. There, we are dealing with not one, but three *almanot*. Often overlooked is the first example of dealing kindly with an *almanah*: Naomi's concern for the welfare of her daughters-in-law. As soon as she, herself a widow, decides to return to Israel, her homeland, she begs Ruth and Orpah, now widows themselves, to return to their mothers' homes, as there is nothing for them in Israel and they will only find hardship there. And once in Israel, Boaz's treatment of both Naomi and Ruth (Orpah had chosen to heed Naomi's advice and return to her home) is legendary.

Furthermore, it is instructive to note that Naomi's concern for the welfare of her daughters-in-law was emotional and social, not financial. Boaz, too, while going out of his way to look after Ruth's financial wellbeing (by instructing his lad to allow her to collect from his fields), was equally concerned for her emotional well-being. Perhaps the most glaring example of this is that Boaz did not chastise or embarrass Ruth when he discovered her sleeping at his feet. And Boaz's marriage to Ruth is a great paradigmatic act of compassion towards an *almanah*.

Another case of the Torah's concern for widows is found in the law of the levirate marriage (yibum).[13] To protect a widow from living alone and without children, if her husband died and she did not yet have children, her late husband's brother is obligated to marry her and care for her.[14]

It is not only in the ancient world that the widow is invoked as one of the most vulnerable categories of people for us to prioritize. Consider Abraham Lincoln's second inaugural address:

> *Both [parties to the war] read the same Bible and pray to the same God, and each invokes His aid against the other. . . The prayers of both could not be answered. That of neither has been answered fully. The Almighty has His own purposes. . . With toward none, with charity for all, with firmness in the right as God gives us to see the right, let us strive on to finish the work we are in, to bind up the nation's wounds, to care for him who shall have borne the*

11. The root of both words, according to Rav Hirsch, is comprised of the letters alef/lamed/mem.

12. Tanach is an acronym for Torah, Nevi'im, and Ketuvim, referring to the three sections of the Hebrew Bible, the Torah (Pentateuch), Prophets, and Holy Writings.

13. Deuteronomy 25:5–10

14. Today the levirate marriage has been fully replaced by *halitzah* (a way out of marrying one's brother-in-law).

battle and for his widow and his orphan, to do all which may achieve and cherish a just and lasting peace among ourselves and with all nations.[15]

Today, we are trying to learn how to recognize that truth, as a value has different valences in different contexts, and how to balance a religious commitment to truth with a social commitment to cultural and moral relativism.

Rav Shagar[16] grappled with this concept:

> Similarly, what is our position regarding *sati*, widow burning, which is still practiced by some in India[17]? From our perspective, this custom is extremely immoral[18], yet some women believe that burning themselves alongside their husbands' bodies is the best thing for the souls of all concerned. The perplexed postmodernist will have "double vision": While railing against the practice he will also be able to see the issue from the point of view of those who practice *sati*. . .To prevent postmodernism from sliding into absurdity, we must set boundaries. Where is the line at which the postmodernist will refuse to accept the other's values? What criteria and methods should be used for setting such boundaries? And can one propose other ways of coping with the paradox of pluralism, which is amplified in the postmodern era?. . . We no longer expect a grand, ultimate justice. Such a justice is unjustifiable and nowhere to be found. The best we can hope for is a specific, weak justice. That justice is generated not by a series of metaphysical arguments, but by human discourse and compromise. As Gurevitz emphasizes,[19] by letting go of the need for hard justice, two rival sides can begin to communicate and resolve profound conflicts pragmatically, by the constant contact struggle between conflicting conceptions of supreme justice. There are several possible models of soft justice, all relinquishing the presumption of absoluteness. Yet, he notes, soft justice has its own limits, and at bottom relies on non-relativistic assumptions, such as the belief in human rationality, whose absence would preclude fertile discourse and accord.[20]

15. Lincoln, "Second Inaugural," 1865

16. Rav Shagar was a 20th-21st century Jerusalem biblical scholar and religious postmodern thinker. Shagar is an acronym for his full name, Shimon Gershon Rosenberg.

17. Sati is associated with a particular caste and not with all Hindus.

18. Those who practice *sati* have a complicated relationship to outside opposition due to British colonialization and the opposition that emerged from the outside.

19. Gurevitz, "The Meaning of Justice in the Age of Frivolity," 167.

20. Rosenberg, *Faith Shattered and Restored: Judaism in the Postmodern Age*, 107—109.

Do we take the culturally tolerant view and respect different societies and their moral norms? Or do we embrace the human rights stance and defend widows?

I believe we must defend widows and find a collaborative way to empower locals in that society to uproot such an evil practice, so that it not be viewed as an outside cultural attack.[21]

The great prophet Isaiah taught: "Seek justice. Relieve the oppressed. Defend orphans. Plead for the widow."[22] This goes beyond financial needs. It means ensuring that those emotionally distressed should receive the attention and love that they need and deserve, as we saw above regarding the book of Ruth. We should seek out those grieving, especially in their later years when they may feel lonelier and more vulnerable, and find ways to show them patience and compassion.

---

21. Afterall, many who practice *sati* (as well as other forms of human sacrifice) believe that their way is not only just but the ultimate, selfless act a widow can take.

22. Isaiah 1:17

#10

Shalom Bayit, Maintaining Peace in the Home

IN JEWISH THOUGHT, THE home is a holy place and the center of our lives. Maintaining and preserving the integrity and sanctity of that home is of utmost importance.

The traditional reason for the importance of lighting Shabbat candles on Friday night was *shalom bayit* (peace in the home), referred to here in the Talmud as "*shalom beito*."[1]

> Rava said: It is obvious to me that there is a fixed list of priorities. When a person is poor and must choose between purchasing oil to light a Shabbat lamp for their home or purchasing oil to light a Hanukkah lamp, the Shabbat lamp for their home takes precedence. That is due to peace in their home; without the light of that lamp, their family would be sitting and eating their meal in the dark. Similarly, if there is a conflict between acquiring oil to light a lamp for their home and wine for the sanctification [*kiddush*] of Shabbat day, the lamp for their home takes precedence due to peace in their home.[2]

We may often have a desire to live our lives in a way that we believe to be authentic, according to our own personal wishes and values. But the rabbis teach that the value of peace in the home matters so much that it can, and at times should, override our personal wishes, and beyond that, even

---

1. The word "*beito*" is the possessive form of "*bayit*," and means "his home" or "one's home."

2. *Babylonian Talmud*, Shabbat 23b

take precedence over a *mitzvah d'rabbanan* (rabbinic *mitzvah*), as in the passage mentioned above.

Similarly, Rabbi Moshe Feinstein writes[3] that one may shave during the *sefirah* period of mourning if his spouse feels strongly about it, for the sake of *shalom bayit*. Rabbi Feinstein generally felt that one should refrain from shaving during this period absent a compelling need such as a job interview. That is to say that he felt this was an example of a strong Jewish custom being overridden in order to keep peace in the home.

The Book of Proverbs teaches:[4] "It is better to eat dry bread and live with peace than it is to enjoy a feast amidst contention."

The home is where we find comfort, an oasis from the tribulations of the outside world. In the home that each of us inhabits, we feel as if everything is under our control, our domain, our mercy. It is prime spot for reflection (and relaxation), but it's also another location in which to actualize holiness. We can see the potentiality of *the home* writ large—and the individual spot that each of us identifies as our home as well—to act as a portal to another realm; a means by which mundanity becomes spiritual and the spiritual becomes tangible.

Like any virtuous concept though, this one too can be misinterpreted. For example, some oppose divorce in the name of "peace in the home." Why would you disrupt your spouse and your children by getting divorced? However, this is a misunderstanding. A home is built on love and trust, and it would be a false peace to remain in a marriage where one (or both) partners were miserable and the relationship was irreparable. This is most certainly true in tragic cases of domestic violence. No one should ever suggest that "peace in the home" is the highest priority when one is at risk of violence or abuse.

Bracketing extreme cases, we generally seek to work out conflicts in the home, because virtually everything of value resides in it. As the soul is the domicile of the Divine essence, our homes are manifestations of our dreams, desires, and domestic needs. We must tend to them carefully, while also keeping them open. The heart of a healthy home is boundless love that is nurtured within it. An unhappy home affects every aspect of a person's life: career, relationships, spiritual life, and even health. Therefore, the nature of home life must be one of positivity, even if it cannot always be expressed to its fullest. So, if a person must cut back on personal pleasures

---

3. Feinstein, *Igrot Moshe*, Orach Chayim 5:120
4. Proverbs 17:1

in order to help bring peace to the home, the emotional investment can be so worthwhile.[5]

Towards this end, many *rashei yeshiva* (spiritual heads of a *yeshiva*) may exempt and perhaps even require newly married students to remain at home with their spouses during the late-night *seder* (study hour) for the first year of marriage, as the foundation of a home infused with *shalom bayit* begins with spouses being there for one another.

The rabbis taught that the Torah allows for the erasure of the holy name of God in order to restore peace to the home.[6] One can nullify a vow that can normally not be nullified, if it can further *shalom bayit*.[7]

The rabbis teach[8] that God lied to preserve shalom *bayit* in the home of Avraham and Sarah:

> It was taught in the school of Rabbi Yishmael: Great is peace, as even the Holy One be Blessed, departed from the truth for it. As initially it is written that Sarah said of Abraham: "And my lord is old" (Genesis 18:12), and in the end it is written that God told Abraham that Sarah said: "And I am old" (Genesis 18:13). God adjusted Sarah's words in order to spare Abraham hurt feelings that might lead Abraham and Sarah to quarrel.

We are told in Pirkei Avot:[9]

> Be like the students of Aaron, loving peace and pursuing peace, loving all creatures, and returning them to the Torah.[10]

Rabbi Ovadia of Bartenura[11] comments on these words that if two people were in an argument, Aaron would tell each of them privately that the other one felt badly and wished to be forgiven, thereby repairing the relationship between them.

---

5. While there are no guarantees of a desired outcome, the effort alone towards *shalom bayit* has the potential to go a long way in paving the path for the future positive home dynamic.

6. *Babylonian Talmud*, Chulin 141a; Nedarim 66b

7. Isserles, *Shulchan Arukh*, Yoreh Deah 228:21

8. *Babylonian Talmud*, Yevamot 65b

9. *Pirkei Avot*, literally meaning "chapters of the fathers," is the original Hebrew name of Ethics of Our Fathers, and contains a list of ethical teachings of the talmudic rabbis.

10. *Pirkei Avot* 1:12

11. Rabbi Ovadia of Bartenura was a 15th-century Italian scholar, perhaps most known for his commentary on the Mishnah.

The Torah teaches that when Aaron died, "they wept for Aaron for thirty days, the whole house of Israel."[12] Rashi taught[13] that this included everyone, the men and women. This could be contrasted with the death of Moshe where only *bnei Yisrael* (the men of Israel) mourned. This is because of Aaron's commitment to bringing peace between wives and husbands that everyone felt Aaron's peaceful presence.

Rabbi Yisrael Isserlin[14] taught that certain *mitzvot* (such as having more children) are superseded by the desire to have a peaceful family.[15]

When a couple gets married, we give them the blessing that they should build a "*bayit ne'eman b'Yyisrael*" (a faithful enduring Jewish home). We hope that they will work through tensions and disagreements in order to find peace and happiness together. And indeed, that is our task toward kindness—to help relieve the tensions of families around us to keep them happily together. We don't, ideally, want divorce or children removed to become foster children. We want, when safe and fruitful, for families to remain together. The Talmud teaches that when there is divorce, "the holy altar sheds tears."[16] The Talmud also teaches that divorce is "really difficult."[17] Just the process of divorce itself can be expensive, exhausting, infuriating, divisive, and lonely, not to mention the challenges of divorced life after the divorce has been complete. Further, we know that the children of divorced parents will suffer and have increased risks.[18]

Rabbi Yona Reiss, the current *av beit din* (head of the Jewish court) of the Chicago Rabbinical Council, however, reminds us that:

> If it is clear to a Bet Din (rabbinic court) that the marriage cannot be saved, then it is incumbent upon each party to cooperate with respect to a *get* (at the request of the other party).[19]

Peace in the Home also intersects with public security. Consider this teaching in the Torah:

---

12. Numbers 20:28–29

13. Rashi on Numbers 20:28–29

14. Rabbi Yisrael Isserlin was a 15th-century German Talmudic scholar, best known for his work *Terumat Hadeshen.*

15. *Terumat Hadeshen* 1:263

16. *Babylonian Talmud,* Gittin 90b

17. *Babylonian Talmud,* Sanhedrin 22a

18. See Robert Emery, *The Truth About Children and Divorce,* 64.

19. Reiss, Yona. "SHALOM BAYIT: THE PARADIGM OF THE PEACEFUL JEWISH MARRIAGE." See Rabbi Chaim Pelagi, *Chaim Ve'Shalom* 2:112; Rav Ovadiah Yosef, *Yabia Omer* 3:18 (13); Rabbi Moshe Feinstein, *Igrot Moshe,* Yoreh Dei'ah 4:15 (2).

> When you build a new house, you shall make a railing for your roof, so that you do not bring blood on your house if anyone should fall from it.[20]

One must turn their home and their property into a peaceful place by ensuring it cannot cause harm to others. This verse is applied to owning a violent pet as well:

> Rabbi Natan says: From where is it derived that one may not raise a vicious dog in their house, and that one may not set up an unstable ladder in their house? As it is stated: "You shall not bring blood on your house" (Deuteronomy 22:8), which means that one may not allow a hazardous situation to remain in his house.[21]

Shalom bayit, then, is as much about physical safety as it is about spiritual and emotional security.

One could easily extend this commitment to gun safety in our day, given the countless needless deaths from gun violence.

So, while *shalom bayit* is primarily about maintaining a joyful, respectful home with one's family, it should also inspire us to be sure that our home is peaceful and safe for those who enter it internally or encounter it externally. Lastly, we're taking for granted here that we're dealing with a situation in which there is a home at all. When there is no physical home to speak of, we must, all the more so, do all we can to ensure that others—the homeless, foster children, refugees, and the like—have homes that they can in turn make peaceful.

We are not learning about "shalom mishpacha" (peace of the family) but "shalom bayit" (peace of the home) and so this is about more than just family. One has an internal home where we can return to spiritual states, "homecomings." But also externally, we can think about the physical structure of "home." How can we rethink how we set up the house so that it brings us more peace? How can we clean and organize before Shabbat to bring more peace into Shabbat? We also have a beit midrash (study home), beit knesset (prayer home), beit hamikdash (holy home), communal "homes" to cultivate together. Even further, a "bayit" can be inter-spatial and inter-relational, creating a home between us in safe shared space.

May we dream of a day when everyone has a home to rest and thrive in, and that these homes emanate a peace that transforms our communities and societies at large.

20. Deuteronomy 22:8
21. *Babylonian Talmud*, Bava Kama 46a

#11

Hiddur Penei Zakein, Respecting the Elderly

IN AN AGE WHERE youth is so deeply celebrated, it can be easy to forget our traditional Jewish teachings regarding respecting the elderly. The Torah wants us to build a just society around our elders:

> Then God said to Moses, "Gather for Me seventy of Israel's elders of whom you recognize as elders and officers of the people, and bring them to the Tent of Meeting and let them take their place there with you.[1]

Of course, we also have the *mitzvah* of honoring our father and mother,[2] which is deeply connected to honoring elders as well. While this value can be found in countless places in the Torah's narrative, the most explicit command in the Torah is:

> Rise up before the elderly, and show respect before an aged; be fearful of your God, I am the Lord.[3]

The Talmud teaches here:

> The Rabbis taught: "Rise up before the presence of the elderly." Could this even be for a *zakein ashmai*[4] (ignorant older person)?

1. Numbers 11:16

2. Exodus 20:12; Leviticus 19:3

3. Leviticus 19:32

4. The term "*ashmai*" is related to the word "asheim" (guilty), and here is a reference to one who is "guilty" of being ignorant or unknowledgeable. This ambiguous term in the talmudic passage quoted here leads to a dispute we will address in the following paragraph.

The Torah says, "elder," and there is no elder other than a wise person, as it says, "Gather for me seventy men from the elders of Israel." Rabbi Yossi HaGalili said, there is no elder except for one who has acquired wisdom, as it says, "God made me as the beginning of God's way, the first of the Divine works of old."[5]

Does this *mitzvah* perhaps apply to a wicked elderly person as well? Regarding the term *zakein ashmai* in the above passage, Rashi comments that this refers to an evil and/or ignorant person. Rabbeinu Tam,[6] however, disagrees, and suggests that it refers only to one who is ignorant, but not wicked.[7]

The Shulchan Aruch supports honoring the ignorant elderly person but rejects honoring the evil elderly person:

It is a positive *mitzvah* to stand before every wise person, even if they are not old, unless they are (so young that they are) still nursing. And even if he is not his teacher, as long as [the sage] is greater than he, it is appropriate for him to learn from him. It is also a *mitzvah* to stand before somebody in their old age, who is [at least] seventy years old, even if he is an ignoramus, as long as he is not an evil person.[8]

A young person may unfortunately come to disrespect an elder with dementia or even with some basic memory loss. Those who care for the elderly with memory loss, be they children caring for their parents or professional care givers, are aware of just how easy it is to lose patience with such a person.[9] The Talmud cautions us against that:

Be mindful of the elderly person who has forgotten their teaching for reasons that are not their fault, as it says [in the Torah] that the broken tablets rested with the [newer] tablets in the ark.[10]

---

5. *Babylonian Talmud*, Kiddushin 32b

6. Rabbeinu Tam, a grandson of Rashi, is one of the most highly regarded Ashkenazi Tosafists. He is perhaps best known for his disagreement with Rashi as to the order of the four biblical passages placed in the *tefillin*.

7. Rabbeinu Tam supports his contention by noting that elsewhere in the Talmud we find that a wicked individual, regardless of his/her age, must be punished for their actions.

8. Karo, *Shulchan Aruch*, Yoreh Dei'ah, Laws of Respect for Your Teacher and Wise Students 244:1

9. Losing patience with an elderly person suffering from dementia is a violation of the *mitzvah* of respecting the elderly.

10. *Babylonian Talmud*, Brachot 8b

The assumption of the Torah seems to be that all elders will have wisdom to offer.

> Remember the days long gone by. Ponder the years of each generation. Ask your father and let him tell you; and your elder, who will explain it.[11]

Furthermore, the Book of Job teaches: "With age comes wisdom, and with length of days brings understanding."[12]

Of course, one can be young and wise and one can be old and foolish, but the assumption is that the more life we've seen and the more experience we have, the more wise a perspective we've been able to accumulate.

But this wisdom of the elderly is not simple. Does it mean that they have the wisdom to be optimistic or pessimistic? Cynical or hopeful? Ideological or pragmatic? More progressive or more conservative? Different elders will have such different viewpoints, and there will therefore be little consistency to the wisdom offered. For this reason, it is important to glean wisdom from as many elderly people as possible, not limited to, for example, one's parents or teachers.

A different approach as to why we must honor the elderly might not be only about their wisdom but about how much they have gone through in life:[13]

> Rabbi Yochanan would stand before the elderly Arameans and say, "How many troubles and experiences have passed over them!"[14]

One might honor the elderly not out of admiration but out of pity, sympathy, or empathy based on their past and perhaps current situation.

There's a powerful teaching in Pirkei Avot about learning and aging.

> Elisha ben Avuya said: One who studies Torah as a child, to what can they be likened? To ink written on fresh paper. And one who studies Torah as an old person, to what can they be likened? To ink written on smudged paper. Rabbi Yose bar Yehudah of Kfar HaBavli says: One who learns Torah from the young, to what can they be likened? To one who eats unripe grapes or drinks unfermented wine from their vat. But one who learns Torah from the old, to what can they be likened? To one

11. Deuteronomy 32:7

12. Job 12:12

13. Arguably, how much one has gone through in life influences the lens through which he/she views the world.

14. *Babylonian Talmud*, Kiddushin 33a

who eats ripe grapes or drinks aged wine. Rabi says: Do not look at the vessel, but what is in it; there is a new vessel filled with old wine and an old vessel that does not even contain new wine.[15]

There is also an entirely different reason to learn from the elderly. The Talmud teaches:

Rabbi Zeira said in the name of Raba bar Zimuna: If the earlier [scholars] were sons of angels, we are sons of men; and if the earlier [scholars] were sons of men, we are like donkeys.[16]

In other words, each generation is less knowledgeable than the previous one.[17] While this teaching may seem counterintuitive, and in many ways is not applicable, it is in fact of great value. After all, previous generations are closer to the original source of their teachings and/or historical events. Children of a Holocaust survivor, for example, may have heard a first-hand account of their parent's experience. The next generation, when hearing about it from their parents, by definition must rely on a second-hand account, and the next generation on a third-hand account. This of course applies to learning about one's own family history as well; my children, for example, will, by definition, know less about my grandparents than I do, simply because I am one generation closer to them.

We must make the best of every opportunity to learn from those emerging from a prior generation while we still have the chance to do so.

In the end, the midrash teaches that by welcoming and thereby honoring the elderly, it is as if we are encountering the Divine.[18]

And God models honoring the elderly in the Torah.

Abraham was now old, advanced in years, and God blessed Abraham with all things.[19]

And yet, many elders feel forsaken. Perhaps they don't have the financial security they had hoped for. Perhaps they never had children or their children have not been there for them in ways they have hoped.

---

15. *Pirkei Avot* 4:20

16. *Babylonian Talmud*, Shabbat 112b

17. This concept is referred to as *yeridat hadorot* (literally meaning "the decline of the generations"). This concept does not refer to advances in medicine or technology, for example, as each generation is more advanced in these areas than the previous one.

18. *Bereshit Rabbah*, Parshat Toldot 63

19. Genesis 24:1

Indeed, King David, in his own fear that humans would forsake him, felt he might turn to God: "Do not cast me off in old age; when my strength fails, do not forsake me!"[20]

Yes, we can display little acts of kindness to the elderly: We can help them across the street, rise in their presence to support them, open doors for them, etc. But we can also build vibrant communities that don't just show honor, but actually engage and recognize seniors in ways that are deeply meaningful to them.[21]

Honor should not solely be due to age but due to trust and virtue as well. Today, however, we see hostility between generations. Older generations often blame the "me generation" for being self-centered. Younger generations often blame the older generations for being racist and destroying the planet. Today, many young folks are willing to walk away from very important relationships because they are "toxic." Of course, one should protect oneself from abuse, but part of honoring elders is not just discarding them anytime we disagree with them, especially when they have sacrificed to raise us.

The last decades of one's life should not be isolating but joyful, and each of us can play our part in helping to make that happen.

20. Psalms 71:9

21. There are many societies where it is built into the culture, even required by law, that the elderly are respected. In Israel, for example, it is a law that individuals over the age of eighty need not wait in line for any services, governmental or otherwise. Similarly, one is required to give up their seat on a bus for the elderly. There are also several retirement communities where the residents themselves lead clubs, teach classes, and participate in synagogue services.

#12

Nichum Aveilim, Comforting Mourners

THE RABBIS TAUGHT[1] THAT Miriam was the provider of the Israelites' water. This miracle was accessible due to her merit, and when this righteous woman died, the miracle had stopped. The 16th-century rabbi Moshe Alshich explains that the Israelites lost the water because they failed to mourn Miriam.[2] Later in this chapter, Aaron dies, and "all the house of Israel bewailed Aaron thirty days."[3] And when Moses dies at the end of Book of Deuteronomy, it says, "And the Israelites bewailed Moses in the steppes of Moab for thirty days."[4] But when Miriam dies, the Torah doesn't say that anyone cried, and so the water of Miriam's merit dries up. The people didn't appreciate who she was.

The *mitzvah* of *nichum aveilim* (comforting mourners) is a quintessential form of kindness in Jewish thought. While of course mourners may need emotional support as soon as their beloved one passes away, and at times even prior to the actual death, the formal process of *nichum aveilim* begins after the burial of the deceased has been completed.[5] Pirkei Avot, for example, teaches: "Do not comfort your friend at a time when their deceased lies before them."[6]

1. *Babylonian Talmud*, Taanit 9a
2. Alshich on Torah, Numbers 20:29
3. Numbers 20:29
4. Deuteronomy 34:8
5. Until the burial is concluded, all funeral procedures, including eulogies and the recitation of Psalms and *kaddish*, while they may be, and should be, comforting and cathartic for the mourners, are actually a fulfillment of a separate *mitzvah* of *kavod hameit*, paying proper respect to the deceased.
6. *Pirkei Avot* 4:18

At the conclusion of a traditional burial, all present form a *shurah*[7] (consisting of two parallel rows) that begins that process as the family leaves the cemetery. The mourners pass through the *shurah*, and those present recite: "May *HaMakom* (the Omnipresent) console you together with everyone who mourns for Zion and Jerusalem."

When the mourners return home from the cemetery, they partake of a *se'udat havra'ah* (a meal of consolation). Others should provide the food for the *se'udat havra'ah*.[8] The reason for this is that one might feel too distracted or distraught to eat, and so we want to be sure we nourish them at that time.

The comforting process continues through *shivah*,[9] the first week of mourning. Oftentimes there will be a *minyan* at the *shivah* house, enabling the *aveilim* to recite *kaddish*.[10] Some comforters may wish to bring food to ensure the mourners have meals prepared for them. In many communities, meals are more formally organized for the entire week.

Comforting mourners is one of the ways that the Talmud explains we are to emulate God.[11]

> God comforts the mourning, as it is written: "And it was after the death of Avraham that God blessed Yitzchak (Isaac) his son."[12] So too must you comfort the mourning.[13]

Maimonides further teaches that one can fulfill the *mitzvah* of *v'ahavta l'rei'acha kamocha* (you shall love your fellows as yourself) through actions of comforting mourners. We might think then that we should comfort others in the way that we would want to be comforted. But that, of course, is not the case. Rather, we should comfort them the way that *they* want to be comforted.

The Shulchan Aruch offers us the traditional approach to not approaching the mourner at their shiva:

7. The word *shurah* literally means "line" or "row."

8. Karo, *Shulchan Aruch*, Yoreh Dei'ah 378:1

9. The term *shivah* comes from the same Hebrew word for the number seven, the number of days for which the process lasts.

10. An *aveil* may indeed attend services at the synagogue if a minyan does not take place in the home. It is best, however, for *aveilim* to remain at home when possible.

11. The idea of emulating God is based on the verse "This is my God and I will glorify Him" (Exodus 15:2). The Talmud relates that one of the ways to glorify God is by emulating His ways.

12. Genesis 25:11

13. *Babylonian Talmud*, Sotah 14a

The consolers are not to speak until the mourner speaks. The mourner sits at the front of the room, and once they nod to indicate that the consolers should leave, they are not permitted to remain any longer.[14]

Why should we give space? Dr. Ron Wolfson comments: "The great wisdom in this insight lies in allowing the mourner to focus on his or her grief, not on the social niceties of formal greetings."[15]

Mourning can be very sad. At the same time, it can be disorienting for many. It is easy to forget this. Comforters may have never lost someone in a way that completely shattered their world, and it may be hard to relate to the emotional processing another is going through.[16] It can also be a time of complicated emotions. Some may only feel sadness, others may feel relief, while some may be immersed in guilt and regret. Some might be thinking of memories. Others may be thinking about theology. While the Jewish tradition takes a humble stance on answering such questions, we surely shouldn't silence someone who is struggling. "It is not within our ability to understand the prosperity of the wicked or the sufferings of the righteous."[17]

The rabbis teach:

> Weep for the mourners and not for their loss, for [those who have passed] have gone to eternal rest, but we [those left behind to mourn] are suffering.[18]

At the same time, while Jewish tradition understands the primary goal of comforting mourners as an act of kindness to the living, it is also considered an act of respect towards the deceased. A comforter should of course seek the right balance, and, as we mentioned above, must honor the wishes of the mourner while paying respect to the relative they are mourning. A comforter may think, for example, that it is appropriate to share a fond memory of the deceased, but the *aveil* may not be interested in memories at

14. *Shulchan Aruch*, Yoreh Dei'ah 376:1. Also see Babylonian Talmud, Mo'ed Kattan 28b

15. Wolfson, *Time to Mourn, A Time to Comfort*, 206

16. It is precisely for this reason that *Pirkei Avot* teaches: "Do not judge another until you reach his/her place" (*Pirkei* Avot 4:2). Rabbi Ahron Soloveichik (the founding *rosh yeshiva* of Yeshivas Brisk, Chicago, and brother of Rabbi Joseph B. Soloveitchik) explained, as reported by his student Rabbi Avram Herzog, that here we are reminded that we never truly know what another is going through. One's loss of a parent, for example, may be quite different from another's loss of a parent, as there are many variables at play. One should be mindful of this teaching of Rabbi Soloveichik when engaging in *nichum aveilim*.

17. *Pirkei Avot* 4:15

18. *Babylonian Talmud*, Moed Kattan 25b

that particular moment.[19] One must be sensitive to the needs and desires of the mourners at all times.

While all of this is true for how we support Jewish mourners, the Talmud teaches that one should comfort and visit non-Jewish mourners as well.[20]

In addition, it is not only a privilege to invite others into one's mourning, but a responsibility as well. A mourner can and should give others the chance to fulfill the *mitzvah* of *nichum aveilim*. In keeping with the theme of sensitivity to the mourners discussed above, the *aveilim* may wish to publicize a schedule of hours for visiting hours in order to give them time to eat their meals, wake up and go to sleep when they choose, or simply have needed alone time for themselves.

One rabbi traces the responsibility to be comforted all the way back to the beginning of the world.

> (After Rabbi Yochanan ben Zakkai's son died), Rabbi Eliezer said: "Adam had a son (Abel) who died, yet he allowed himself to be comforted. And how do we know that he allowed himself to be comforted? For it is said, 'And Adam knew his wife again'" (and they had another son).[21] You too must let yourself be comforted.[22]

As mentioned above, as comforters take leave of the mourners, they refer to God as *HaMakom* (the Place). One reason for this is because God is omnipresent. Another explanation is that we, as people, are to cultivate a "space" where Divinity can be felt; a healing "space" where one feels less alone.

There is yet another beautiful reason provided for referring to God as *HaMakom*. Rabbi Joseph B. Soloveitchik suggests[23] that we refer to God as *HaMakom* precisely when one may think that God is in no place, that God is simply absent. The mourner may reason, "Where is God? How could God take my beloved?" At such a time, Rav Soloveitchik explains, we tell

---

19. Similarly, while when sitting *shivah* mourners are technically not supposed to stand for a comforter as they arrive or depart, even a close friend or important figure, at the same time one should not correct a mourner who does so. Sensitivity to the mourner and his/her state of mind outweighs the technical execution of such minutiae.

20. Karo, *Shulchan Aruch*, Yoreh Dei'ah 367:1

21. Genesis 4:25

22. *Avot d'Rebbe Natan* 14:6

23. This thought of Rabbi Joseph B. Soloveitchik has been shared orally by many of his students. It is also recorded in Rabbi Yosef Adler's haggadah, a haggadah with commentary based on the teachings of Rabbi Soloveitchik.

the mourner that while it may seem that God is no place, in fact God is out there some place. The mourner may not be feeling that right now, but the very knowledge that God is indeed out there some place may provide some level of comfort.

We learn from the Book of Job that we are to sit with mourners rather than stand in their presence.

> When they saw him (Job) from a distance. . .they broke into loud weeping; each one tore their robe and threw dust into the air [and] onto their head. They sat with him on the ground for seven days and seven nights. None spoke a word to him, for they saw how very great was his suffering.[24]

It is important for family, friends and community members to be deeply supportive and responsive. It's also important to remember that people can say and do otherwise abnormal things in times of pain.

The Talmud teaches:

> A person is not held responsible for what they say while in pain.[25]

Still, it is also important for mourners themselves to try as best as possible to not be judgmental of others who don't make it to the *shivah* house or who show up in ways that may rub the mourners the wrong way.

One of the reasons that we want to fully embrace the burial, the *shivah*, the *shloshim*, *kaddish*, and the year-long *aveilut* for parents, etc., is that our tradition wants us to stop there. Yes, there is an annual *yahrtzeit*, but we need to get back to life, and ultimately be strengthened, not weakened, by our loss. The rabbis instructed us not to add on to the periods of mourning.[26] The best way to not add, the rabbis believed, is to max out the spiritual opportunities of grieving, remembering, and celebrating within the cycle structure we've inherited.

Life is all too short, and death, no matter how prepared one can be,[27] is all too startling. As humans, we strive to make meaning of our lives and deaths, and as Jews, we add a rich tradition of wisdom to that inquiry and search process. There is no one right way to feel, no one right way to mourn and grieve, and there is no one right way to offer comfort. Each of us can cultivate the emotional intelligence and the spiritual imagination to

24. Job 2:11–13

25. *Babylonian Talmud*, Bava Batra 16b

26. *Babylonian Talmud*, Mo'eid Katan 27b; Karo, *Shulchan Aruch*, Yoreh Dei'ah 394:1

27. In truth, many who have lost a relative will attest to the fact that they thought they were ready and prepared, and only upon the death realize that they in fact were not. It may be true that one is never fully prepared for a relative to die.

creatively offer the best of what we have to offer. It doesn't all have to be at a graveside or during *shivah*. We have weeks, months, and years to be of support to others. Mourning is not a one week or one year journey but a lifetime journey. My teacher Rabbi Avi Weiss shared a helpful way for me to think of it. When your parent dies, a light goes off in your home. That light never turns back on, but over time, you learn how to get around in the dark.

May we all be comforters and may we all be comforted.

#13

Diyun L'Chaf Zechut, Judging Favorably

WE NOW TRANSITION FROM our first section about "kindness to specific individuals" to this new section about "kindness to all individuals." Kindness to everyone is quite difficult, because we simply may feel more attracted toward helping some people over others. The word "kindness," some linguists have suggested, emerges from the old English word *cynd*, which refers to kinship. It is easier to be kind to our kin. A psychologist in the UK, Penelope Campling, wrote: "Kindness implies the recognition of being of the same nature as others, being of a kind, in kinship. . .It implies that people are motivated by that recognition to cooperate, to treat others as members of the family, to be generous and thoughtful."[1]

Taking care of one's parent when sick, helping one's neighbor when their car is stuck, listening empathetically to one's child after a hard day, these are exhausting but perhaps natural. It is our nature to take care of those in our most inner circles. When it comes to showing kindness toward those who are not our "kin," or our "kind," this can be more challenging. Yes, we all know how to hold a door for a stranger, or say hello to a passerby, or make an online donation to a group of vulnerable people, but deep, radical kindness for strangers? That's more difficult.

Albert Einstein writes:

> A human being is a part of the whole, called by us [the] "Universe," a part limited in time and space. He experiences himself, his thoughts and feelings as something separated from the rest — a kind of optical delusion of his consciousness. This delusion

---

1. Campling, "Reforming the culture of healthcare: the case for intelligent kindness." (BJPsych Bulletin)

is a kind of prison for us, restricting us to our personal desires and to affection for a few persons nearest to us. Our task must be to free ourselves from this prison by widening our circle of compassion to embrace all living creatures and the whole of nature in its beauty. Nobody is able to achieve this completely, but the striving for such achievement is in itself a part of the liberation and a foundation for inner security.[2]

In this new section, we won't look at actions that make the news: an anonymous $50,000 gift to a homeless person, or a family who adopts five vulnerable siblings, and the like. We will look at the humble every day, indeed every moment opportunities that we are presented with. Perhaps the most humbling place to start is "judging favorably," because each of us fails at this daily, some in small unnoticeable ways and others in catastrophic ways.

In the Torah, we learn that when we sit in judgment, we should do so "with righteousness."

> You should not commit a distortion of justice [as a judge in court]. You should not favor the poor, nor honor the great. With righteousness you should judge your fellow.[3]

Based on this verse, the Talmud teaches us to be *dan l'chaf zechut* (to give the benefit of the doubt to others):

> "With righteousness you must judge your fellow"[4]—This means that you should judge your fellow favorably.[5]

Rashi comments here:

> "Judge your fellow favorably"—This does not refer to judging litigants in court. Rather, it refers to someone who observes another person doing an action that could be interpreted as either a wrongdoing or as a neutral act. You should not suspect him of a wrongdoing; rather, assume he is innocent.[6]

For the Sefer HaChinuch,[7] this applies not only in the social realm but also in the courtroom. His view could be taken as a step beyond the idea of being "innocent until proven guilty." In his words:

2. Sullivan, Walter. "The Einstein Papers. A Man of Many Parts." (New York Times)
3. Leviticus 19:15.
4. Ibid.
5. *Babylonian Talmud*, Shavuot 30a.
6. Rashi on Talmud, Shavuot 30a.
7. *Sefer HaChinuch*, literally meaning "a book of education" or "a book of direction"

> There is a mitzvah to judge with righteousness . . . which means treating the litigants fairly and equally . . .[8]

To presume that someone is innocent until proven guilty is to recognize the importance of the *Talmudic* dictum *hamotzi meichaveiro alav hara'aya* (if one wants to take from another, the proof is upon that person). That is, someone who wants to prove that someone else is guilty or liable—a plaintiff in a civil case or the prosecution in a criminal matter—bears the burden of proof. To view someone's actions always in a positive light adds another layer of favorable treatment.

For some commentators, there is an interesting intersection between justice and love.

> If one truly loves another as a father loves a son, he will very naturally have a positive outlook toward that person. He will see everything that person does in a positive light and judge him positively.
>
> Thus, the *mitzvah* of judging positively is really an outgrowth of the *mitzvah* to "love your fellow as yourself." The extent to which one judges others positively is a good indicator of his love for others.[9]

For this *mussar* teacher, judging favorably is about loving others. The spiritual shift required here is to move from just observing an action to inspiring oneself to assume that another person's actions are motivated by positive inclinations. Similarly, Rabbi Shlomo Wolbe[10] taught:

> Someone who judges others favorably *really hopes* that his fellow man is guiltless. He seeks ways of understanding the other's actions as good.
>
> This is the extent to which one must regard another person with a positive attitude, and wish to see his actions as issuing from a good source. . . This is the opposite of what most people usually do, which is to immediately notice another person's shortcomings and ignore his strong points.[11]

---

is of anonymous authorship, written in 13th-century Spain. It lists the biblical *mitzvot* in the order of their appearance in the Torah, and attempts to provide a rationale for each *mitzvah*.

8. *Sefer HaChinuch*, Mitzvah 235.

9. Rabbi Dovid Kronglass, *Sichot Chochmah U'Mussar*, Vol. I, 82.

10. Rabbi Shlomo Wolbe was a 20th-century teacher of the *mussar* movement. He lectured at Yeshivas Be'er Ya'akov as well as others.

11. Rabbi Shlomo Wolbe, *Alei Shur*, Vol. II, p. 207.

This idea of judging others favorably has precedent in the *Mishnaic* tractate Pirkei Avot (Ethics of the Fathers).

> Yehoshua ben Perachya says, "Establish a rabbi for yourself, acquire a friend, and judge every person favorably."[12]

Rambam (Maimonides) comments here:

> "Judge every person favorably"—This refers to someone whom you do not know, and therefore cannot tell if he is a *tzaddik* [an upright person] or *rasha* [habitual wrongdoer].
>
> In such a case, if you see him doing something or saying something that could be interpreted in two ways, one good and one bad, you should give him the benefit of the doubt and assume the action was good . . . This approach is praiseworthy.[13]

Rambam is addressing three categories: Someone we know to be righteous; someone we know to be wicked; and someone we do not know at all. When it comes to the third category, someone we do not know, that is where we need to make this leap toward "the benefit of the doubt."

On the other hand, we have another teaching from Pirkei Avot on this matter:

> "Do not judge your fellow until you have reached their place."[14]

This source does not seem to distinguish between the righteous and the wicked. Rather, we are not positioned to be judgmental at all since everyone is different, in a different place, at a different time, with different genes, a different background, and in a unique scenario. Human perspectives and experiences are so radically diverse[15] that we might never be able to fully understand one another, and therefore should try to refrain from judging each other.[16]

The commentator Rabbi Ovadia of Bartenura[17] limits this to a specific challenge:

12. *Pirkei Avot* 1:6.

13. Rambam on *Pirkei Avot* 1:6.

14. *Pirkei Avot* 2:4

15. When trying to console another, it is not uncommon to hear one saying, "I know what you're going through." In truth, as well meaning as the friend may be, he/she cannot truly know what the other is going through. There are simply too many variables for two seemingly equal experiences to actually be equal.

16. Of course, a judge and jury are called upon to do just that, but every precaution should and must be taken to judge favorably and honestly.

17. Rabbi Ovadia (of) Bartenura is best known for his commentary to the Mishnah. He is also known by his acronym, Ra'av.

If you see someone else fail a challenge, do not judge him until you have undergone the same challenge and overcome it.[18]

Rabbi Yehoshua Leib Diskin[19] offers a brilliant psychological insight here about how judging others favorably not only is more empathetic to others but how it also helps keep our own behavior in check and holds *us* accountable.

> [Consider the following:] A town has ten Jewish people living in it. If one person commits a transgression, he breaks down the fence of embarrassment, which had prevented people from sinning until now. If a second person sins, he does not need to break this barrier, and he does not need as much brazenness, because the second person is only sinning in front of eight others, and he has [the other sinner as] his accomplice. If a third person sins, he [requires] even less brazenness...
>
> ... In telling us to "judge every person positively" (Pirkei Avot 1:6) the Sages are giving us wise advice. This advice is in order that we should not break down the internal barriers of embarrassment that hold us back from transgressions. When we view every person as being righteous, then we will hold ourselves back from transgressing [since we will think that no one else is transgressing, so how could we be the first?!] However, when one sees the negative in every person, then he is likely to stumble [since he will think others are transgressing, and therefore it becomes more acceptable in his mind to transgress].[20]

We can now shed light on the *mitzvah* of tending to the needs and burial of the deceased. It is only this particular *mitzvah* that is referred to as *chessed shel emet* (true, or completely pure, kindness). This *chessed* is traditionally explained as *emet* because it simply cannot be repaid by the deceased. Perhaps we can add another meaning to *chessed shel emet*. Every person, upon their death, is entitled to, and receives, the same treatment. There is no distinction between one individual and the next. Tending to the burial and other rites of the deceased, then, compels us to set aside any preconceived judgment of the individual, and in that sense is kindness in its purest form.

For the Sefer HaChinuch, there is a related but different goal here: to build community.

18. Rabbi Ovadia Bartenura's commentary on *Pirkei Avot* 2:4.

19. Rabbi Yehoshua Leib Diskin was a 19th-century Talmudist. Born in Belarus, he served as a rabbi in many communities, culminating in Israel.

20. Rabbi Yehoshua Leib Diskin (Maharil Diskin), *Teshuvot Maharil*, end of Vol. I

> The *mitzvah* of judging favorably serves as a catalyst for achiev-
> ing peace and friendship between people.
>
> Therefore, the main purpose of this *mitzvah* is to direct
> communities in establishing fair judicial systems, and to bring
> peace between them, by removing the suspicion between one
> person and another . . .[21]

By judging favorably, we develop social trust, foster positivity, and
build a more peaceful coexistence.

For Rambam, this should be a priority for a learned person who will
be serving as a public model.

> A scholar should not shout like an animal when he speaks with
> people. Neither should he raise his voice. Rather, he should
> speak calmly with everyone . . .
>
> He should make sure to take the initiative to greet every-
> one first, so that he is pleasant to be around. He should judge
> people positively, and speak favorably about others, never
> speaking negatively of them. He should love and pursue peace
> . . . In general, he should always speak words of wisdom and
> loving-kindness.[22]

Another theological layer informs how we should treat others. The
Talmud teaches:

> If one judges one's fellow positively, they will be judged posi-
> tively by the Omnipresent."[23]

The way that we judge will determine the way that God judges us. The
Ba'al Shem Tov takes this approach to another whole level:

> We have a tradition that no verdict is ever passed on a person
> until he himself issues that verdict. How so? The person is
> shown someone else doing what he himself is guilty of, and his
> reaction to that person's flaw is what determines the judgment
> of his own misdeeds.[24]

For the Ba'al Shem Tov,[25] every moment and activity, as well as its
interpretation, is about both others and us. It is all intertwined. Everything

---

21. *Sefer HaChinuch*, Mitzvah 235

22. Maimonides, *Yad Hachazakah*, Hilchot Dei'ot (Laws of Conduct) 5:7

23. *Babylonian Talmud*, Shabbat 127b. Also see Chafetz Chaim, *Shmirat HaLashon*,
Sha'ar HaTevunah, Chapter 4

24. *Ba'al Shem Tov Al HaTorah*, Vayikra 19:15.

25. The title Ba'al Shem Tov, to whom the approach underlying the modern Hasidic

comes back to our interpretation and to our personal reality (i.e., the way we judge external events affects the internal events that occur to us).

For Rabbi Moshe Cordovero,[26] this is less about self-interest and self-protection; rather, it's about Divine emulation. God restricts Divine harsh judgement, and so should we. God is merciful, and we should be too.[27]

So, a very strong case can be made for not being judgmental. Clearly, it is an important spiritual way to live. On the other hand, we are called upon to be advocates for justice, to be discerning about good vs. evil, and to speak out against evil. We are to learn how to identify the righteous from the wicked, and we are bidden to associate with the righteous and to distance ourselves from the wicked. We are to prevent moral boundaries from being crossed and to speak out to advocate for the downtrodden. We must assess and judge fairly but also critically. Only if we can judge injustice done by others and learn from it, can we be aware of what we must guard ourselves from.

So how do we hold a spiritual consciousness of being non-judgmental alongside a social justice consciousness of being a public ambassador for what is just, thereby providing a critique of what is unjust? The answer to this seeming paradox is that we must slow down and not bandwagon on rapid social shaming and jump on campaigns without facts. It means we must not equate not liking someone with them being evil. It means that we cannot and must not confuse ideological diversity with a stark categorization of people as good and evil. Perhaps we can be suspicious of those whose attitudes and actions harm others, but at the same time we must try to give the benefit of the doubt to everyone who deserves it.

There is a lot at stake here: how we are to judge others fairly; our own spiritual health; the way we ourselves will be judged; and how we can sustain communities and society. We will need to take stock of our defense mechanisms of fearing our own judgment and thus channeling that fear by turning our judgement upon others. In addition to healing ourselves with less judgement, we can heal our relationships by ensuring others feel less judged. This intellectual and spiritual work is some of the most challenging, yet most elevating, we will encounter.

Let us always be mindful of being *dan l'chaf zechut*. We must make that our endeavor. We must rise to the occasion.

---

movement is attributed, literally means "one of a good name." He is also known by his acronym, Besht.

26. Rabbi Moshe Cordovero was an influential 16th-century kabbalist in Safed.

27. Cordovero, *Tomer Devorah* Ch. 1, Eighth Attribute.

#14

Dibbur Yafeh, Speaking Kindly

HERE WE RETURN TO the basics. Virtually every child is taught not to hit other children and to use kind words such as "please" and "thank you." But few are taught the nuances of the full power of speech to destroy or redeem others, to tear down or build up.

For the Talmudic rabbis, Divine speech has enormous power. In the creation story, we see God speak and a world created,[1] and so they teach: "The world was created through ten statements."[2] Human speech is to be used cautiously and creatively modeled off this Divine speech.

Some rabbis teach that the above insight regarding creation was not merely a historical phenomenon but is still in place today. Rabbi Chaim of Volozhin[3] taught:[4]

> Each one of God's statements during Creation is the soul and life-force of the thing that was created with it. All the various species or types of that thing, as well as the *mazalot* (constellations) and angels in charge of that thing [are also brought into being through these statements].
>
> From the moment of the original Creation throughout all of history until the present time, the word of God keeps all things in existence every moment and in all different situations . . . We are not sensitive to this phenomenon, since we only see with physical eyes.

1. Genesis 1:1–29

2. *Pirkei Avot* 5:1

3. Rabbi Chaim of Volozhin was a 19th-century Lithuanian scholar and founded the famed Yeshiva of Volozhin, from which many noted rabbis emerged.

4. *Nefesh HaChaim* 3:11

Onkelos,[5] the great Talmudic-era translator and commentator, translated the culmination of the creation of man episode, *Vayehi ha'adam l'nefesh chayah* (literally meaning "man became a living being")[6] as "man became "a speaking being."[7] Humans are beings of mind, body, and soul, but for Onkolos, it is our capacity for speech which was so unique to our creation. Judaism is a very speech-oriented religion as there is such heavy emphasis upon prayer, Torah study, and the ethics of speech. Rashi, following Onkelos' translation, emphasizes that the most significant difference between humans and other creatures is the power of speech.

The Maharal[8] expands on this idea and writes that the essence of a human is not found in body or in soul, but in our power of speech, since it's a place where body and soul meet.[9] For the Maharal, like Rashi and Onkelos, it is the capacity for speech that makes us uniquely human. Angels have souls but no bodies. Animals have bodies but lower souls. But humans, through speech, play a unique role in the Divine plan for creation.

Human speech, indeed a gift from God, has enormous power. We know for example that the spiritual union of a husband and wife is not completed until the verbal recitation of the *sheva brachot* (seven blessings under the *chuppah*). The Mishnah states:[10] "A bride is forbidden to her husband until the *sheva berachot* are recited."

Also, consider the power of *nedarim* (verbal vows). The Torah teaches:

> Moshe spoke to the heads of the tribes of the Children of Israel saying, "This is the thing that God has commanded: If a man takes a vow to God or swears an oath to establish a prohibition upon himself, he shall not violate his word. According to whatever comes from his mouth shall he do."[11]

Similarly, King Solomon wisely advised in Ecclesiastes:

> It is better not to take a vow than to take a vow and not fulfill it.

---

5. It is fascinating to note that while Onkelos was a convert, it is his translation of the Torah (into Aramaic) that made its way into the Shulchan Aruch (the 16th-century Code of Jewish Law). The Shulchan Aruch writes that one is required to read the weekly Torah portion twice, along with the translation of Onkelos. While today Aramaic is no longer the vernacular for most, many still maintain this practice, either instead of or in addition to reading a modern-day translation in their vernacular.

6. Genesis 2:7

7. Onkeles on Genesis 2:7

8. Maharal, Rabbi Yehudah Loew, was a 17th-century Polish mystic and philosopher.

9. *Netivot Olam*, Netiv HaLashon, chapter 2, first paragraph.

10. *Mishnah* Tractate Kallah 1:1

11. Numbers 30:2–3

There are Jewish laws around *shemirat halashon* (guarding the tongue) too. For example, we must avoid *lashon hara* (evil speech) and *rechilut* (tale bearing). The Jerusalem Talmud couldn't make clearer how serious this is:

> There are four transgressions for which one pays in this world and in the next: idolatry, sexual immorality, and murder.[12] And *lashon hara* is equivalent in severity to them all.[13]

Psalms advises us that guarding our tongue from evil speech is the pathway toward life and blessing.

> Who is the one who desires life, who loves days of seeing good? [If this is what you desire,] Guard your tongue from evil, and your lips from speaking deceit.[14]

The Rambam teaches[15] about the damage of speech that causes shame or pain to another:

> We are instructed not to engage in *ona'at devarim,* causing emotional distress to each other with our words. This includes statements that cause another person pain, anger, or embarrassment. . .
>
> The source in the Torah is, 'Do not aggrieve your fellow, and you shall fear your God' (Leviticus 25:17). The Talmud tells us that the verse is referring to causing emotional distress with our words.

But in addition to avoiding inappropriate speech, what about actively thinking about kind speech?

Shem MiShmuel teaches:[16]

> According to Rabbeinu Yonah,[17] if one guards their tongue and is careful about what they say, then their mouth is considered to be a holy vessel [on par with the vessels used in the Temple]. Just like a holy vessel confers holiness upon whatever [non-holy] item is placed in it, so too all words that are issued from such a mouth are holy.

---

12. Idolatry, sexual immorality, and murder are the three cardinal sins for which one must give up his/her life rather than transgress them.

13. *Jerusalem Talmud,* Pe'ah 1:1

14. Psalm 34:13–14

15. *Sefer HaMitzvot,* negative mitzvah 251

16. *Shem MiShmuel,* Parshat Matot, 5670

17. Rabbeinu on *Pirkei Avot* 1:17

It is so easy to see the negative in everything and in everyone around us. Our brains almost seem hardwired to focus on problems and to think critically about everything and everyone. Rabbeinu Yonah further taught,[18] however, that a righteous person will work to see the positive in everything.

> 'And amongst upright people, [one can find] acceptance,'[19] because a righteous person covers over people's shortcomings and always praises whatever is deserving of praise . . . It is related that once a wise man and another individual were walking together when they came across a carcass. The latter commented, "How disgusting is this carcass!" The wise man countered, "How white are its teeth!"

So how can we get there? For starters, we are implored to constantly remember one of the most central teachings of Jewish ethics:

> "And you shall love your fellow as you love yourself; I am God."[20]
> This is taught to be a central principle of the Torah.[21]

Similarly, the Talmud tells a fascinating story:

> The story is told of a gentile who approached Shammai. He said to him: 'Convert me on the condition that you teach me the entire Torah while I stand on one foot.' Shammai pushed him aside with a building beam he had in his hand. [The gentile] came before Hillel, [and Hillel] converted him. [Hillel] instructed him: 'What is despised by you, do not do to another. That is the entire Torah; the rest is explanation. [Now] go and study.[22]

The Sefer HaChinuch directly connects the above teaching to how we use speech.[23]

Perhaps, before seeing the good in all, we'll need to practice removing our anger and critique of all. The 20th-century *mussar* teacher, Rabbi Shlomo Wolbe, suggested the following formula towards achieving this goal:[24]

> We will train ourselves to be patient. We will fix a specific amount of time every day—for example, approximately fifteen minutes—in which we will strive to bear with patience all that

18. *Sha'arei Teshuvah* 3:217
19. Proverbs 14:9
20. Leviticus 19:18
21. *Midrash Sifra* 2:12
22. *Babylonian Talmud*, Shabbat 31a
23. *Sefer HaChinuch*, Mitzvah 243
24. Wolbe, *Alei Shur*, Vol. II, p. 215

we see and hear, even when things may be upsetting to us, and even if they are hurtful to us, without losing our composure at all. In cases where it is necessary or obligatory to react, we will do so with measured, calm words, without becoming overly emotional.

It is instructive to note that Rabbi Wolbe stresses the importance of improving our behavior towards others with small steps. An all-or-nothing approach to changing our behavior is not only not necessary, but usually does not work. A healthy approach, by which we can achieve our goal, is to begin with a mere fifteen minutes each day, increasing that timeframe steadily.

We can think more carefully about how we use our speech with others at home, socially, at work, in stores, and of course on social media. We should create a plan each day for how we'll speak in ways that help others, comfort others, empower others, and bring dignity to others. It will require more than a vague commitment. Indeed, this practice is an art and skill that needs to cultivated daily to ensure we can lift up others through our speech.

The contemporary author and educator Dasee Berkowitz shares a teaching from the Sefat Emet about how we experience our voices and the voices of others.[25]

> There's a teaching by the Sefat Emet,[26] a Hasidic master from the nineteenth century, on the difference between speech (*dibur*), and voice (*kol*). With speech we can express ideas, feelings, and practical communication. We say "Well done!" to a colleague and "I love you" to our children. We also say firm words such as "No, not now!" when we want to set a boundary. Speech is important. It allows us to communicate; it's efficient. But it can also be insufficient.

Words alone cannot convey the fullness of what we want to express.

This is where *kol*, the voice, comes in. Speech is generic, but each person's voice is unique. If I close my eyes, I can hear my grandmother's voice, its tone and singsongy lilt. I can hear the voice of my younger daughter when she calls "*Imma!*" (Mommy) amid throngs of other children. Her voice is immediately recognizable; it's just *her*.

---

25. *Becoming a Soulful Parent*, pp. 3–4

26. *Sefat Emet* was authored by Rabbi Yehudah Aryeh Leib Alter, a 19th-century Polish scholar and biblical commentator.

Our voice, says the Sefat Emet[27], and the voice of those we love, is more than a thing to be cherished; it is redemptive. Only one voice sounds just like yours. Only one voice can sing your unique song.

We can reflect not only on our *dibbur*, the words we say and how we say them, but also on our *kol*, the unique authenticity that we bring to that speech. Let us use both our *dibbur* and *kol*—our power of speech and our unique voice—to bring our inner world into the outer world to build up others and spread kindness.

27. *Sefat Emet*, Pesach 5633, on Exodus 14

#15

Ahavat Rei'acha, Loving Your Neighbor

THERE CONTINUES TO BE fascinating research regarding the psychological capacity for empathy. More and more it has philosophical implications, as well, for how we think about the human being as a moral agent. The Harvard philosopher and cultural commentator Professor Susan Neiman writes:

> Even further, one leading neurologist, V.S. Ramachandran, has described the mirror neurons that react equally to pain in one patient and the observation of pain in another as 'Dalai Lama cells.' These neurons (mirror neurons) were dissolving the barrier between the self and others—showing that our brains are actually "wired up" for empathy and compassion. Notice that one isn't being metaphorical in saying this; the neurons in question simply can't tell if you or the other person is being poked. It's as if the mirror neurons were doing a virtual reality simulation of what's going on in the other person's brain—thereby almost "feeling" the other's pain. If research continues to support the idea that we are hardwired for empathy, it would be powerful confirmation of the naturalist view the eighteenth century acquired without access to primate or neurological research. Moral sentimentalists like Hutcheson, Smith, and Hume argued that we are naturally endowed with feelings of sympathy and concern for others that move us to act in their behalf. Strict Kantians may hold that without being founded on principle, such actions are not fully moral, an objection that has been raised to De Waal's claims about the moral capacities of apes.[1]

1. Neiman, *Moral Clarity*, 271–22

John Rawls, the great 20th-century Harvard philosopher, designed a thought experiment for cultivating empathy and for setting policy, in which he suggested that citizens determine a moral problem and its solution collectively, but without knowing what role each citizen would have in its implementation. In this "veil of ignorance," one could end up the CEO of a Fortune 500 company or a minimum wage earner. One would, and should, vote to construct a society so that wherever one were to randomly end up on the totem pole, they would consider it fair and their needs would be satisfied.

What evokes empathy? Often, simply the face of another! The Hebrew language seems to have known this. *Panim* literally means face but also means interiority. When the prefix *"bi"* (resulting in *bifnim*) is added to the word *panim*, it means inside,[2] and is the literal opposite of *bachutz*,[3] meaning outside. When we see another's face, to a certain degree, we see their internal world. One's *bifnim* is awakened through the exteriority of the *panim* of another, invoking empathy within. In fact, the Torah describes Moshe's unique relationship with, and closeness to, God, as *"asher yidao Elokim panim el panim"* ("which God knew him face to face").[4] These words are meant to be understood allegorically, not literally, conveying to the reader that God knew Moses intimately in a way God knew no other.

This empathy for another (as opposed to just pity or sympathy) enables one to see the other in oneself and see oneself in the other. In blurring the boundaries of the self and the other, a space for love opens up.

The Biblical *mitzvah* *"v'ahavta l'rei'acha kamocha"* ("love your fellow as you love yourself")[5] is described by Rabbi Akiva as being "a fundamental principle of the Torah."[6] This concept is taken a step further in the Talmud:[7]

> There is a story about a gentile who came before Shammai and said to him, "I will convert if you teach me the entire Torah while I stand on one foot." Shammai pushed him away with the measuring stick that was in his hand. The gentile then went to

2. Similarly, the prefix *"li"* (resulting in *lifnim*) means before or in front of. The idea here is that with the addition of a prefix the word *panim* is transformed from a word referring to a mere physical body part to one describing a spatial/relational concept.

3. This, despite the fact that *chutz* only means outside and is not a body part at its core.

4. Deuteronomy 34:10

5. Leviticus 19:18

6. *Midrash Sifra* 2:12

7. *Babylonian Talmud*, Shabbat 31a

Hillel, who converted him. Hillel told him, "Whatever is hateful to you do not do to your friend. This is the entire Torah. The rest is its explanation. Go and study."[8]

The Sefer HaChinuch teaches us how this *mitzvah* works on a social level:

> The elements included in this *mitzvah* follow the general principle that one should treat another person in the way they would treat themself, e.g., protecting their property, preventing them from being harmed, speaking only well of them, respecting them, and certainly not glorifying oneself at their expense. The Sages have said regarding this last point, "One who glorifies themself at the expense of their fellow has no share in the World to Come." Whereas one who behaves with others in a loving and peaceful manner fulfills the verse, "Israel, by whom I am glorified. . ." . . .The basis for this *mitzvah* is well known, namely that a person will respond in kind to the way that they are treated. Fulfilling this *mitzvah* can bring peace to all living beings.[9]

The Sefer HaChinuch[10] adds that to love another is not just about them but their belongings as well:

> [It means]to love each member of Israel with a "soul love," i.e., that one should have compassion for a Jew and their property just as one has compassion for themself and their own property. As the verse states, "And you shall love your fellow as you love yourself."[11]

And so, loving another not only includes positive actions toward them but also avoiding negative actions toward them. We are to treat others how we'd want to be treated, and not treat them how we'd not want to be treated.

The Maharsha[12] offers an interesting insight here. Aware that we might be confused and think that we must do as much for others as we do for ourselves, he cautions against this:

8. It can be argued that, according to Hillel, the entire purpose of the *mitzvot bein adam laMakom*, laws between man and God, such as Shabbat and kosher observance, is to assist one in improving upon and enhancing their sensitivity to *mitzvot bein adam lachaveiro*, laws pertaining to interpersonal relationships.

9. *Sefer HaChinuch*, Mitzvah 243

10. *Sefer HaChinuch*, Mitzvah 243

11. Leviticus 19:18

12. Maharsha, an acronym for Moreinu Harav Shmuel Eliyahu (Our Teacher Rabbi Shmuel Eliyahu Eidels) was a 16th-century Polish Talmudic scholar. His glosses appear in the back of the standard set of Talmud.

"Whatever is hateful to you, etc." This refers to that which is written in the Torah, "And you shall love your fellow as you love yourself. . ." We can ask why Hillel altered the *mitzvah* by phrasing it in the negative, i.e., "Whatever is hateful to you, do not do unto your friend. . ."

The answer is that the *mitzvah* itself is a type of prohibition just like the other *mitzvot* in this verse, e.g., not taking revenge and not bearing a grudge. "And you shall love your fellow as you love yourself" is not an imperative to bestow an equal amount of goodness upon another, which we know from the legal principle of *chayecha kodmin*[13] (your own life comes first.)[14]

Rabbi Shneur Zalman of Liadi, known as the Alter Rebbe (the first Lubavitcher Rebbe), taught that most people are not purely good or purely evil. This has implications for how we love others while still keeping our values in place.

Regarding that which is stated in the Talmud—that it is a mitzvah to hate someone who sins—this refers to someone who is your equal in learning and deeds, and whom you have properly rebuked. But if they do not fit this description, Hillel the Elder has taught us, "Be like the disciples of Aaron, loving peace, pursuing peace, loving God's creatures and drawing them close to Torah." Those who are far from God's Torah must be drawn close with strong bonds of love. Thus, the *mitzvot* to love and to hate co-exist. It is a *mitzvah* to hate the evil that exists within a person while loving the hidden spark of godliness that resides within them.[15]

The goal in loving others is not just taking care of others but ultimately fostering a lasting peace in the broader world. The Sefer HaChinuch teaches:

The basis for this *mitzvah* is well known, namely that a person will respond in kind to the way that they are treated.[16] Fulfilling this *mitzvah* can bring peace to all living beings.[17]

13. *Babylonian Talmud*, Bava Metzia 62a

14. Maharsha, Chiddushei Aggadot, Shabbat 31a. See Section III B.
Maharsha here is emphasizing that just as the prohibition of taking revenge is not quantifiable, neither is refraining from mistreating another, the very definition and manifestation of *v'ahavta l'rei'acha kamocha.*

15. Rabbi Shneur Zalman of Liadi, *Tanya*, Ch. 32

16. It has been suggested that Hillel's principle of "what is hated by you do not do unto others" was born out of the care he himself received when he was down and out. See Babylonian Talmud, Yoma 35b, for an incident relating this point.

17. *Sefer HaChinuch*, Mitzvah 243

We are socialized, easily influenced, and habituated by certain behaviors. Pirkei Avot similarly teaches:

> Ben Azai says: You should run towards a light *mitzvah* [with the same diligence] as a stringent *mitzvah*, and you should flee from an *aveirah* (transgression); for one *mitzvah* leads to another *mitzvah*, and one *aveirah* leads to another *aveirah*.

Now, while Jews most certainly have moral duties to gentiles, this particular *mitzvah* was taught by the Rabbis to be about *ahavat Yisrael* (love for our fellow Jews). In Onkelos' translation of our original verse, he writes: "And you shall have compassion for your fellow Jew as you have for yourself; I am God."[18]

But why is this specific *mitzvah* about the relationship between Jews and Jews? The answer lies in the fact that Judaism teaches and stresses that our relationships towards and with the other are different based on who that other is. We should not treat our mother the same way we treat our brother. And we should not treat our brother the same way we treat a stranger.[19] We have a familial relationship and hence an obligation to family members above and beyond the relationship and obligation to others. So too, we have a unique relationship with Jews as a spiritual family. Justice is of course for all humanity. Moral responsibility is for all humanity. But this unique love for a spiritual family is reserved for Jews. It does not detract from our universalism but enhances it. "Universal love" is at times weak and confusing about moral priorities. Being in a community while never forgetting about our role within the broader community can strengthen us all. Our particularism will feed our universalism.

May our love for our fellow Jews inform and enhance our love for all humankind.

18. Onkelos on Leviticus 19:18

19. This concept does not negate the biblically mandated *mitzvah* of (Deuteronomy 10:19) "*Va'ahavtem et hageir*," ("You shall love the stranger").

#16

Arvut, Taking responsibility for our Community

WHAT IS THE CORE essence of Judaism? Is it primarily a personal religious conviction, or a communal one? Is it a series of epistemological contentions, or an emotional journey? To be sure, these rhetorical questions are never-ending and are at the heart of our great tradition. Learning how to reconcile these different ideals into a common reality is enough to warrant a call to action towards the grand notion of *arvut,* that we are responsible for one another.

Jews are vital in the spiritual enterprise of learning the values imbued by Torah. The Sages taught that a wise individual is someone who can learn from anyone,[1] and in their consummate wisdom of the enigmatic, the Kabbalists taught that every Jew represents a single letter of the Torah. And just as if one letter of the Torah scroll is missing, the entire Torah is rendered invalid, so too every Jew is needed and informs the entire entity of Am Yisrael. Thus, although we may be individuated with distinct personalities, wants, and desires, at some point, we all converge as a great nation. We are each crucial to the spiritual development of our fellow and community, though we may not always know it.

It is not for naught that the Sages noted that the one occasion in the Torah in which B'nei Yisrael achieved complete *arvut* was at Sinai, just prior to the Revelation and pronouncement of the Ten Commandments. The Torah tells us: *"Vayichan sham Yisrael"* ("The Israelites camped there").[2] It is

---

1. *Pirkei Avot* 4:1
2. Exodus 19:2

instructive to note that the word *vayichan* is written in the singular form; in every other mention in the Torah it is written in the plural form. Rashi, quoting the midrash on this oddity, comments:

> *Vayihan sham Yisrael: K'ish echad b'leiv echad* (as one person with one heart). All other encampments were with infighting and disagreement.[3]

It's as if Rashi is informing us that *arvut* is a prerequisite to the receiving of the Torah!

In our pursuit of *arvut* we are not limited to our ideals alone. To sustain spiritual growth, so vital to the health of the soul (if not the body), people have to journey beyond familiar comforts. Responsibility towards humanity means taking up the critical mantle of creating communities where there are gaps, filling the vacuum with respect for the inherent dignity of all people, regardless of status or station. Pluralistic understanding is the key, though disagreements as to its application will surely arise. Being aware of this means that building communities is not dependent on picayune differences of ideology or ritual (let's say), but on mutual regard for deeply-held convictions. For even if we do not agree with one other, the shared destiny of the Jewish people rests on the sacred integrity and wisdom that has been cultivated for countless generations.

Modernity, indeed post-modernity, raised serious questions about our role in caring for one another. The increasingly prominent role of digital anonymity has created a sense of distance in human interactions, nearly to the point of abstraction. But people aren't made of bits of code. The blood and sinew which was created from upon High binds our collective fates, and it can inspire us to reflect on the monumental role we have to play in stewarding succeeding epochs of humanity towards the path that is most just. For without this in mind, we doom ourselves to irrelevancy and the void of indifference. This is the antithesis of *arvut*, the antithesis of leading a life guided by Torah values.

We have been chosen for a singular and crucial mission: to bring holiness to the world. The task, though immense, is part and parcel of the Divine contract which was struck by our ancestors, eons ago with the Divine. To fulfill the terms, we must be absolutely unequivocal about our commitment to respect, to tolerance, to the perspicacity we need to ensure that all people, not only Jews, can thrive in the world. It is our eternal task; it is our constant spiritual test. And perhaps, it is our most important link to all of creation.

3. Rashi, ad loc.

The primary value that should guide every agency in our individual communities and society at large is *arvut*. We are diverse and will thus have different views; nonetheless, we must take care of one another.

Looking at the Purim story, Haman approached Achashveirosh and told him that the Jewish people were *"mefuzar umeforad bein ha'amim"* ("scattered and separated among the peoples").[4] Haman was demonstrating the vulnerability of the Jewish people because there was no *achdut* (unity), collective responsibility, or shared purpose. Each year at Purim, while we celebrate our diversity, we must also re-commit to our mission of preserving and building our cherished eternal people. This is why Esther and Mordechai implemented the *mitzvot* of *mishlo'ach manot* and *matanot la'evyonim* (giving food portions to our neighbors and charity to the poor) as part of the celebration of the holiday of Purim. Indeed, two of the four *mitzvot* of Purim, a full 50%, demonstrate our sense of *arvut*. This is also why Esther insisted that if she does indeed go to the king without being summoned, thereby risking her life, that everyone else fasts for her. She understood that the key to her success in her mission was our acting *k'ish echad b'leiv echad*.

As fragmentation and enmity perpetuate, this sacred task is more crucial than ever before.

Why did the rabbis have so much faith in individuals? Why did they believe that we are capable of such heroism? Are we taught to embrace collective responsibility because we want to empower others, or because we are responsible for their wrongs and have the power to inspire them to do right? Going deeper, is Judaism primarily an individualistic religion, accountable primarily to oneself, or a collectivist one where the benefits for all are paramount? For us to wrestle with these questions, we have to consider carefully the contextual and epistemological obstacles that Jews are forced to face. The divide between Israeli and Diaspora Jews, between collective struggles and individualistic liberty, is present and real. But learning to reconcile these different dreams into a reality of common cooperation for Jews, indeed all peoples, is beyond a philosophical imperative: It's a call to action.

While Jews are commanded to show compassion to all human beings (*ahavat ha'briyot*), there is also a unique *mitzvah* to love our fellow Jews (*ahavat Yisrael*) and take responsibility for them (*arvut*). This principle is concerned primarily with helping others to actualize *mitzvot*[5] but also with preventing *aveirot* (wrongs):

---

4. Esther 3:8
5. *Babylonian Talmud*, Sanhedrin 27b; Rosh Hashanah 29a; Sotah 37b

> Regarding all sins in the Torah, a person is punished for what they did, and here [regarding an oath taken in vain], they are punished for what they did and for what the whole world did. . . And regarding all the sins in the Torah, this is not so? But surely it is written: "And they shall fall, each upon his brother"[6]— each person because of the sin of their fellow. This teaches that all of Israel are responsible one for the other! That is where they could have objected, but they failed to do so.[7]

Further, the Jewish people are held accountable for collective wrongs:

> Whoever can prevent their household [from sinning] but does not, is seized for [the sins of] his household; [if they can prevent] their townspeople, they are seized for [the sins of] their townspeople; if [they can prevent] the whole world, they are seized for [the sins of] the whole world. . .[8]

Not only do we need to help one another, we need to learn from one another, foster relationships, and act in solidarity when the times call for it. All Jews are needed in the spiritual enterprise of learning Torah, whether in the study halls or out on the streets. Rabbi Yehuda HaLevi explained that all Jews are like instruments. To make a symphony, you can't only have a piccolo, a kazoo, and some violas. You need timpani and trumpets, oboes and xylophones, tubas and pianos; you need heart and soul. Rav Yoel Sirkis[9] taught that the verse "*v'tein chelkeinu b'Toratecha* ("give us our share of Your Torah")[10] means that every individual has a specific and special portion that only he or she can reveal. Each individual is crucial to the collective.

The late Rabbi Aharon Lichtenstein argued[11] that now that Jews have returned to the land of Israel and achieved sovereignty, our responsibility towards *arvut* has increased. This raises interesting questions about our era. Perhaps other factors of modernity and post-modernity—the decreasing proximity we have to people on the other side of the world—have raised the stakes of our responsibility as well. To continue growing spiritually, we have to journey beyond the familiar. Our first steps are to create pluralistic communities where any and all Jews can learn from one another while honoring the diverse values inherent in any community. The second step

6. Leviticus 26:37

7. *Babylonian Talmud*, Shevuot 39a–b

8. *Babylonian Talmud*, Shabbat 54b

9. Rav Yoel Sirkis, 16th-17th-century Polish scholar, is also known by the name Bach, his magnum opus.

10. *Avot* 5:20

11. Based on the *Jerusalem Talmud*, Sotah 7:5

is to build our community and work to repair the world together. Further, we are to cultivate love for one another and stand up for one another when attacked. Even if we do not agree with each other on virtually anything, the shared fate and destiny of the Jewish people rests on the sacred integrity and wisdom we have cultivated for millennia.

We have been chosen for a unique and crucial mission in the world: not merely to survive but to thrive in fulfilling our global mission to make the world more just and holy. Never again should Haman be equipped to argue that we are vulnerable to outside threats due to our internal arrogant pettiness. We may oscillate between embracing diversity and striving for unity, but we must be absolutely unequivocal about our commitment to a culture of respect, tolerance, and collaboration.

There is no freedom without responsibility. We are not free simply because we are "free from," but also because we are "free to." When we commit, when we take responsibility, we actualize our freedom. Not only is our freedom found in our responsibility but so is our uniqueness. The 20th-century French philosopher Emmanuel Levinas writes powerfully:

> The trauma I experienced as a slave in the land of Egypt constitutes my humanity itself. This immediately brings me closer to all the problems of the damned on the earth, of all those who are persecuted, as if in my suffering as a slave I prayed in a prayer that was not yet oration, and as if this love of the stranger were already the reply given to me through my heart of flesh. My very uniqueness lies in the responsibility for the other man; I could never pass it off to another person, just as I could never have anyone take my place in death: obedience to the Most-High means precisely this impossibility of shying away; through it, my 'self' is unique. To be free is to do only what no one else can do in my place. To obey the Most-High is to be free.[12]

Even once we determine our unique responsibility, we may still have little clarity about how to act next. As the late Rabbi Walter Wurzburger taught, each of us has our own holy work that we must do, since there is a plurality within the complexity of Jewish values:

> The pluralism of Jewish ethics manifests itself in the readiness to operate with a number of independent ethical norms and principles such as concern for love, justice, truth, and peace. Since they frequently give rise to conflicting obligations, it becomes necessary to rely upon intuitive judgments to resolve the conflict. There is, however, another dimension to the pluralism

12. Levinas, *Beyond the Verse*, 142.

of Jewish ethics: it is multi-tiered and comprises many strands. It contains not only objective components such as duties and obligations, but also numerous values and ideals possessing only subjective validity. Moreover, the pluralistic thrust of Jewish ethics makes it possible to recognize the legitimacy of many alternate ethical values and ideals.[13]

When we determine how we must take responsibility, learning the "ability" of "response," we will see that we are also taking *achrayut* (responsibility).[14] Within achrayut, we have both the words *ach* (our sibling) and *acher* (the other) showing how our responsibility is to those like us and those unlike us. But in taking responsibility for the other, we also bring wholeness to the self. Rabbi Irving (Yitz) Greenberg said it this way: "Tzedakah means taking responsibility for life. One shares one's own possessions in order to take responsibility for the needs of others because life is indivisible. My life cannot be whole while others' lives are not."[15]

For Rav Yitz, it is precisely due to God's invisibility in our time that our responsibility has increased so greatly.

> God was now limiting the visible divinity in history—*less manifest but more present*—in order to summon human beings to a higher level of responsibility in realizing the goals of the covenant.[16]

It is beneficial to reflect every hour of the day on how we are receiving and emanating spiritual energies. To be sure, we have a responsibility to battle the darkness within us and around us. God forbid we dismiss such holy work. But it can't weigh us down spatially, temporally, or existentially. Our efforts to zoom out and remain positively charged, actualizing our unique life missions, and emanating holy light, must be our daily obsession for bringing all people together in solidarity and peace.

As humans, often full of guilt or shame, it is all too easy to deny injustices right before our eyes. The Kedushat Levi[17] taught that Cain was not only a murderer of his brother but also a heretic for his reply, "Am I my brother's keeper?" Denying his responsibility to stand for justice was akin to rejecting the Creator! Abandoning moral agency is abandoning

13. Wurzburger, *Ethics of Responsibility*, 5

14. It is instructive to note that the word *achrayut* shares its Hebrew root with the word *acheir* (the other).

15. Greenberg, *The Jewish Way*, 369

16. Greenberg, *Sage Advice*, Preface xi

17. Kedushat Levi is the name of the eminent work authored by the 18th-century Polish Hasidic master Rabbi Levi Yitzchok of Berditchev.

everything! As Rabbi Abraham Joshua Heschel wrote: "Few are guilty, but all are responsible."

Kant spoke about universal human duties. Hume spoke about responsibility based upon emotion. The Torah adds a third important dimension: memory (Do not oppress a stranger, because you were slaves in Egypt).[18] We are responsible to ourselves, to God, to our family, to our community, to humanity, and to all of life. It can only be sustainable and not completely overwhelming if we hold it all together.

May we be blessed with *gevurah* (strength) and with a sense of *chesed* (gentle love and kindness) throughout our journey towards maximizing our *arvut*.

18. Exodus 22:20

#17

Rodeif Shalom, Pursuing Peace

IN CHAPTER 10, WE discussed *shalom bayit* (peace in the home). Now we're going to explore *rodeif shalom* (pursuing peace) more broadly. The rabbis teach that the greatest of heroes is "one who turns an enemy into a friend."[1] Afterall, it says in the Torah:

> When you encounter your enemy's ox or donkey wandering, you must take it back to them. When you see your enemy's donkey sagging under its burden and would [otherwise] refrain from raising it, you must nevertheless raise it with them.[2]

If this is not enough, the Talmud goes even further!

> If the animal of a friend needs unloading and an enemy's needs loading, you shall first help your enemy—in order to discipline your evil inclination.[3]

And the rabbis suggest that this has actually worked:

> Rabbi Alexandroni said: Two donkey drivers who hated each other were traveling along the same road. The donkey of one of them fell down. The other saw it but passed him by. After he had passed by, [the other] said, "It is written in the Holy Scriptures, 'If you see your enemy's donkey . . .'" Forthwith he went back to help him with the load. The other began to think things over and said, "So and so is evidently my friend and I didn't know

1. *Avot d'Rabbi Natan* 23:1
2. Exodus 23:4–5. Also see Deuteronomy 22:1,4
3. *Babylonian Talmud*, Baba Metzia 32b

it!" The two went into a roadside inn and had a drink together. What led them to make peace? One of them looked into the Torah.[4]

If this is true for enemies, how much more so should it be true for those who are not our enemies. We do not wait passively to resolve tensions but move eagerly toward them. Rabbi Chaim of Volozhin, of the late 18th and early 19th centuries, taught:

> When it says, "seek peace,"[5] it means that you should want there to be peace between you, even if in your opinion the other person wronged you. Nevertheless, you should "pursue it"—you should be the *rodeif shalom* (pursuer of peace), rather than waiting for the other to reconcile with you [first].[6]

So what is the psychological work involved here? The Torah instructs us not to hold grudges:

> You shall not take revenge, nor shall you bear a grudge against the members of your people.[7]

Rambam elaborates:

> You shall blot [any offenses against you] out of your mind and not bear a grudge. For as long as one nurses a grievance and keeps it in mind, one may come to take vengeance. The Torah therefore emphatically warns us not to bear a grudge, so that the impression of the wrong shall be completely obliterated and no longer remembered. This is the correct principle, [for] it alone makes civilized life and social interaction possible.[8]

Another teaching of Rambam[9] gets to the heart of what the entire Torah is ultimately about:

> If such a poor person has to choose between oil for both a house lamp [on Shabbat] and a Chanukah lamp, or oil for a house lamp [on Shabbat] and wine for the *kiddush*, the house lamp

---

4. *Midrash Tanhuma Yashan*, Mishpatim, cited in Nechama Leibowitz, Studies in the Weekly Parsha, p. 433.

5. Psalms 34:15

6. *Sefer Ruach Chayim*, commentary on Pirkei Avot 1:12

7. Leviticus 19:18

8. Maimonides, *Mishneh Torah*, Hilchot Dei'ot 7:12

9. Based on *Babylonian Talmud*, Gittin 59b

should have priority, for the sake of peace in the household,[10] seeing that even a Divine Name may be erased to make peace between husband and wife.[11]

Great indeed is peace, forasmuch as the purpose for which the whole of the Torah was given is to bring peace upon the world, as it is said, 'Its ways are ways of pleasantness, and all its paths are peace.'[12][13]

For many, *darchei shalom* (the ways of peace) means that we should support gentiles even in, and perhaps especially in, eras and cultures with enormous antisemitism, simply to save ourselves. If others continue to accuse us of only being for ourselves, it will fuel their fires of hatred and violence toward us.

But for Rambam, we follow *darchei shalom* not for a practical survivalist reason but for a deep theological and moral reason:

> Even with respect to gentiles, the rabbis bid us visit their sick, bury their dead along with the dead of Israel, and maintain their poor with the poor of Israel in the interests of peace, as it is written: 'The Lord is good to all, and God's tender mercies are upon all God's works.'[14] And it is also written: 'Its ways are ways of pleasantness, and all its paths are peace.'[15][16]

Aside from meaning peace, Shalom is also a name of God, and so we pursue peace so that we can emulate a loving, peaceful God. We are to pursue peace within the home, within communities, and within society at large.

A well-known verse from Tehillim (Psalms) speaks to this idea of pursuing peace: "May there be peace within your walls, serenity within your palaces."[17] Translated this way, this verse is a prayer, a hope. But there is another way to read the verse: "If you wish for there to be peace within your walls (referring here to city walls), there must be peace within your palaces." In other words, the well-known adage is correct; peace begins in the home. First, we must make every effort towards *shalom bayit*. We must ensure that

---

10. *Babylonian Talmud*, Shabbat 23b
11. *Devarim Rabbah* 5:15
12. Proverbs 3:17
13. Maimonides, *Mishneh Torah*, Hilchot Megillah v'Chanukah 4:14
14. Psalm 145:9
15. Proverbs 3:17
16. *Mishneh Torah*, Laws of Kings 10:12
17. Psalms 122:7

we have peace on a micro level. Only then can we be impactful in pursuing peace on a macro level.

It can be powerful to just be a "truth speaker," but it can often be wiser to be a pursuer of peace. Sometimes we must learn to hold our truths a little looser for the welfare of others. This is a virtually a lost virtue today, as so many are not willing to budge on anything at all that they feel is right.

When it comes to war, Judaism at its core should neither be read as hawkish nor as totally pacifist. There is a right and duty of self-defense, but also a duty of restraint. We yearn for messianic times of no violence, about which Isaiah famously foretells: "The wolf shall dwell with the lamb"[18] and of which Micah similarly teaches: "Nation shall not take up sword against nation; they shall never again know war."[19] But until then we will need to figure out how to survive in a world of violence.

In reality, the Torah even instructs us to engage in offensive wars, but as seen below, peace is built into the charge:

> When you approach a town to attack it, you shall offer it terms of peace. If it responds peaceably and lets you in, all the people present there shall serve you at forced labor. If it does not surrender to you, but engages in battle with you, you shall lay siege to it. And when the Lord your God delivers it into your hand, you shall put all its males to the sword. You may, however, take as your booty the women, the children, the livestock, and everything in the town—all its spoil—and enjoy the use of the spoil of your enemy, which the Lord your God gives you.[20]

The rabbis emphasize how serious this call for peace must be. The Midrash teaches:

> God commanded him (Moses) to make war on Sihon. . . but he did not do so. God said to him: 'I have commanded you to make war on him (Sihon) but instead you begin with peace! By your life, I will confirm your decision; every war upon which Israel enters, they shall begin [with an attempt to bring] peace, as it is said, *when you come near to a city to fight against it, then proclaim peace unto it.*'[21][22]

---

18. Isaiah 11:6

19. Micah 4:3

20. Deuteronomy 20:10–18

21. Deuteronomy 20:10

22. *Devarim Rabbah* 5:13

In another famous, and disturbing, biblical text, we see just how seemingly violent God's demand could be:

> Samuel said to Saul. . . 'Thus said the Lord of Hosts: I am exacting the penalty for what Amalek did to Israel, for the assault he made upon them on the road, on their way up from Egypt. Now go, attack Amalek, and proscribe all that belongs to him. Spare no one, but kill alike men and women, infants and sucklings, oxen and sheep, camels and asses. . .' Saul destroyed Amalek. . . He proscribed all the people, putting them to the sword; but Saul and the troops spared Agag and the best of the sheep, the oxen. . .
>
> The word of the Lord then came to Samuel: 'I regret that I made Saul king, for he has turned away from Me and has not carried out My commands. . .' As Samuel turned to leave, Saul seized the corner of his robe, and it tore. And Samuel said to him, 'The Lord has this day torn the kingship over Israel away from you and has given it to another who is worthier than you. . .'[23]

The rabbis also struggled with this text.

> 'And he [Saul] fought [Amelek] in the valley' (I Samuel 15:5). Rabbi Mani said: Because of what happens in the valley. When the Holy One be blessed, said to Saul, 'Now go and strike down Amalek,' he [Saul] said: 'If on account of one person the Torah said: 'Perform the ceremony of the cow whose neck is to be broken, how much more [ought consideration to be given] to all these persons! And if human beings sinned, what have the cows done? And if the adults have sinned, what have the children done?' A divine voice came forth and said: 'Be not righteous overmuch.'[24]

Even built into the laws of Shabbat, we learn how instruments of war and violence are to be viewed:

> A person should not go out on Shabbat, not with a sword, or a bow, or a shield, or a mace or a spear. And if they did, they are liable for a sin offering. Rabbi Eliezer says: They are just an adornment for him (like jewelry). But the sages say: They (the instruments of war) are a disgrace. For the verse states (Isaiah 2:4): 'They shall beat their swords into plowshares and their

23. I Samuel 15:1–11

24. *Babylonian Talmud*, Yoma 22b

spears into pruning hooks. Nation shall not take up sword
against nation, nor shall they train for war anymore.'[25]

While we dream of a pacifist utopia, after the Holocaust we can never
again be so naive. Rabbi Dr. Yitz Greenberg writes:

> The Holocaust made manifest a fundamental shift in the bal-
> ance of power between victims and aggressors. Thanks to the
> extraordinary concentrations of power made possible by mod-
> ern cultural technology and science, forces of evil have unlim-
> ited power available to carry out their designs. Death now has
> the capacity to stamp out life.

The lesson of the Holocaust was that in the face of overwhelming con-
centration of power, acts of self-sacrifice and spiritual demonstrations had
little or no effect on the murderers. Classic moral traditions—martyrdom
in Judaism, satyagrapha in Hinduism, the cross and turning the other cheek
in Christianity—were shattered in the Holocaust. Nor did the norms developed by modern society—humanitarianism, liberalism, universal rights,
rule of law—protect the Jews. Nor did established sources of aid to victims
(religion, taboos on killing) prove any more capable of blunting the force
of the Nazis' murderous fury. Only the transfer of power to potential victims—power enough to defend themselves—can correct the new imbalance
of power. . .

> The State of Israel was designed to place power in the hands of
> Jews to shape their own destiny and to affect or even control the
> lives of others. Creating the state meant that Jews took on major
> responsibility for saving their own lives. With this decision, use
> of prayer alone or Torah study alone—heretofore the pillars of
> authentic Jewish response—henceforth became an evasion of
> covenantal responsibility. If one seeks out one moment that
> symbolizes the transition, it might well be the Haganah drafting
> able-bodied males in Mea Shearim (a Haredi, ultra-Orthodox
> neighborhood) to build defenses for the Old City in the battle
> for Jerusalem in 1948.

For Rabbi Greenberg, after the Holocaust, it is a sin to be powerless.
Yes, power must be used responsibly, but we must never be powerless again.
Yet, Rabbi David Hartman emphasizes how much we must not build this
state to be like other states:

---

25. *Babylonian Talmud*, Shabbat 63a

> Israel is not a return to a religious or political ghetto where
> Jewish particularity and universality conflict, where symbolic
> religious ritual and the passion for social justice are unrelated
> expressions of loyalty to traditional Judaism. Israel represents
> the birth of a healthy society that seeks to create a nation like
> all other nations. The demythologization of the Jewish people
> is one of the great gifts of Israeli society to the Jewish people...

It may be easy, albeit painful, to be powerless. But to have power is also very difficult, as one now has enormous responsibilities both to protect oneself and one's people while also showing enormous restraint and pursuing peace. Everyone with power will ultimately fail, but to be a Jew means that we cannot tolerate our own failure. We must defend ourselves. At the same time, we must be total lovers of peace, for to love peace and pursue peace is one of the greatest demands in emulating the ways of God.

Let us be like Aaron, about whom we are taught:

> Hillel said: Be among the students of Aaron, who loved peace
> and pursued peace; he loved [all] creatures and drew them near
> to the Torah.[26]

26. *Pirkei Avot* 1:12

#18

Gemilut Chasadim, Random Acts of Kindness

WE KNOW HOW TRANSFORMATIVE our consistent, planned, and intentional acts of *chesed* (kindness) can be. But how about spontaneous and random acts of kindness? There are infinite opportunities each day to lend a hand, elevate a soul, give joy to another. But with the full list we've been learning about, does the Torah want us to consider these as well? The Rambam taught:

> It is a rabbinic positive precept to visit the sick, comfort the mourners, escort the dead, dower the bride, accompany the [departing] guests. . . as well as to cheer the bride and groom, and to assist them in whatever they need. Even though all these precepts are of rabbinic origin, they are implied in the biblical verse: "You shall love your neighbor as yourself" (Leviticus 19:18); that is, whatever you would have others do to you, do to your brothers in Torah and precepts.[1]

Essentially the Rambam is teaching that acts of *chesed* even not listed among the 613 biblical *mitzvot* are indeed still a part of the Torah's highest commitment toward love, empathy, and kindness. Another way to root kindness in the Torah is not directly through loving our neighbor but through emulating the Divine.

1. *Mishneh Torah*, Laws of Mourning 14:1

We are commanded to emulate God, as it is written, "And you shall go in God's ways. . ." This implies emulating the good actions and good attributes that are used to describe God.[2]

The rabbis taught that acts of kindness sustain the world.

The world rests upon three things: Upon Torah study, upon Divine service, and upon the practice of acts of kindness.[3]

Psalms teaches: "The world will be built through kindness."[4] Although the rabbis listed three things that sustain the world, the Maharal[5] teaches of the centrality of kindness.

Why does the world stand specifically upon these three things and not others?. . . The reason is that everything that was created only deserves to exist in as much as it is inherently good. It is the goodness in each object that allows it to exist . . . For this reason, we find that after the creation of each object during the six days of Creation, it is written that God saw that it was good . . .

People's capacity for goodness can be divided into three parts: God's own intrinsic goodness; a person's goodness in relationship with God; and a person's goodness in relationships with fellow human beings . . .

Chesed corresponds to this third aspect of one's life; for it is eminently clear that when one performs kind deeds for one's fellow without expecting any reimbursement, they are being good towards them. There is, in fact, no greater good than when one bestows kindnesses upon others from their own volition—in doing so they are truly and really "good."[6]

The Talmud teaches that acts of chesed are even greater than giving tzedakah.

The rabbis taught: Gemilut chasadim is greater than tzedakah in three ways: Tzedakah is with one's money, whereas gemilut chasadim is with one's body and with one's money; tzedakah is for the poor, whereas gemilut chasadim is for the poor and the

---

2. *Sefer Hamitzvot*, positive command #8. Also see Babylonian Talmud, Sotah 14a.

3. *Pirkei Avot* 1:2

4. Psalms 89:3

5. Maharal is the Hebrew acronym for the 16th-century scholar and mystic Rabbi Judah Loew, also known as the Maharal of Prague.

6. Maharal on *Pirkei Avot* 1:2

wealthy; *tzedakah* is for the living, whereas *gemilut chasadim* is for the living and the dead."[7]

In fact, the act of burying the dead and tending to all their needs is referred to as *chesed shel emet* (truest kindness), as the dead cannot repay another for their acts of kindness.

The Talmud further picks up on the fact that the Torah begins and ends with an act of *chesed*.

> Rabbi Simlai deduced: The Torah begins with *gemilut chasadim* and ends with *gemilut chasadim*, as it is written: "God made for man and his wife garments of skin and dressed them.[8]" It ends with *gemilut chasadim*, as it is written: "God buried him in the valley[9]."[10]

The Talmud is stressing here that the Torah is bracketed by acts of *chesed* performed by God Godself, as if to suggest that we, too, are to infuse our entire observance of Torah, from beginning to end, with acts of kindness. It follows that the observance of *mitzvot*, even, or perhaps especially, *mitzvot bein adam laMakom* (*mitzvot* between people and God, e.g., *kashrut, shabbat*) without a commitment to *chesed*, is lacking a key element of what God is asking of us as Torah engaged Jews.

Perhaps one of the greatest acts of kindness one can bestow upon another is helping to lift their self-esteem. Afterall, so many people around us have a low self-esteem and need support in being lifted up to see their own goodness. Consider this story from Rabbi Abraham Twerski.

> Goodness tends to propagate itself. It's apt to form a chain. A story occurs to me of a man named Avi. I first met him while I was in Tel Aviv speaking before a group of ex-convicts in recovery who were coming into our Israeli rehabilitation program. When I began to speak of self-esteem, this man interrupted me. "How can you talk to us of this? I've been in and out of jail for half of my 34 years. I've been a thief since I was eight. When I'm out of prison I can't find work and my family doesn't want to see me."

I stopped him and asked if he'd passed by a jewelry store lately. "Consider the diamonds in the window," I said. "Try and think what they look like when they come out of the mine—lumps of dirty ore. It takes a person

---

7. *Babylonian Talmud*, Sukkah 49b

8. Genesis 3:21

9. Deuteronomy 34:6

10. *Babylonian Talmud*, Sotah 14a

who understands the diamond to take the shapeless mound and bring out its intrinsic beauty. That's what we do here, we look for the diamond in everyone; we help the soul's beauty come to the surface, we polish it until it gleams. We're all like that dirt-covered ore and our business is to find the diamond within and polish it until it grows."

Two years passed. Avi had graduated from the treatment center, and was integrated into the community, working in construction. One day, Annette, who manages our halfway house, received a call from a family whose elderly matriarch had died and wanted to donate her furniture. Annette called Avi and asked him to pick up the furniture. When he went to pick it up, he saw that it wasn't worth saving, but not wanting to insult the family, he hauled it anyway.

While Avi was laboring to carry the shabby sofa up the stairs to the halfway house, an envelope fell from the cushions. After getting the couch inside, Avi retrieved the envelope, in which he found five thousand shekels (about $1,500). Avi called Annette and told her about the envelope. Annette said it must be reported to the family.

> The family was so gratified by Annette and Avi's honesty that they told her to keep the money for the halfway house. As a result, the halfway house was able to buy one more bed and provide room for one more guest, creating another opportunity for recovery. And Avi wasn't a thief anymore. Another year went by and I returned to the halfway house. There was a sign hanging above the entry. It read: "Diamonds Polished Here."[11]

The opportunities are everywhere. Rav Shlomo Wolbe wrote:

> Chesed is not limited to money. A nice word, a smile—these can give new life to someone who has given up on themselves! A word of encouragement can bring joy. These are such small things [yet so significant!]. In general, there are so many acts of chesed that are easily within our reach—if only we would notice that they are needed![12]

The prophet Micah sought to describe the Torah in one verse. He wrote:

> [God] has told you, man, what is good and what God demands of you: Only to do justice, to love chesed, and to walk modestly with your God.[13]

---

11. Twerski, *Do unto Others*, 3–4
12. Wolbe, *Alei Shur*, 93
13. Micah 6:8

One of the most prevalent Jewish theologies around why God desired, or perhaps even needed, to create a world was to do enormous acts of kindness. So too, one might suggest that we exist as human beings in order to do acts of kindness. Imagine if we challenged ourselves each day to do new acts of kindness, those that others expect from us and those that are random, or above and beyond and not expected.

At every moment, there are more kind acts than cruel acts occurring. Yes, the news tells us of all the tragedies. But we don't hear as much about each teacher patiently teaching a listen, each nurse compassionately offering comfort, each hospice worker holding the hand of a dying stranger. And small random acts of kindness can truly change lives in ways we'll never know. A colleague shared with me that she was deeply suicidal and right at her worst moment, the car in front of her paid for her coffee. She said this simple act changed her worldview and truly saved her life.

We are not looking to save others, but rather to be saved together. Our fates our bound up together, as givers and receivers. Lila Watson wrote: "If you have come here to help me you are wasting your time. But if you have come here because your liberation is bound with mine, let us work together." Some suggest that kind acts should be anonymous to avoid bringing shame upon the receiver and to inspire humility among the giver. But others might suggest that giving in relationship can, at times, be more appropriate and empowering when power dynamics are mitigated and relationships are deepened.

Perhaps the most exciting way to live is not in seeking the thrill of a new vacation or a new food (although those pleasures can, and perhaps should, surely be enjoyed) but in the excitement in seeking out new ways each day to lift up others, to repair little bits of brokenness, and to add joy to others. Then we will have actualized our existence and our purpose.

#19

Derech Eretz, Displaying Good Manners

MOST OF US ARE already working really hard to live lives of kindness. Taking on new major projects might not work. But there are little moments all the time where we can do a little more. Yes, people in poverty need more money, sick people in hospitals need more visits, and the elderly need better care. There are big, hefty lifts that we need to make to be agents of kindness in supporting those who are suffering. But there are also little, kind gestures we can make for every person we encounter no matter what their situation may be. We are all taught, as children, to be polite, to say please and thank you, to hold doors for others, and to have dinner table manners. But how can we take this further?

More than us being "religious," God, according to the Jewish tradition, wants us to be decent. The prophet Hoshea says: "For it is kindness that I desire and not sacrifice."[1] On this verse the rabbis taught:

> Once, as Rabbi Yochanan ben Zakkai was coming from Jerusalem, Rabbi Joshua followed him, and beheld the Temple in ruins. 'Woe unto us!' Rabbi Joshua cried, 'that this, the place where the sins of Israel were atoned for, is laid waste.' 'My son,' Rabbi Yochanan said to him, 'be not grieved. We have another atonement as effective as this. And what is it? It is acts of lovingkindness, as it is said, *"For it its kindness that I desire and not sacrifice."*[2]

Consider, for example, the value of respect. A *midrash* teaches:

1. Hosea 6:6
2. *Avot d'Rabbi Natan* Ch. 4

118

The wise person does not speak before one who is greater than them in wisdom or in age. This refers to Moshe, as it says, "And Aharon spoke all the words which the Lord had told Moshe, and [he] performed the signs in the sight of the people.[3]" And who was most fitting to speak, Moshe or Aharon? Surely Moshe! For Moshe heard [the words] from the mouth of the Almighty while Aharon heard them [only] from the mouth of Moshe. But thus said Moshe [to himself]: "Shall I then speak while my older brother is standing by?" He therefore told Aharon to speak, and it is for this reason that it is said, "Aharon spoke all the words which the Lord had told Moshe."[4]

This form of respect goes beyond just those whom we deem to be wiser or older than us.[5] Further, we can work to cultivate our emotional intelligence and sensitivity and be empathic with those in front of us. The rabbis taught: "One should not rejoice among those who are crying, nor cry among those who are celebrating."[6]

Rabbi Eliyahu Dessler, the famed 20th-century *mashgiach ruchani* (spiritual advisor) of the Ponovezh Yeshiva in Israel, reinforced how our relationships can be transformed by being kindlier in touch with others.

If you make an effort to help everyone you meet, you will feel close to everyone. A stranger is someone you have not yet helped. [By] doing acts of kindness for everyone, you can fill your world with friends and loved ones.[7]

Perhaps the most religious project is to emulate the ways of the Divine. The contemporary Jewish philosopher Alan Mittleman wrote:[8]

---

3. Exodus 4:30

4. *Avot D'Rabbi Natan* Ch. 37

5. Rabbi Avi Herzog reports that he once observed Rabbi Gedalia Dov Schwartz, ob"m, the Av Beit Din (Rabbinic Head) of the Rabbinical Council of America and the Chicago Rabbinical Council, exhibiting this same behavior as Moshe in the above cited *midrash*. A member of the congregation where Rav Schwartz regularly prayed approached Rav Schwartz and asked him an *halachic* inquiry. Motioning to the much younger rabbi of the synagogue, Rav Schwartz said, "In here, he's the rabbi. I can only answer *sh'eilot* (*halachic* questions) outside the building." The man again approached Rav Schwartz once they were outside, and only when they were off the shul property did Rav Schwartz agree to answer the question.

6. *Derech Eretz Rabbah* 7:7

7. Morinis, *Every Day, Holy Day*, 214

8. Mittleman, *Human Nature & Jewish Thought, Judaism's Case for Why Persons Matter*, 92

To achieve intellectual apprehension of God, it is necessary to emulate His attributes of loving-kindness, judgement, and righteousness.[9] When Moses asks God to reveal His (presence) *kavod* to him (Exodus 33:18), God reveals His goodness (*tuv*).[10] To know God is to know which values are ultimate.

Indeed, the *Talmudic* rabbis stressed this same idea in explaining the well-known verse "This is my God and I shall glorify Him:"[11]

Abba Sha'ul says [on the verse] 'This is my God and I shall glorify him:' Be similar to Him. Just as He is kind and merciful, so too should you be kind and merciful.[12]

What if we all were to take our very next human interaction and add a bit more joy and kindness into the moment? It can be so contagious! When someone sends light to us, our soul captures it but then craves sharing it! If we can all embrace these little sacred moments, we can radically transform ourselves and the world.

A contemporary teacher of *mussar*, Alan Morinis, shares:

In the five Books of Moses, the word kindness (*chesed*) appears 248 times.[13] Generosity, compassion, grace, patience, and love are all held up as divine qualities we are meant to embody in our own lives.[14]

The Zohar teaches: "There are 248 limbs in the body, and each word of Shema serves to protect one of them.[15]" If we have 248 limbs and *chesed* appears 248 times in the Torah, it fits to reason that each limb is a vote of confidence in our ability to use our full being for kindness. And in turn, our faith (the recitation in the Shema) will protect us and strengthen us in our service of others.

---

9. Maimonides, *The Guide of the Perplexed*, 2:638.

10. Exodus 33:19

11. Exodus 15:2

12. *Babylonian Talmud*, Shabbat 133b
It is perhaps instructive to note that the rabbis chose to deduce this point from the opening words of Moses' and the Israelites' bursting into song as they successfully crossed the Red Sea. It can be further deduced, then, that the greatest way for one to demonstrate gratitude towards God is to emulate God's ways.

13. Interestingly enough, the number 248 also corresponds to the number of *positive* mitzvot in the Torah.

14. Morinis, *With Heart in Mind*, 4–5

15. *Zohar*, Chadash, Ruth 97b

And yet, sometimes we're so busy and so distracted that we don't see what's happening right in front of our eyes. My young son was once speaking nonsense! Or so I thought. So I tuned him out for a few minutes. Then I tuned back in and realized he was explaining the mechanics of how his love for me could travel through invisible tubes, through walls from his heart at school to my heart at work. We can hit our chests for the sin of not listening.

Political advocacy has its place and is one way to work for change, but it can be quite limiting and can't replace acts of kindness. Outrage at injustice can't replace being a *mensch*. Identity markers can't replace introspection and self-work. And righteous indignation can't replace regret and apologizing. Having the "right" ideology can't replace praying, donating, repenting.

Derech Eretz is about doing, not simply espousing.

Yes, we can win with service, social entrepreneurship, grassroots organizing for local causes, bridge-building, community building, sustainable development, and education. We can't, of course, fully abandon political advocacy, but we need to open hearts and minds, and we need to do so now. We need to shift our consumer behaviors to live according to the values we advocate for. We need to bring kindness to every interaction. We need to build compassionate communities. We need to think more creatively and expansively about alternative models of social change. The opportunities for winning are literally everywhere!

But we can't lead from the darkness of anger. We need to lead from our inner light! Rabbi Elazar taught:[16]

> The reward for acts of justice [and] charity (*tzedakah*) depends upon the degree of loving-kindness (*chesed*) in them, as it is written, 'Sow righteousness (justice, charity, *tzedakah*, for yourselves; reap according to (your) goodness (*chesed*)."[17]

I recently had some conversations with the Spinka Rebbe[18]. In one, I asked him what the most important *midah* (moral/spiritual character trait) to master is. He said, "*Chesed* (kindness). Master *chesed*, and all other *midot* will flow from there!" I definitely think he's right. If we come to care for others and cultivate compassion for them, it will be harder to be angry at them and easier to be patient with them.

Consider, for example, this teaching from Rav Kook:

---

16. *Babylonian Talmud*, Sukkah 49b

17. Hosea 10:12

18. There are many Spinka Rebbes (in Kiryas Yoel, Williamsburg, Israel, etc.). This one is from Brooklyn.

The general conception of striving for equality, which is the basis of kindness and the pure love of people, is seen in the mystical interpretation as bringing up the sparks that are scattered among the husks of unrefined existence, and in the great vision of transforming everything to full and absolute holiness, in a gradual increasing of love, peace, justice, truth, and compassion.[19]

Rav Kook continuously urged us to strive for social progress. This was not a political endeavor at its core, but a spiritual revolution. In seeing the holy sparks in everyone and everything, and working in solidarity to elevate them, we can move closer each day to living in a redeeming world that is overflowing with "love, peace, justice, truth, and compassion!"

I've started tracking the number of unplanned acts of kindness I do each day that have a significant impact on others in need, and I am so completely ashamed and embarrassed at myself. Try tracking it for yourself. I'm sure you'll come out better than me, but you might also realize how many more opportunities there are each day to embrace intentional giving.

In synagogues around the world, we read the Creation story (the first chapters of Genesis) each year. But the Creation story is not merely a 6-day project relegated to the confines of history, but is rather a story that continues to play out today! The Sages taught: When a person chooses to perform a good deed without any obligation to do so, G-d looks down and says, 'For this moment alone it was worth creating the world!'

Many people speak rudely to customer service agents on the phone forgetting their humanity based on their invisibility. I think of my wife Shoshana who routinely laughs with customer service agents on the phone and floods them with kindness. Our teachers can be all around us. Derech Eretz, meaning the way of the earth, is a reminder that we are all earthlings, all interconnected on this land. "Good etiquette" can be formulaic and dictatorial. It can also be dehumanizing for all those without access to "the proper rules" or decorum. Nazi Germany was very "proper" (clean, organized, formal, punctual, etc.). There is much more to respect than etiquette. The type of derech eretz we need to cultivate is not one of formal rules but one of radical kindness and empathy that is truly responsive to the other.

Let us continue to justify the creation of the world through our acts of *derech eretz!* Let us continue to expand the creation story as we creatively and compassionately beautify the world together! Afterall, we have all been chosen to be G-d's partners in Creation!

---

19. Kook *Orot HaKodesh* 2

#20

Rodeif Emet, Pursuing Truth

> "Beauty is truth, truth beauty, that is all
> Ye know on earth, and all ye need to know."[1]

There are few values that feel as obviously Jewish as pursuing truth. What is religion about if not the quest for truth? In addition to being an epistemological pursuit as we strive to comprehend the cosmos, it is a moral pursuit as we strive to live with integrity. While truth would not be an absolute commitment as Immanuel Kant would have it,[2] nonetheless the commitment to truth is a very high priority in Jewish thought.

The Torah teaches us: *"Mid'var sheker tirchak"* ("Distance yourself from falsehood.")[3] It is not only that we should speak truth and not lie, but that we should actually distance ourselves from falsehood. The Sefer HaChinuch, focusing on the phrase "distance yourself," emphasizes this point:

> The root of this *mitzvah* is well known: falsehood is abominable
> and corrupt in the eyes of all. There is nothing more abhorrent

---

1. Keats, "Ode on a Grecian Urn"

2. There are times when Judaism calls for not being completely truthful. When Joseph and his brothers return from burying their father Jacob, they are concerned that Joseph may take revenge upon them, and they inform him: "Your father commanded before his death, saying, 'Tell Joseph [to] please forgive the sins of your brothers.'" Yet Jacob apparently never made such a request. In fact, this episode is considered to be the basis of the permission to lie for the sake of *shalom bayit* (peace within the home) and, indeed, to bring about peace between any two individuals. See *Babylonian Talmud*, Yevamot 65b, for further treatment of this subject.

3. Exodus 23:7

than it. Desolation and curse [are found] in the home of those
who love falsehood . . .

And blessing is only found and will only take effect upon those who
emulate God in their actions: to be truthful just as the Lord is a God of
truth; to have compassion, as it is known that God is compassionate; to do
acts of loving-kindness, just as God abounds in loving-kindness[4].

> For this reason, the Torah cautions us to distance ourselves
> exceedingly from falsehood, as it is written: "Distance your-
> self from falsehood.[5]" In stating the *mitzvah*, the Torah uses
> the word "distance" [as a verb], which it does not do regard-
> ing any other *mitzvah*, to [indicate] the disgusting nature [of
> falsehood].[6]

Even further, we may feel that as long as we're not the speaker of lies,
we may associate with others who are. The Sefer HaChinuch teaches here:

> An aspect of "distancing" is not to incline one's ear at all to [hear]
> anything that one believes to be falsehood, even if [the listeners]
> do not know for certain that this particular matter is a lie . . .[7]

Additionally, it's not only that we don't want to give those who lie
credibility but also that we may inadvertently be influenced by them.[8]
Indeed, we are warned that *"aveirah goreret aveirah"* ("one wrong leads to
another").[9]

The rabbis taught: "Truth stands, falsehood does not stand."[10] In
the end, falsehood will be exposed; it cannot endure. Furthermore, we are
told: "Rabban Shimon ben Gamliel taught: 'The world is sustained by three
things: justice, truth, and peace.'"[11]

Rabbeinu Yonah teaches that our commitment to truth is not only
religiously meaningful and morally imperative, but necessary for the health
of the soul.

---

4. c.f. Rashi, Deuteronomy 11:22

5. Exodus 23:7

6. *Sefer HaChinuch*, Mitzvah 74

7. *Sefer HaChinuch*, Mitzvah 74

8. *Babylonian Talmud*, Shavuot 30b

9. *Pirkei Avot* 4:3. While this is a general aphorism about all sins, lying is clearly
included here.

10. *Babylonian Talmud*, Shabbat 104a

11. *Pirkei Avot* 1:18

Misleading people and lying . . . is in a sense more serious than theft. This is because speaking falsehood is an act of self-destruction, for truthfulness is one of the foundations of the health of the soul. Therefore, we are obligated to stay within the parameters of truth.[12]

We may think that when we're unsure if we should speak up in a given situation that we should just remain silent, but the rabbis teach[13] that silence may also be a form of lying.

From where [do we know] that if a student is sitting before their teacher [who is the judge], and [the student] sees a supporting argument for the poor litigant, or an argument against the rich litigant [that their teacher missed], that they may not sit quietly? The Torah states, "Distance yourself from falsehood."[14]

Of course, there are some very rare cases where other values outweigh the value of perfect truth. Consider how Rabbeinu Yonah teaches this when he defines nine categories of falsehood.

The fourth category is: one who intentionally lies in relating a story that they heard and changes [the facts] around a little. They have no benefit from their lies, and it does not damage anyone else. . . This category of falsehood was made permissible [by the Rabbis] in order to: first, fulfill a *mitzvah*; and second, also, for the pursuit of good and peace.[15]

The Talmud teaches how preserving a marriage also may matter more than perfect truth.[16]

Abraham and Sarah were informed by three guests that they would miraculously have children even though they were old. Sarah expressed disbelief at the news, claiming that both she and her husband were incapable of producing children. When God related the incident of Sarah's disbelief to Avraham, He omitted the fact that Sarah had implied that her husband was old and incapable of having children.

The School of Rabbi Yishmael taught in a Baraita: "Great is peace, for even The Holy One be Blessed, alters [words] for its sake. Originally, it is written, "[Sarah said: after I have withered

12. Rabbeinu Yonah, *Shaarei Teshuvah* 3:184

13. *Babylonian Talmud*, Shavuot 31a

14. Exodus 23:7

15. Rabbeinu Yonah, *Sha'arei Teshuvah* 3:181. See footnote 2 above.

16. *Babylonian Talmud*, Yevamot 65b

and become old shall I again have delicate skin and give birth?!]
And my husband is old!" But in the end [when God quotes
Sarah's words to Avraham] it is written, "and *I [Sarah]* am old."[17]

In addition to performing a *mitzvah* and preserving a marriage, the
rabbis talk about altering truth for the sake of the dignity of the other:[18]

> The Rabbis taught in a *baraita*: How do we dance before the
> bride?[19]
> Beit Shammai says, "[We praise and describe] the bride as she is."
> But Beit Hillel says, "[In all cases we give praise and say] that the
> bride is beautiful and kind."
> Beit Shammai said to Beit Hillel, "Now, if she were lame or blind
> do we say about her that she is a beautiful and charming bride?
> But the Torah has said: 'Distance yourself from falsehood!'"
> Beit Hillel said to Beit Shammai, "According to your view, if
> someone made a bad purchase in the market [and he asked your
> opinion on the purchase, and he had no way of returning the
> item] should one praise it in the purchaser's eyes or denigrate it?
> Of course, you would say that one should praise it in his eyes.
> [We should therefore praise even a homely bride]."[20]

There are other situations that may warrant exemption from refraining
from lying, such as acting humbly[21] or protecting oneself from extortion.[22]
But Jewish tradition requires one to be on a very high level to engage in such
behavior. One has to have total clarity that one's altering of truth is not for
their own benefit, is not going to cause harm to another, will not influence
another to lie or to believe that lying is acceptable, etc.

> Today, truth is under attack. It's under attack from the far-right
> who claim all is "fake news" and who discredit election integrity
> and medical expertise. It's under attack from the far-left who
> throw out empirical data to fit their ideology. It's under attack
> from post-modernists who claim that all truth is relative. It's
> under attack from fundamentalists who claim that all truth is
> simple, accessible, and in their control. It's under attack by those

---

17. Genesis 18:12–13

18. *Babylonian Talmud*, Ketubot 16b-17a

19. This question is a euphemism for "how do we praise the bride?"

20. In this case, Hillel seems to be interested in protecting both the dignity of the
bride and the groom.

21. *Babylonian Talmud*, Bava Metzia 23b

22. *Mishnah*, Nedarim 27b

who think the goal of life is happiness at all costs and do not include a rigorous pursuit of truth.

Aside from being truthful in our words and refraining from lying, there is a different type of truth which we should pursue. Rav Kook teaches how indeed there are multiple conflicting truths we can live with, and how only in a time to come will all of these truths come to fit together in a sensible and meaningful way.

> The abundance of peace means that all sides and opinions will become evident, and it will become clear how there is room for all of them, each according to its own standing, place, and substance. On the contrary, even matters that appear superfluous or contradictory will become evident when the truth of wisdom in all its facets is revealed. For only through an assemblage of all the parts and all the particulars, all the dissimilar ideas and all the diverse disciplines—only through them will the light of truth and justice shine, as well as knowledge of God, love and awe of God, and the true light of Torah.[23]

We cannot let our different theological truths divide us. Rabbi Jonathan Sacks wrote:

> Nothing has proved harder in the history of civilization than to see God, or good, or human dignity in those whose language is not mine, whose skin is a different colour, whose faith is not my faith, and whose truth is not my truth.[24]
>
> Biblical monotheism is not the idea that there is one God and therefore one truth, one faith, one way of life. On the contrary, it is the idea that unity creates diversity.[25]

Some may approach me and say: "Rabbi, prove to me that God exists." But this is a flawed question. We don't use a cheap mathematical or scientific proof to demonstrate the deepest truth of the universe. In fact, we cannot prove, in the absolute sense, that God exists. Nor should we. God is to be experienced, not proven. So too, I hear: "Rabbi, prove to me that Judaism is true." But here too, this is a flawed question. Judaism is not proven through a quick axiom but rather through its story. Rabbi Sacks added:

> Judaism is a faith. But it is the faith of a particular people. It is more than a set of truths and commands. It is a people to whom

23. Kook, *Olat Re'ayah,* volume 1, 330
24. Sacks, *The Dignity of Difference,* 65
25. Sacks, *The Dignity of Difference,* 53

those truths and commands are addressed and in whose lives they are embodied. The future of the covenant depends on the future of the people of the covenant. Theology, in Judaism, is dependent on demography.[26]

And so, while we are so committed to pursuing truth, we also know how much bloodshed there has been in the name of truth. Rabbi Sacks speaks up here too and reminds us of how we must change this course:

> For life to be livable, truth on earth cannot be what it is in heaven. Truth in heaven may be platonic—eternal, harmonious, radiant. But man cannot aspire to such truth, and if he does, he will create conflict, not peace. Men kill because they believe they possess the truth while their opponents are in error. In that case, says God, throwing truth to the ground, let human beings live by a different standard of truth, one that is human and thus conscious of its limitations. Truth on the ground is multiple, partial. Fragments of it lie everywhere. Each person, culture and language have part of it; none has it all. Truth on earth is not, nor can it aspire to be, the whole truth. It is limited, not comprehensive; particular, not universal. When two propositions conflict it is not necessarily because one is true [and] the other false. It may be, and often is, that each represents a different perspective on reality, an alternative way of structuring order, no more and no less commensurable than a Shakespeare sonnet, a Michelangelo painting, or a Schubert sonata. In heaven there is truth; on earth there are truths. Therefore, each culture has something to contribute.[27]

May we be rigorous pursuers of peace, dignity, and humility, but may we do everything possible to uphold the deepest commitment to truth alongside these other virtues. Living with truth is a kindness enabling us to give others a sense of stability. It allows us to build trust, to deepen relationships, and to create spaces where we can all be more vulnerable in bringing our authentic truthful selves wherever we go.

---

26. Sacks, *Tradition in an Untraditional Age*, 101

27. Sacks, *The Dignity of Difference*, 64–65

#21

Savlanut, Being Patient

NONE OF US ARE born patient. Watch any young child and they just can't wait for their food, for their toy, or for their birthday party. True, some of us may be more naturally inclined to be patient, but, nonetheless, all of us need to work on cultivating that patience.

The Talmudic rabbis teach a lesson in how anyone in an educational role needs extraordinary patience:

> Our rabbis learned: What was the procedure of the instruction in the oral law? Moses learned from the mouth of the Omnipotent. Then Aaron entered and Moses taught him his lesson. Aaron then moved aside and sat down on Moses' left. Thereupon Aaron's sons entered and Moses taught them their lesson. His sons then moved aside, Eleazar taking his seat on Moses' right and Ithamar on Aaron's left. (R. Judah stated: Aaron was always on Moses' right.) Thereupon the elders entered and Moses taught them their lesson, and when the elders moved aside all the people entered and Moses taught them their lesson. It thus followed that Aaron heard the lesson four times, his sons heard it three times, the elders twice, and all the people once. At this stage Moses departed and Aaron taught them his lesson. Then Aaron departed and his sons taught them their lesson. His sons then departed and the elders taught them their lesson. It thus followed that everybody heard the lesson four times. From here R. Eliezer inferred: It is a person's duty to teach [the lesson to] his pupil four times. For this is arrived at a minori ad majus: Aaron, who learned from Moses who [himself] learned it from the Omnipotent, had to learn his lesson four times; how

much more so an ordinary pupil who learns from an ordinary teacher.[1]

To hammer home the point, the rabbis go even further:

Yet we find that Rabbi Preida had a student with whom he reviewed each lesson *four hundred* times. As a reward for this, four hundred extra years were allotted to his life, and everyone in his generation was guaranteed a place in the World to Come.[2]

We learn that God is the ultimate model of one who is slow to anger and compassionate and gracious with patience. The rabbis taught:

There were ten generations from Adam to Noah. This shows how great was God's patience, for every one of those generations provoked God continually until God brought upon them the waters of the Flood.[3]

God is willing to be insulted and not lash out until God feels there is no alternative. Rabbi Moshe Cordovero[4] writes:

This attribute refers to the Holy One be Blessed, as a tolerant King Who bears insult in a manner beyond human understanding. Without doubt, nothing is hidden from God's view. In addition, there is not a moment that a person is not nourished and sustained by virtue of the Divine power bestowed upon them.

Thus, no one ever sins against God without God, at that very moment, bestowing abundant vitality upon them, giving them the power to move their limbs. Yet even though a person uses this very vitality to transgress, God does not withhold it from them. Rather, the Holy One be Blessed, suffers this insult and continues to enable their limbs to move. Even at the very moment that a person uses that power for transgression, sin, and infuriating deeds, the Holy One be Blessed, bears them patiently. . .

This, then, is a virtue man should emulate—namely, tolerance. Even when he is insulted to the degree mentioned above, he should not withdraw his benevolence from those upon whom he bestows it.[5]

---

1. *Babylonian Talmud*, Eruvin 54b

2. Ibid. This number (four hundred) should perhaps be understood as a metaphor for R. Preida being as patient with his pupil as he felt necessary.

3. *Pirkei Avot* 5:2

4. R. Moshe Cordovero was a famed 16th-century kabbalist.

5. Cordovero, *Tomer Devorah*, Who *is Like You God? (Mi Kel Kamocha?)*

It is instructive to note that the word *savlanut* shares the same Hebrew root as the word *sevel* (suffering or affliction). One suffers, at times in patience, sitting in the gray area waiting for clarity. Further, the trait of *savlanut*, in its fullest manifestation, demands more than just being patient with others. It requires taking the time to discern what is troubling them, what is holding them back, and how they would like to be helped, if at all, before acting. Indeed, the Torah informs us that prior to Moshe's striking the Egyptian, *"vayar b'sivlotam"* ("he took notice of their [the Israelites'] affliction"). It seems that Moshe only discerned the proper course of action, killing the Egyptian, after internalizing just how deeply the Jews were suffering. Going further in the connection between patience and suffering, it may be that we're not suffering in our patience but that our patience enables us to more deeply see another's suffering.

The Book of Proverbs reminds us that patience is not simply a kindness we should display toward others, but that we will, ourselves, make better decisions if we are patient. "The patient person shows much good sense, but the quick tempered one displays folly at its height."[6]

Consider also how shortcuts in our interactions with others might actually not get us where we want to go.

> R. Joshua b. Hananiah remarked: No one has ever had the better of me except a woman, a little boy and a little girl. . .What was the incident with the little boy? I was once on a journey when I noticed a little boy sitting at a cross-road. 'By what road,' I asked him, 'do we go to the town?' 'This one,' he replied, 'is short but long, and that one is long but short.' I proceeded along the short but long road. When I approached the town, I discovered that it was hedged in by gardens and orchards. Turning back, I said to him, 'My son, did you not tell me that this road was short?' And he replied, 'Did I not also tell you: 'but long?' I kissed him upon his head and said to him, 'Happy are you, O Israel; all of you are wise, both young and old.[7]

The Jewish people needed to go the long way to Israel: forty years in the desert! But God was instructing that the long path was the way needed to arrive properly and prepared. Specifically, regarding Torah, itself, the Tanya teaches:

> Based on the verse, "For it is exceedingly near to you, in your mouth and in your heart, to do it"- [this is written] to explain

---

6. Proverbs 14:29

7. *Babylonian Talmud*, Eruvin 53b

clearly how it is exceedingly near, in a long and short way, with the help of God, be blessed.[8]

It doesn't just take age and experience to be wise; rather it takes work, and patience, to achieve wisdom. The Talmud teaches:

> Rabbi Yitzchak said: If a person tells you, "I have toiled and I have not found," don't believe them. If they say, "I have not toiled and I have found," don't believe them.
> If they say, "I have toiled and I have found," believe them.[9]

A big part of the wisdom of patience is knowing what's in our control (where we must push at times) and what is not in our control (where we must surrender at times). The Serenity Prayer famously teaches:

> God, grant me the serenity to accept the things I cannot change,
> Courage to change the things I can,
> And wisdom to know the difference.[10]

Rabbi Menachem Mendel Lefin[11] made a similar point:

> Woe to the pampered one who has never been trained to be patient. Either today or in the future they are destined to sip from the cup of affliction. . .When something happens to you and you did not have the power to control it, do not aggravate the situation further through wasted anxiety or grief.[12]

Each of us is tempted to make rash or poor decisions. God said to Cain: "Sin crouches at the door, its urge is toward you, yet you can be its master."[13] If we don't pause with patience, we can make quick, poor decisions based on temptations. Victor Frankel reminds us of how we can take control of our lives, through our freedom, one moment at a time:

> Between stimulus and response there is a space. In that space is our power to choose our response. In our response lies our growth and our freedom.

---

8. *Tanya*, Title Page. *Tanya*, an important work of hasidic philosophy, was written by Rabbi Shneur Zalman of Liadi, the first rebbe of the Chabad Lubavitch movement.

9. *Babylonian Talmud*, Megillah 6b

10. Reinhold Neibuhr, "Serenity Prayer"

11. Rabbi Menachem Mendel Lefin of Satanov (Ukraine) was an 18th-century scholar, author, and translator.

12. Rabbi Menachem Mendel Lefin of Satanov, *Cheshbon Ha-Nefesh*

13. Genesis 4:5–7

If we wish to be more reflective and more intentional, we will need to bear the burden of our emotions; we will sometimes need to suffer through waiting instead of rushing.

In activism, the work requires a very calculated and sensitive balance between patience and alacrity. On the one hand, one must have the patience for teaching and engaging the apathetic and the uninformed. On the other hand, one must also have the alacrity to respond to crises and injustices at the most crucial time. Most often the precise timing that necessitates immediate action precedes the completion of the essential education and mobilization of the public. This is one of the reasons why the uninformed segments of the public at times view the activist as radical. One must have the courage to act in the name of *shalom* (peace) and *tzedek* (justice) while maintaining patience and respect for more passive critics from one's own constituency.

This *savlanut* (patience) is required for one who believes deeply enough in their convictions and also cares enough about his or her students and constituents joining to pursue justice for social change. Both Pinchas[14] and Moshe[15] serve as our quintessential Jewish models of *kinah* (zealotry) and *zerizut* (alacrity).[16] Moshe's core identity and community were transformed by his courageous decision to protect the abused. Similarly, the way that Avraham greeted his guests[17] teaches us that one must develop the emotional intelligence to be in touch with another's needs to the point that one can indeed respond to situations that demand immediate and urgent responses with care.

Meditation can be an important tool to slow us down and help us become more present to the moment. We can practice patience and through habituation and biological conditioning, extend the seconds or minutes that we can learn to wait. We can learn to befriend, rather than fight, our impatience. Afterall, our impatience is there to help us. Our inner impatience may be screaming at us "Life is short!" "Achieve your goals!" "Help others now!" Rather than fight the voice of impatience, we can befriend them and calm them down. We can book a little less in our schedule, if possible, and move a little more thoughtfully rather than frantically.

14. Numbers 25:7–13

15. Exodus 2:11–12; Ibid. 32:19–20

16. Moshe demonstrated *zerizut*, as we mentioned earlier in this essay, in his smiting the Egyptian. He once again demonstrated this same alacrity later in life when he broke the tablets upon seeing the Israelites worshipping the Golden Calf. Pinchas is considered the paradigm of *zerizut*, as he killed Zimri, a Jew from the tribe of Shimon, and Kozbi, a Moabite, who had publicly engaged in lewd behavior.

17. Genesis 18:2

We must be patient with ourselves, our family members, our students, and our constituents. We must also live with urgency. Through experience, wisdom, and partnership, we can all learn which trait is required at which time. The Israelites needed to be patient to be freed from slavery, then patient waiting in the dessert to enter the promised land. So too, we have our tests and those challenges can produce growth.

Leo Tolstoy, the great Russian writer, famously noted that "the two most powerful warriors are patience and time." There is a time for *savlanut* and a time for *zerizut*. Balancing these two warrior traits requires self-awareness, courage, partnership, and sensitivity. May we develop this necessary balance of order to lead and create social change.

#22

Hakarat HaTov, Expressing Gratitude

THE HEBREW TERM FOR expressing gratitude, *hakarat hatov*, literally means "recognizing the good." This is precisely what God modeled right at the beginning of the Torah: "And God saw the light that it was good, and God separated between the light and between the darkness."[1] Later, Leah is the first person in the Torah[2] to orally thank God: "And she [Leah] conceived again and bore a son, and she said, "This time, I will thank the Lord! Therefore, she named him *Yehudah* (Judah),[3] and [then] she stopped bearing."[4]

In fact, the Hebrew term *Yehudim* (Jews)[5] is derived from the name Yehudah. While we are historically called Yehudim because the earlier kings of Israel beginning with David[6] were from the tribe of Yehudah, it is possible to suggest that with our name comes a charge to express our gratitude both to God and to others.

It turns out that living with gratitude is not only a deeply Jewish value but is also good for us:

1. Genesis 1:4

2. *Babylonian Talmud*, Berachot 7b.
While others prior to Leah displayed their gratitude towards God, e.g., Noah, and similarly, Abraham, by building altars and monuments to God, Leah was the first to verbalize this thanks.

3. The root of Yehudah (the Hebrew name of Judah), hei-dalet-hei, means thanks. Leah used the same root when she declared, "*Hapaʾam* odeh *et Hashem*" ("This time I will thank God").

4. Genesis 29:35

5. The English term Jew is also derived, albeit indirectly, from the name Judah.

6. Saul, the first king, was from the tribe of Benjamin.

Cultivating an "attitude of gratitude" has been linked to better health, sounder sleep, less anxiety and depression, higher long-term satisfaction with life and kinder behavior towards others, including romantic partners. . . as a culture we have lost a deep sense of gratefulness about the freedoms we enjoy, a lack of gratitude for all the material advantages we have. . .[7]

Hakarat hatov is also the pathway to becoming rich! "Ben Zoma says: 'Who is rich? One who is content with their own lot.'"[8] (and thereby recognizing the good with which they are blessed). Becoming grateful means turning off one of the greatest curses of our time: insatiability. For some, they can simply never be enough or have enough.

Cultivating gratitude enables us to "see" others, even those we cannot actually see physically. Consider that the author of the teaching in Pirkei Avot we shared above also lived accordingly:

He [Ben Zoma] used to say: What does a good guest say? 'How much trouble my host has taken for me! How much meat he has set before me! How much wine he has set before me! How many cakes he has set before me! And all the trouble he has taken was only for my sake!' But what does a bad guest say? 'How much, after all, has my host put himself out? I have eaten but one piece of bread, I have eaten but one slice of meat, I have drunk only one cup of wine! All the trouble which my host has taken was only for the sake of his wife and his children!'[9]

The Sefer HaChinuch teaches that the reason we should honor our parents is also rooted in the trait of gratitude.

The essence of this commandment [to honor one's father and mother] is that one should recognize and do kindness to those who have done good to them. For one should not be ungrateful, for that is a negative trait and an utter abomination before God and humankind. And one should take to heart that their father and mother are the reason for their being in the world, so it is incumbent upon them to do them all the honor and good they can, because they brought them to the world, and also exerted themselves many times for them in their childhood. And when one can internalize this in their soul it will lead them to

7. John Tierney, *A Serving of Gratitude May Save the Day*, New York Times, Nov 21, 2011

8. *Pirkei Avot* 4:1

9. *Babylonian Talmud*, Berachot 58a

recognize the good of God be Blessed, that God is his cause and
the cause of all the ancestors back to Adam. . .[10]

Prayer, too, can help us get there. Rabbi Abraham Joshua Heschel taught:

> To pray is to take notice of the wonder, to regain a sense of the
> mystery that animates all beings, the divine margin in all attain-
> ments. Prayer is our humble answer to the inconceivable sur-
> prise of living. . .. It is gratefulness that makes the soul great.[11]

Indeed, our daily prayers begin with *hakarat hatov*, as the first prayer we
recite every morning is *Modeh Ani*,[12] in which we thank God for restoring our souls. The *Shacharit* service then continues with a series of blessings known as *Birchot HaShachar* (Morning Blessings), in turn followed
by Pesukei D'Zimrah (Verses of Gratitude). Even the silent *Amidah* prayer,
which consists mainly of requests, begins with three blessings of gratitude.

And for this reason, this form of prayer must last. A *midrash* teaches:
"[In the time to come] all prayers will cease, but the prayer of thanksgiving
will not cease."[13]

In addition to daily blessings expressing gratitude, we have a special
blessing, *Birkat HaGomeil*,[14] that one recites when they feel God has res-
cued them.

> Rabbi Yehudah said in the name of Rav: "Four (individuals) are
> required to express gratitude: Those who go down to the sea
> (i.e., travel by boat), those who traverse the desert, one who was
> ill and recovered, and one who was imprisoned and freed.[15]

The rabbis taught that we should recite one hundred blessings a day.
They learn this from a verse:[16]

> And now, O Israel, what does your God demand of you? Only
> this: to revere your God, to walk in God's ways, to love and to
> serve your God with all your heart and soul.[17]

10. *Sefer HaChinuch*, the commandment of honoring one's parents (mitzvah 33)

11.. Heschel, *Man's Quest for God*

12. The literal translation of the words *modeh ani* is "I thank."

13. *Leviticus Rabbah* 9:7

14. The word *hagomeil* literally means "the One Who bestows (goodness upon me)."

15. *Babylonian Talmud*, Berachot 54b. This talmudic dictum is the source for a
woman to recite *birkat hagomeil* after giving birth. Some also recite it after travelling by
airplane, likening it to traveling by boat.

16. Deuteronomy 10:12

17. While the one hundred daily blessings are not comprised only of blessings of

The Hebrew word for "what" (used in the verse cited above) is *mah*, and is phonetically similar to the word *mei'ah*, meaning one hundred. So, according to the Talmud, the verse can be understood as saying: "Now, Israel, *one hundred* does the Lord, your God, ask of you," suggesting that we should strive to recite one hundred blessings.

Rav Shlomo Wolbe, the famed 20th-century *mussar* teacher, shared an insight as to how to cultivate more gratitude:

> "If one appreciates that all the needs one has fulfilled [by others] are truly goodness and kindness, one most certainly increases love and friendship in the world and comes to realize that one exists in a world of kindness. When one hides from this recognition, the world is grey. [One's perception is that] every person is only doing their job, each merchant only wants to profit, the doctor only wants the payment, the educator only the salary— there is no goodness, no kindness and no friendship. The world is sucked dry. No! We want to live in a bright world, a world full of goodness and kindness, love and friendship! This illuminated world is built through showing gratitude to all."[18]

As we mentioned earlier, the very first prayer that many say in the morning is *Modeh Ani*, in which we thank God that we are alive. Wake up this morning? Of course. But did you really *wake* up? Or are you still sleep-walking? To be awake, we must stir our inner being and be prepared to encounter all that truly comes before our eyes and be grateful for it.

Our lives are remarkably short, and we need spiritual activities to constantly remind us of this truth. A person who lives to eighty years old will take about 672,768,000 breaths in a lifetime. Consider the shofar, which only makes a noise if someone blows their precious breath into it. So too, our soul only prays if we allow God to breathe through us.

Consider tapping into the Divine breath that breathes through you like a Divine shofar. Feel the gratitude and intimacy. Only then the soul can start to shake, to dance, to sing!

When we encounter others, we must see beyond the surface, which will in turn enable us to be truly grateful. Rav Alexandri taught:[19]

> If a common person uses a broken vessel, it is considered a disgrace. But not the Holy One, blessed be God. All of God's vessels are broken. "God is near the brokenhearted."[20]

---

thanks and gratitude, the above prooftext does reflect this concept.

18. Wolbe, *Alei Shur*

19. *Pesikta d'Rav Kahana*

20. Psalm 34

To emulate the Divine, one should be adamantly focused on the most powerless rather than the most powerful, the most broken rather than the most privileged and fortunate; we must witness the suffering right before our eyes. A Chassidic story hits home:

> The Sassover Rebbe entered a hotel and sat beside two local peasants. As the two peasants sat at the bar and drank, they began to fall into a drunken stupor. One turned to his friend and said, "Tell me, friend, do you love me?" His colleague responded, "Of course I love you. We're drinking companions. Naturally I love you." Then the first one said to his friend, "Then tell me, friend, what causes me pain?" His colleague said, "How should I know what hurts you? I'm just your drinking buddy." The other said, "If you loved me, you would know what causes me pain."

To achieve such a level, we must gain more elevated freedom. Many who consider themselves free are, from the Torah's perspective, still enslaved. Rav Kook explains that there are intelligent slaves whose being is full of freedom and there are free individuals whose being consists of the spirit of a slave. The real slave is one who lives in conformity seeking to be honored by others. The free individual experiences inner individuality and is focused on the eternal illumination of the image of God within oneself. Only such a person can free themself of the need to be honored and recognized by others and can instead honor and recognize them.

The opportunities to truly see ourselves and others are right before our eyes. Therein lies our freedom, indeed our dignity. This can all be rooted in *hakarat hatov*, which is good for our health. It can help sustain our Jewish spiritual lives, can bring us closer to others and to God when we express our gratitude, and can be a source of our moral responsibility, seeing how much our gratitude can be channeled into giving back to others.

#23

Ichpatiyut La'Acheirim, Reaching Out to Others

SOMETIMES, SOMEONE'S NEED FOR support is clear. They are calling us, asking us, knocking on our door. Other times, there are people who don't ask for help. Some don't even know that they need help. Being a person of kindness means that we're not only reactive to requests but that we actively reach out. We ask others what they need. We reach out without being begged.

Dr. Martin Luther King Jr. famously asked: "Life's most persistent and urgent question is, what are you doing for others?"[1] We cannot only combat the great challenges of our day. We also need to leave room for the smaller, positive acts of service. The 20th-century Russian-British philosopher and historian Isaiah Berlin wrote:

> Injustice, poverty, slavery, ignorance—these may be cured by reform or revolution. But [people] do not live by only fighting evils. They live by positive goals, individual and collective, a vast variety of them, seldom predictable.[2]

The great Catholic teacher Mother Teresa said: "Do not wait for leaders. Do it alone, person to person."[3] This is existential for us, and sometimes achieving something "small" is not so small at all. Emily Dickinson wrote:

> If I can stop one heart from breaking,
> I shall not live in vain;

---

1. Ryan, *Random Acts of Kindness Then & Now*, 15
2. Ryan, *Random Acts of Kindness Then & Now*, 40
3. Ryan, *Random Acts of Kindness Then & Now*, 52

If I can ease one life the aching,
Or cool one pain,
Or help one fainting robin
Unto his nest again,
I shall not live in vain.[4]

And so, we can, and must, master a practice of proactively reaching out to others. So many are isolated and suffering from loneliness. Rabbi Jonathan Sacks writes:[5]

> . . .A similar state of affairs exists in the United States. A 2018 Cigna survey showed that 46 percent of Americans always or sometimes feel alone, and 47 percent feel left out. One in four rarely or never feel that there are people who really understand them. Forty-three percent feel that their relationships are not meaningful and that they are isolated from others. Fifty-four percent feel that no one knows them well. These most distressed by loneliness were young people between eighteen and twenty-two years of age.[6] The phenomenon is not confined to the West. In Ukraine, Russia, Hungary, Poland, Slovakia, Romania, Bulgaria, and Latvia, 34 percent of the population declared themselves lonely.[7]

These numbers are striking and disheartening. Rabbi Sacks continues to explain[8] the pain of loneliness and the benefits of socialization and connectedness.

> Simply playing cards with friends once a week, or getting together over a cup of coffee, adds as many years to life expectancy as giving up a pack-a-day smoking habit.[9] People with active social lives recover faster after illness. A study done by the University of California in 2006 showed that of three hundred women with breast cancer, those with a large network of friends were four times as likely to survive as women with few social connections.[10]

4. Ryan, *Random Acts of Kindness Then & Now*,114

5. Sacks, *Morality: Restoring the Common Good in Divided Times*, 2021, p. 27

6. "Loneliness in America," Cigna, May 1, 2018

7. Yang, Victor, "Age and Loneliness in 25 European Nations," (Ageing and Society), 1368–88

8. Yang, Victor, "Age and Loneliness in 25 European Nations," (Ageing and Society),

9. *Participating in Activities You Enjoy*, National Institute on Aging, U.S. Department of Health & Human Services, October 23, 2017

10. *Social Networks, Social Support and Survival after Breast Cancer Diagnosis*,

Similarly, in The Book of Forgiving, Archbishop Desmond Tutu and his activist daughter Mpho Tutu share:[11]

> Dr. Lisa Berman, chair of the Department of Society, Human Development and Health at the Harvard School of Public Health, studied seven thousand men and women. According to her findings, people who were socially isolated were three times more likely to die prematurely than those who had a strong social web. Even more astonishing to the researchers, those who had a strong social circle and unhealthy lifestyle (smoking, obesity, and lack of exercise) actually lived longer than those who had a weak social circle but a healthy lifestyle.[12] A separate article in the journal Science concluded that loneliness was a greater risk factors for disease and death than smoking.[13]

Former US Senator John McCain, who spent over five years as a POW in Vietnam, described just how destructive forced solitude can be. He said it "crushes your spirit and weakens your resistance more effectively than any other form of mistreatment."[14]

All of this points to just how crucial it is for us to reach out to others in need, not only in need of physical and financial assistance, but emotional support and friendship as well.

Rabbi Harold Kushner writes:

> This is the terrible paradox of loneliness: the more it forces us to focus on our own needs, the harder it becomes for us to be [alerted] to the needs of others, until we become our own worst enemies, chasing people away with our unrelenting focus on ourselves. . . .. True religion teaches us not how to win friends but how to be a friend, to be concerned with alleviating the loneliness of others, learning to hear their cry instead of wondering why no one hears ours. When we have learned those lessons, connecting with other people around us becomes much easier.[15]

Journal of Clinical Oncology, March 2006

11. The Book of Forgiving, Desmond Tutu and Mpho Tutu (Douglas C. Abrams, ed), Harper One, New York, 2014, p. 19

12. Lisa F. Berman and Lester Breslow, Health and Ways of Living: The Alameda County Study (New York: Oxford Univ. Press, 1983)

13. Greg Miller, Why Loneliness Is Hazardous to Your Health, Science 14 (January 2011) vol. 333, no. 6014: 138–40

14. Atul Gawande, Hellhole, New Yorker, March 23, 2009

15. Kushner, Who Needs God, 98–99

Perhaps the codifiers of *halachah* had this very paradox in mind when instituting an oft-overlooked detail of the *mitzvah* of *mishlo'ach manot* (the giving of gifts of food) on the holiday of Purim. We are informed: "If one does not have (the means to give *mishlo'ach manot*), two people should exchange food portions in order to fulfill the dictum of '*mishlo'ach manot* to one another.'[16][17] At face value, this *halachah* seems pointless, as at the end of the day each ends up with no more or less than they had before. But as we have seen above, there is dignity in the act of giving, and this minor detail of the *mitzvah* of gift-giving provides every individual with that opportunity.

"And a man found him, when he was wandering in the field, and the man asked him, 'What are you seeking?' And he said, 'I am seeking my brothers'" (Genesis 37:15). This story about Joseph strikes me so deeply. As a child who moved to different cities every few years, I constantly felt like I was seeking "my brothers." To some degree, we are all wandering in search of our "brothers." Friendship is a challenging virtue to cultivate, even more challenging in our transient times. Yet, in an age that is increasingly interdependent, our culture is strangely moving toward an illusion of independence. Cultivating spiritual friendship ensures we remain grounded in the types of human relationships that cultivate virtue.

Transience is not even the biggest barrier to the cultivation of friendship today. Our Web-based society has weakened the strength of our relationships, and the fast-paced, self-interested nature of these relationships has become more transactional. One can "friend" or "defriend" someone with the click of a finger on Facebook. There are many "friends" created through social networking, but the social bonds are very weak. Web-based friendships may be interesting, entertaining, and enhance social capital, but they rarely create strong dependent bonds that foster more moral and spiritually inspired living. Friendship sadly becomes more about the taking than the giving.

Today, we are witnessing increased individualism, decreased institutional affiliation, and more talk about social networks than about relationships. While this helps our emerging micro-communities, it diminishes our traditional communities. True friendship is on the decline. Cornell University sociologists found that adults have only two friends they can discuss "important matters" with—down from three in 1985. Half of those surveyed said they had only one, and 4% had none. Friendship may still be social, but it is less confidential and intimate.

---

16. Esther 9:22

17. *Shulchan Aruch*, Laws of Purim 695:4

Further, more Americans are living alone. In major U.S. cities, 40% of households contain a single occupant. In Manhattan and Washington, D.C., nearly 50% of homes consist of only one person. Singles are marrying later, divorce is on the rise, and more individuals prefer to live in privacy than within a community. Increasingly, we live alone in a lonely society.

Without deep friendships, we lack adequate self-knowledge and awareness of our blind spots. lack of friendships can also lead to arrogance, as we become less able to recognize our need for others. To acquire most of our world knowledge, we must rely upon what others have shared with us in order to supplement our own experience. We look to experts for technical knowledge and to friends for subjective knowledge. *When we fail to cultivate friendships, we fail to cultivate ourselves.*

Aristotle suggests that there are three kinds of friendship—pleasure, utility, and virtue.[18] Each of these can have value for those suffering from isolation. The word for friendship in Aramaic (*chavruta*) means more than just a relationship; it is the primary model of Jewish learning. A *chavruta*, in its truest sense, is a challenger, (*bar plugta*), not one who merely supports us, but also challenges us.

The Talmud teaches that in religious learning and growth, a friend is even more important than a teacher: "I have learned much from my teachers, but from my friends more than my teachers."[19] A friend of virtue can be more connected to our intimate life pursuits more than any teacher can be. Thus, the rabbis teach that "one is not even to part from one's friend without exchanging words of Torah."[20] A friend, on the highest level, is primarily a learning partner, a partner in life.

Similarly, Maimonides explains that "man requires friends all his lifetime."[21] And it is the strong advice of the rabbis to "acquire for yourself a friend."[22] Like any other moral effort, doing so does not come naturally, but requires deliberation and toil.

My commitment to supporting the cultivation of virtue-based friendships is motivated by Jewish values. To be sure, one clear and important value of friendship is utilitarian; friends help each other in times of distress. As Ecclesiastes teaches: "Two are better than one because they have a good reward for their labor. For if they fall, the one will lift up his fellow; but woe

---

18. Aristotle, *Nicomachean Ethics*, Book VIII

19. *Babylonian Talmud*, Ta'anit 7a

20. *Babylonian Talmud*, Berachot 31a

21. Maimonides, *Guide for the Perplexed*, 3:49

22. *Pirkei Avot* 1:6

to him that is alone when he falls, for he has not another to help him up."[23] The Bible, too, consistently reminds us to protect the stranger. In friendship, we can move the other, and ourselves, from alienation into a social network and friendship.

Rabbi Joseph B. Soloveitchik valued both a *"haver li-de'agah,"* a person in whom one can confide both in times of crisis, when distress strikes, and in times of glory, when one feels happy and content, and a *"haver le'dei'ah,"* a friend in whom he or she has absolute trust and faith.[24] A friend is an emotional partner in our high and low journeys. Sometimes friendship is manifest in lifelong commitment. Other times, we can offer moments of the gift of friendship. One is never lonely if they are willing to connect to whomever they encounter. Every moment can be seen as an opportunity for spiritual presence and friendship.

In addition to support, Rabbi Soloveitchik explains (based upon the book of Job) that there is a vital spiritual purpose to friendships. "Job certainly did not grasp the meaning of friendship. . . Real friendship is possible only when man rises to the height of an open existence, in which he is capable of prayer and communication. In such living, the personality fulfills itself."[25] It is not until Job realizes the importance of opening himself spiritually to others that he truly comes to understand the virtue of friendship: "And the Lord returned the fortunes of Job when he prayed for his friends; and the Lord gave Job twice as much as he had before."[26]

Living a good, happy life without deep friendships was unfathomable to the rabbis. According to one Talmudic story, Honi, the legendary miracle-worker, was depressed from social isolation. He prayed for death, that he might be released from his despair. And Rava, a great 4th-century Talmudic sage, utters tersely that one must choose "either friendship or death."[27] The lesson is that we cannot thrive in our life missions without companionship. In the extreme, without companionship, one may choose death.

When friendship is just about having a good time on a hike or at a movie, it is not impactful or enduring. But when friendship is about the cultivation of virtue, the opportunity to pursue the good, the exploration of life, and the search for meaning, it is transformative and enduring. As the rabbis teach, "Any love that is dependent upon a specific cause, when the cause is gone, the love is gone; but if it does not depend on a specific cause,

23. Ecclesiastes 4:9–10

24. Soloveitchik, *Family Redeemed*, 27–28

25. Soloveitchik, *Out of the Whirlwind*, 154

26. Job 42:10

27. *Babylonian Talmud*, Ta'anit 23a

it will never cease."[28] Friendships of pleasure and utility are fun but end as our needs and wants evolve. Friendships of virtue are not whimsical, as they are attached to our pursuit of the just, holy, and good.

A friend is more than another who shares our experiences, values, or narratives. To friends, we have special duties that arise from our relationships. To become virtuous citizens committed to moral and religious excellence, life partners are crucial.

But we need not be one's friend to reach out to them. We can care about others who are not friends and who we don't wish to be social friends. It just requires the empathy and the planning to work to see others who are often not seen and to hear those who are often not heard.

28. *Pirkei Avot* 5:16

#24

Shituf Pe'ulah, Sharing

WE RECENTLY BOUGHT A new blanket for our home, and all the kids flocked to it to be wrapped up. Quickly that became difficult and divisive. We had a conversation about the importance of sharing, and we discussed different ways of sharing. Perhaps we could share the blanket all at once? Perhaps we could take turns, making sure that everyone had a turn? It's all so difficult to share when something is new and exciting and when everyone feels some level of entitlement.

But the truth is that sharing doesn't become any easier as we get older. There are family break-ups, lawsuits, even wars, over issues of sharing. There are siblings divided when a parent's estate is allocated. The distribution of resources can be incredibly emotional and even contentious. So what should be our basis for distributive justice? How would a good family or a good society distribute goods in a way that is fair to all?

Rabbi Jonathan Sacks writes:

> The voluntary sector differs from the state and the market in one vital respect. The state is about the production and distribution of power. The market is about the production and distribution of wealth. But power and wealth are, at any given moment, zero-sum games. If I have total power and then I share it with nine others I am left with only a tenth of what I had. If I had a thousand pounds and then share it with nine others, again I have only a tenth of the amount with which I began. Politics and economics are about competition—they are arenas of mediated conflict. But there are other goods—among them love, friendship, trust—which are different. The more I share them, the more I have. Indeed, they only exist in virtue of being shared.

That is why communities, neighbourhood groups and voluntary organisations are vital to the health of society. They are not arenas of conflict, but rather the seedbeds of co-operation.[1]

For Rabbi Sacks, it seems we will never figure out a perfect plan as it pertains to the distribution of goods. Politics and the marketplace will always be competitive, divisive, and perhaps unfair. We cannot have a monarchy or communism or totalitarian control. If the masses are free, then there will be some order of chaos, even with different degrees of regulation. He argues that the arena for sharing is in communities, built not on competition but on cooperation, and that the goods are not money but virtues. We can share virtues like "love, friendship, trust" with one another in intimate, safe spaces of communities.

But beyond that, how are we to understand the rabbinic view of sharing? The Talmudic rabbis taught:

> There are four types of people: One who says 'Mine is mine and yours is yours'—this is the average type; and some say, this typifies Sodom; (One who says) 'Mine is yours and yours is mine' is an am ha'aretz (ignoramus); (One who says) 'Mine is yours and yours is yours' is a pious person; (And one who says) 'Mine is mine and yours is mine' is a wicked person.[2]

When it comes to property law as we know it today, we witness too much of "Mine is mine and yours is yours." It seems almost laughably obvious. According to some rabbis, this is indeed normal or "average." But according to the second view this is Sodom. This is the worst place on earth that is worthy of being destroyed. The rabbis teach that Sodom was destroyed because it was a place that hated and criminalized sharing:

> They issued a proclamation in Sodom saying, "Everyone who strengthens the hand of the poor and the needy and the geir (stranger)[3] with a loaf of bread shall be burnt by fire.[4]

It is fascinating and instructive to note that Abraham, who himself prayed for the salvation of Sodom despite its inhabitants' corruption, was an exemplar of the opposite approach, of "Mine is yours and yours is yours." Abraham demonstrates this when three malachim (messengers or angels) suddenly appear at his doorstep. He runs to greet them and bows, he has

1. Sacks, *The Power of Ideas*, 60

2. *Pirkei Avot* 5:10

3. Alternatively, the term *geir* can be understood as referring to a convert.

4. *Pirkei D'Rebbe Eliezer* 25

water brought to them to rinse their feet, he gives them to rest under the shade of a tree, and together with his wife Sarah, he prepares for them an elaborate meal.[5] He engages in five acts of kindness towards strangers, culminating in sharing, in giving generously.

Furthermore, a common misunderstanding is that Abraham was chosen by God as the first Jew because he was the first monotheist. But the Torah itself informs us that he was chosen to be our founding father for an entirely different reason: "For I know of him that he will instill in his children and household after him to keep the ways of God and engage in acts of *tzedakah* and *mishpat* (kindness and justice)."[6] Abraham inherently understood that to give is to fulfill what God asks of us.

God didn't create the world for each person to own whatever they wish as long as they earned it themselves. Rather God created a world of love, and we are to emulate and express that love by seeing our purpose in giving to others.

What do we own? Theologically, God is the owner of all. Of course, as far as modern law goes, we should understand and obey property laws, but there is clearly a deeper truth here. The Torah teaches: "The land shall not be sold in perpetuity, for the land is Mine; for you are foreigners and temporary dwellers with Me."[7] We also learn: "For we are like foreigners before You, and like temporary dwellers, as were all of our forefathers—our days on earth are like a shadow, and there is no hope."[8]

One Talmudic passage relates a story of a king who decided that sharing was his spiritual priority.

> A story concerning King Munbaz:[9] Now King Munbaz decided to give away all the wealth of his kingdom. His brothers sent him a message [stating], "Your fathers spent much time acquiring wealth and expending the treasury which they had inherited from their predecessors. What gives you the right to spend it all?" Munbaz replied, "I am stockpiling wealth in heaven while my predecessors only stockpiled wealth on this earth. I am stockpiling wealth where no one can access it while my predecessors stockpiled wealth where anyone can take it away. My predecessors stockpiled treasures of money while I am

5. Genesis 18:1–8
6. Genesis 18:19
7. Leviticus 25:23
8. Chronicles I 29:15

9. King Munbaz was the son (or perhaps the brother) of Queen Helena of Adiabene, a region in Northern Mesopotamia. Queen Helena and her family converted to Judaism.

stockpiling treasures of souls. I am stockpiling wealth for myself and for the next world while my predecessors stockpiled wealth for others and in this world."[10]

Consider today, also, how some billionaires have taken "the billionaire's pledge." Warren Buffet explains:

The reaction of my family and me to our extraordinary good fortune is not guilt, but rather gratitude. Were we to use more than 1% of my claim checks on ourselves, neither our happiness nor our well-being would be enhanced. In contrast, that remaining 99% can have a huge effect on the health and welfare of others. That reality sets an obvious course for me and my family: Keep all we can conceivably need and distribute the rest to society, for its needs. My pledge starts us down that course.[11]

Sharing is one of the greatest challenges of our lives, whether one is a billionaire or living in poverty. Most of us feel an entitlement to what we have and more. We reason that "we deserve what we have, regardless of how we earned it. And we deserve even more." We need a spiritual revolution to awaken a deeper spirit of kindness that will enable us to both feel worthy of what we have but also feel a sense of sufficiency and humility so that we can continue to see sharing not as a loss but as a gain.

We recite in the Ashrei prayer: "You open Your hand and satisfy the desire of every living being."[12] We can and must emulate God Who decided to share life with all creatures and then to continue and supply others with their needs and desires. In fact, Ecclesiastes describes one who takes the alternative, miserly approach, as a fool: "The fool folds their hands together, and eats their own flesh."[13]

We would do well to remember how interconnected we all are. Rabbi Moshe Cordovero[14] taught: "All souls are united, and each soul contains a part of all others."[15] This concept is explained more fully and eloquently by Rabbi Cordovero's disciple, Rabbi Eliyahu de Vidas:

Even though your body's material substance separates you from your friend, the soul of both of you is a spiritual entity, and the

10. *Babylonian Talmud*, Bava Batra 11a

11. Buffett, "My Philanthropic Pledge," (CNN)

12. Psalms 145:16

13. Ecclesiastes 4:5

14. Rabbi Moshe Cordovero was a 16th-century leader of the Kabbalah movement in Safed.

15. Cordovero, *Tomer Devorah*, Chapter 1, part 3

tendency of the spirit is to make you cleave to your friend with unbroken unity. When your soul becomes aroused to love a friend, your friend's soul will be equally aroused to love you in return, until both of your souls are bound to form one single entity.[16]

Let us recommit to sharing what we have. Let us follow the lead taken by our founding father Abraham. Doing so not only allows us to demonstrate to others that we care about them, but also goes a long way towards realizing our aspiration that we are truly one!

16. *Reishit Chochmah*, Sha'ar Ha'Ahava

#25

Meni'at Nekamah, Not Taking Revenge

WHY WOULD NOT TAKING revenge be a kindness? We may feel we are hard wired to believe that those who hurt us ought to be hurt, or at very least that we have a right to take revenge upon those who hurt us. And perhaps we may even think that the only true justice is for us to directly hurt them. We feel revenge is just and deserved. Why, then, should refraining from taking revenge be considered a *chesed*, a "pearl of kindness?"

The Torah does allow for (or at least not punish) one who avenges the life of one who accidentally killed someone, while they are fleeing to an *Ir Miklat* (City of Refuge)[1]. But this is an extreme case that merely allows the passion crime of the avenger to be a mitigating factor. It is still far from ideal. But what is the ideal?

In order to address this question, we need to first explore the negative commandment itself. The Torah is clear about the mandate to avoid revenge: "You shall not take vengeance or bear a grudge against the people of your nation."[2] Interestingly enough, the verse just before that one is: "You shall not hate your brother in your heart."[3] Perhaps this juxtaposition and order of verses is hinting to us that one of the goals of removing hate from the heart is to remove it from action. Conversely, perhaps the Torah is telling us that in order to prevent hate from turning to action, we must first remove it from our heart.

Furthermore, we intuitively know that we should react to every action against us from a place of measured reason with a commitment to justice,

1. Numbers, Chapter 35
2. Leviticus 19:18
3. *Ibid.*, 19:17

rather than from an unstable place of anger. The Talmud addresses this very point, distinguishing between the two prohibitions mentioned in the above verse, taking revenge and bearing a grudge:

> 'I will not lend [my item] to you, just as you refused to lend me your sickle.' This is *nekamah* (revenge). 'Here is [my item]. I am not like you, who would not lend me what I asked for.' This is *netirah* (bearing a grudge).[4]

Both examples of *nekamah* and *netirah* provided by the rabbis are reactions out of anger and resentment. Reacting in such a manner may be understandable, and may not even be viewed as overreacting, but is forbidden just the same.

Restraining our desire to take revenge may benefit not only the subject of our wrath but also ourselves. We may refrain from taking revenge for own sake, as revenge has the ability to destroy a person. It's a pernicious emotion, an all-encompassing, infinitely heavy shackle.

Maimonides teaches us about how destructive anger can be and how cautious we must be, codifying Jewish law to oppose its destructive use. He writes:

> There are certain character traits that one must distance oneself from in the extreme. In fact, it is forbidden to take [the standard approach of] the "middle path" regarding these character traits...
>
> Anger is an extremely negative character trait, and it is fitting for a person to distance oneself from it to the opposite extreme. One should train oneself never to become angry, even regarding things for which anger might be justified...
>
> ... Those who frequently become angry have no quality of life; therefore, [the Sages] instructed us to distance ourselves from anger to the farthest degree, until a person acts as though they do not sense even those things that would justifiably anger a person.[5]

Maimonides' words certainly apply to the examples of revenge given by the Talmudic rabbis, as they can be viewed as non-extreme, yet are nonetheless strongly discouraged.

Indeed, the Talmud says that one loses their wisdom in a state of rage just as a prophet loses their prophecy.[6] Furthermore, *sinat chinam* (baseless

---

4. *Babylonian Talmud*, Yoma 23a—23b

5. Maimonides, *Mishneh Torah, Hilchot Dei'ot* 2:3

6. *Babylonian Talmud*, Pesachim 66b. Also, on the destructive nature of anger, see

hatred) is considered the catalyst for the destruction of the Temple, akin to the worse offenses: idolatry, sexual immorality, and murder.[7]

The Talmud relates a well-known story to illustrate this point:

> Jerusalem was destroyed on account of Kamtza and bar Kamtza. There was a certain man whose friend was named Kamtza and whose enemy was named bar Kamtza. He once made a large feast and said to his servant: 'Go bring me my friend Kamtza.' The servant went and mistakenly brought him his enemy bar Kamtza. The man who was hosting the feast came and found bar Kamtza sitting at the feast. The host said to bar Kamtza: '. . . You are my enemy. What then do you want here? Arise and leave.' Bar Kamtza said to him: 'Since I have already come, let me stay, and I will give you money for whatever I eat and drink.   J u s t do not embarrass me by sending me out.' The host said to him: 'No, you must leave.' Bar Kamtza said to him: 'I will give you money for half of the feast; just do not send me away.' The host said to him: 'No, you must leave.' Bar Kamtza then said to him: 'I will give you money for the entire feast; just let me stay.' The host said to him: 'No, you must leave.' Finally, the host took bar Kamtza by his hand, stood him up, and took him out.
>
> After having been cast out from the feast, bar Kamtza said to himself: 'Since the sages were sitting there and did not protest the actions of the host, although they saw how he humiliated me, learn from it that they were content with what he did. I will therefore go and inform against them to the king. He went and said to the emperor: 'The Jews have rebelled against you. . .'[8]

In response to *sinat chinam*, Rabbi Abraham Isaac Kook profoundly suggests that we go the opposite direction and seek to cultivate *ahavat chinam* (baseless love).[9]

With this in mind, we are now able to understand how refraining from taking revenge can be categorized as an act of *chesed*.

We are to try to emulate God's ways even when, and perhaps especially when, we have been hurt. The Torah mandates us to *"v'halachta b'drachav"* ("walk in God's ways"). Just as God is forgiving, so must we be forgiving. In the *selichot* (penitential prayers) we recite each year leading up to the High Holidays, in articulating the thirteen attributes of God, we recite, by way of introduction, a description of the justice of God's actions: "God deals

---

BT Kiddushin 40b-41a, Sanhedrin 105b, and Pirkei Avot 2:11.

7. *Babylonian Talmud*, Yoma 9b

8. *Babylonian Talmud*, Gittin 55b-65a

9. Kook, *Orot Hakodesh* 3:324

righteously with all and does *tzedek* (justice), pardoning *chotim* (careless wrongdoers), and forgiving *poshim* (intentional wrongdoers)." Forgiving others here is connected to *tzedek*; forgiveness of those who have erred is a fulfillment of justice, an act of healing both individual relationships and the broader social fabric. Furthermore, one of God's thirteen attributes is *chesed*! Part of what it means to be righteous and kind is to be a forgiver, to understand that humans are fallible, and to therefore be loving of others who stumble, even in their actions towards us. We work toward restorative justice which is to show compassion and sensitivity toward all parties and toward individual and collective healing.

Rabbi Yisrael of Rizhin[10] distinguishes between two different types of forgivers: The *solai'ach* is one who *occasionally* forgives, and the *solchan* is one who forgives *habitually*, time and time again. To perpetuate opportunities to forgive and to repair relationships is to be a *solchan*. Some people hurt us so much that we cannot merely forgive them one time; rather, we need to forgive them in our hearts time and time again in order to achieve full forgiveness. This helps us not only to heal but also to cultivate a very deep virtue of being a forgiver.

This process has another step. Just as we are obligated to forgive others, so too are we commanded not to bear a grudge (*lo titor*). Not bearing a grudge is an outgrowth of *ahavat chinam* and forgiveness. In fact, the second half of the verse regarding *nekamah* and *netirah* is comprised of the famous quote "*v'ahavta l'rei'acha kamocha*" ("love your neighbor as yourself").[11]

Forgiving another is about deeds of the past; removing a grudge, on the other hand, is about a present, and perhaps even a future, sense of indebtedness. To truly love another, we must move *beyond* entitlement and release our grudges.

How does this apply to our daily lives on a global scale? About a month before his assassination, in his second inaugural address, President Abraham Lincoln famously said:

> With malice toward none, with charity for all. . . to bind up the nation's wounds, to care for him who shall have borne the battle and for his widow and his orphan, to do all which may achieve and cherish a just and lasting peace. . ."[12]

---

10. Rabbi Yisrael of Rizhin (also known as Ruzhin) was a 19th-century Ukrainian hasidic rabbi and founder of the Rizhiner hasidic sect.

11. Leviticus 19:18

12. Second Inaugural Address of Abraham Lincoln (March 4, 1865) https://www. ourdocuments.gov/doc.php?flash=false&doc=38&page=transcript

We observe historic choices as to whether to seek forgiveness and thereby to achieve its dramatic consequences. To be forgiving is to be courageous and takes much work, and leaders who try to heal long-standing conflicts often sadly pay with their lives.

Another more contemporary example of taking Leviticus 19:18 seriously and pursuing a path of forgiveness is embodied in the recent history of South Africa. In 1994, bolstered by its political and religious leaders, Archbishop Desmond Tutu and soon-to-be-president Nelson Mandela, South Africa conducted peaceful elections to elect its first black-majority government. Then, in spite of predictions that this government would unleash a vengeful bloodbath against the former apartheid white rulers, the Truth and Reconciliation Commission, chaired by Nobel laureate Tutu, helped bring healing to the country. Instead of putting all the perpetrators—mostly white—on trial, or granting a general amnesty that would do nothing to defuse the hatred, South Africa tried a different course. Archbishop Tutu wrote:

> They saw the process of the Truth and Reconciliation Commission, when perpetrators of some of the most gruesome atrocities were given amnesty in exchange for a full disclosure of the facts of the offence. Instead of revenge and retribution, this new nation chose to tread the difficult path of confession, forgiveness, and reconciliation.[13]

As long as the torturers and murderers would acknowledge their crimes and ask for forgiveness, the victims would in turn forgive them, and the state would not pursue further action against their actions. Incredibly, this tactic avoided the violence that gripped so many other nations such as Robert Gabriel Mugabe's[14] Zimbabwe and Mozambique, formerly a Portuguese colony.

Forgiveness is hard, and sometimes seemingly impossible. However, before we decide that we cannot forgive, we should consider the price of not seeking forgiveness, and try to be the *solchan* who follows the command of *lo titor*. As Archbishop Tutu points out, "Retribution leads to a cycle of reprisal, leading to counter-reprisal in an inexorable movement, as in Rwanda, Northern Ireland, and in the former nation of Yugoslavia. The only thing that can break that cycle, making possible a new beginning, is forgiveness. Without forgiveness there is no future."

13. Tutu, *Let South Africa Show the World How to Forgive*. Accessed March 26, 2020. https://www.sol.com.au/kor/19_03.htm

14. Robert Mugabe was the former president of Zimbabwe.

There really is no better way to say it than in Archbishop Tutu's insightful words: "Without forgiveness there is no future." It may feel more just to take revenge, but we cannot build a world of kindness if everyone gets what they deserve and/or have coming to them.

In Rashi's commentary on the first verse of the Torah, he explains that this world cannot be sustained on justice alone but also on compassion:

> Elokim created- It doesn't say that Hashem created.[15] This is because in the beginning God intended to create with the attribute of strict justice. God saw that the world could not be sustained this way, and therefore God preceded it with the attribute of compassion and joined it with the attribute of justice, as it says later on in Genesis 2:4: ". . . on the day that Hashem Elokim made the heaven and the earth."[16]

As partners of the Divine, we too need to learn that it takes kindness to sustain this all too-broken-world. And with this compassion, we will at times be slighted and wish to mete out justice, but barring a few extreme exceptions, we must embrace and bear those injustices without seeking revenge, thereby doing our part to make this a better, kinder world. Sometimes learning to forgive others starts with learning to forgive ourselves. In doing so, we can be a bit more vulnerable and allow this deep compassion to transform our lives and the lives of those around us.

---

15. The name Elokim refers to God acting through strict justice, whereas the name Hashem (a euphemism for Adonai) refers to God acting with compassion.

16. Rashi on Genesis 1:1

#26

Meni'at Michshol, Not Placing a Stumbling Block Before the Blind

THE TORAH TEACHES: "YOU shall not place a stumbling block before a blind person."[1] This transgression is generally referred to as *lifnei iveir*.[2] We are left with many questions here. What would constitute "a stumbling block?" Does "the blind" in this verse include others who are not physically blind? If so, who?

Indeed, Rashi applies this verse more broadly:

> "You shall not place a stumbling block before a blind person:" Before someone who is 'blind' in a particular matter, do not give them advice that is inappropriate for them.[3]

Rambam (Maimonides) goes even further:

> . . . Similarly, anyone who causes a person who is blind with regard to a certain matter to stumble and gives them improper advice, or who reinforces a transgressor (who is spiritually blind, for he does not see the path of truth, due to the desires of their heart) transgresses a negative commandment, as Leviticus 19:14 states: "Do not place a stumbling block before a blind person." When a person comes to ask advice from you, give them proper counsel.[4]

1. Leviticus 19:14

2. "*Lifnei iveir*" literally means "before a blind person." This phrase comprises the first two words of the transgression in the biblical Hebrew text.

3. Rashi's on Leviticus 19:14

4. Maimonides, *Mishneh Torah*, Hilchot Rotsei'ah uShmirat Nefesh 12:14

It is instructive to note that the very first drama in the Torah centers around *lifnei iveir*. The Torah relates:

> Now the serpent was the shrewdest of all the wild beasts that God had made. It said to the woman, "Did God really say: You shall not eat of any tree of the garden?"

The woman replied to the serpent, "We may eat of the fruit of the other trees of the garden. It is only about fruit of the tree in the middle of the garden that God said: 'You shall not eat of it or touch it, lest you die.'"

And the serpent said to the woman, "You are not going to die, for God knows that as soon as you eat of it your eyes will be opened and you will be like divine beings who know [to distinguish between] good and bad."

> When the woman saw that the tree was good for eating and a delight to the eyes, and that the tree was desirable as a source of wisdom, she took of its fruit and ate. She also gave some to her husband, and he ate.

Placing a stumbling block before "the blind," as illustrated in the above narrative, can have devastating results, even to the extent of altering God's intended course for humankind.

One area where we apply *lifnei iveir* is to theft.[5] The Talmud teaches:

> And Rabbi Yehudah said, "A typical shepherd is not accepted as a witness" [because a thief cannot testify, and a shepherd is presumed to act as a thief by allowing his animals to graze on other people's property] . . .. This is only true if the shepherd is taking care of his own animals, but not if he is taking care of the animals of others [in which case we assume that the grazing does not involve theft]. For if you do not acknowledge that distinction, how could we give our animals to a shepherd? For it is written (Lev. 19:14), "Do not place a stumbling block before the blind."[6]

We might wonder how as investors or businesspeople or consumers, this might apply to us today. When we know that goods are produced through exploitation and theft, what are our new responsibilities in this interconnected global marketplace? And when one buys and sells stocks, may one engage with companies that are known to exploit their workers?

---

5. In fact, the serpent story itself can be viewed as involving theft, as the forbidden fruit, in a sense, belonged solely to God.

6. *Babylonian Talmud*, Bava Metzia 5b

Consider this teaching from the economist Meir Tamari:[7]

> Giving, selling or even advertising goods that are harmful to physical, mental or spiritual health, either because of the obligation on the buyers not to cause damage to their own bodies or because of their infringing the Torah's commandments [violates *lifnei iveir*] . . . An example . . . is the *issur* (ban) against the trade in cigarettes (attributed to Harav Ovadia Yosef). Jewish trade in harmful food or drink, drugs and pornography would similarly seem to transgress *lifnei iveir*.[8]

Tamari's application of *lifnei iveir* to harmful goods and services seems to be rooted in the Mishnah:

> We do not sell to them [i.e., to idolators] bears or lions, or anything else that is harmful to the public. We do not build a . . . stadium with them."[9]

Rambam explains:[10]

> It is forbidden to sell idolators any weaponry. We may not sharpen weapons for them or sell them a knife, chains that are put on the necks of prisoners, fetters, iron chains, raw Indian iron, bears, lions, or any other object that could cause danger to people at large. One may, however, sell them shields, for these serve only the purpose of defense. . . Every article that is forbidden to be sold to an idol worshipper is also forbidden to be sold to a Jewish robber, for by doing so one reinforces a transgressor and causes them to sin.

Lifnei iveir also applies to the issue of taking bribes. The Torah teaches: "You shall not pervert justice; you shall not show favoritism, and you shall not take a bribe."[11] Rambam teaches here:

> Just as the recipient [of a bribe] transgresses a negative commandment, so, too, does the giver, as [Leviticus 19:14] states: "Do not place a stumbling block before the blind."[12]

---

7. Meir Tamari is a 20th-21st-century economist whose work is in the field of Jewish business ethics.

8. Tamari, *Spiritual & Ethical Issues in the Stories of Sh'mot* http://www.ou.org/torah/tt/5767/chukat67/navi.htm

9. *Mishnah*, Avodah Zarah 1:7

10. Maimonides, *Mishneh Torah*, Hilchot Rotsei'ah uShmirat Nefesh 12:12, 12:14

11. Deuteronomy 16:19

12. Maimonides, *Mishneh Torah*, Hilchot Sanhedrin 23:2

Furthermore, *lifnei iveir* can also apply to loans. The Talmud teaches:

> Rav Yehuda said in the name of Rav: One who lends money without witnesses present violates "And you shall not place a stumbling block before the blind."[13]

On this verse "violates *lifnei iver,*" Rashi explains: "in that the borrower will be tempted to deny the debt."[14]

Professor Hershey H. Friedman writes:

> Mortgage brokers who counseled poor people to take on mortgages that they would have no way of repaying a few years down the road, and — because of their own greed — not even warning customers of the potential dangers, were clearly violating the principle of *lifnei iveir.*[15]

But we needn't be responsible beyond reason. The rabbis therefore place limitations on *lifnei iveir*:

> Rav Ashi owned a forest, and then sold it to the temple of fire worship. Ravina said to R. Ashi, "But there is [the verse in Lev. 19], 'You shall not place a stumbling block before the blind?'" Rav Ashi said to him, "Most trees are used for heating [rather than idol worship]."[16]

Here we see a limitation placed upon the heavy demands of this prohibition. This first consideration we just saw in the Talmud has to do with quantities. Is the majority of something used in a problematic fashion or is it in the minority?

A second limitation emerges from a different Talmudic tractate:

> How do we know that a person shall not extend a glass of wine to a Nazirite, or a limb from a live animal to non-Jews?[17] The Torah says (Lev. 19:14), "And you shall not place a stumbling block before the blind." And behold, here the [Nazirite or non-Jew] could take the forbidden food or drink for themselves without assistance, and yet [the facilitator nevertheless] violates

13. *Babylonian Talmud*, Bava Metzia 75b

14. Rashi's on Talmud, Bava Metzia 75b

15. Hershey H. Friedman, *Placing a Stumbling Block Before the Blind Person: An In-Depth Analysis*
http://www.jlaw.com/Articles/placingstumbling.html

16. *Babylonian Talmud*, Nedarim 62b

17. It is forbidden for a Nazirite to drink wine and for a gentile to partake of a limb from a live animal.

"You shall not place a stumbling block before the blind"! [No,] we are dealing with a case where the two people are on opposite banks of a river [such that the Nazirite or non-Jew needs help to obtain the forbidden item].[18]

If one asks for a problematic item that they could get themselves then it may not be a problem. But if the person doesn't have access to that problematic item but can only get access from you (as if you're on the right side of the river and they're on the wrong side) then it's more problematic.

We don't see that *lifnei iver* requires us to intervene in every evil. Rather, difficult questions are raised around our enabling of wrongs, our complicity. Further, it is often about actions rather than mere words. One doesn't need to preach to an alcoholic not to drink but one should not buy them an alcoholic drink.

One industry, of many, that has hard questions to ask today is the marketing industry. Is the marketing promoting an ethical product? Is the marketing making an item look better than it is or over-promising on what it can do for one's life? Is the marketing tapping into fear or misleading in any ways? Consumers have many blind spots and are those exploited at times?

On another level, while we want to point out blind spots, we also want to leave room for others to stumble, learn, and grow. Sometimes, a parent, mentor, or coach might choose not to intervene but give room to the other. Rebbe Nachman went so far to not only see challenges (and perhaps stumbles from blind spots) as positive growth opportunities but as seeing God within the obstacle itself. These stumbles are spiritual opportunities for realization and Divine encounter.

How might we also extend *lifnei iveir* toward a basic kindness orientation? Perhaps by realizing that each of us has our "blind spots." We can choose to exploit or mock another's blind spots or we can help them, gently, to recognize them. We can build trust and care for one another by helping each other see what we may not be able to see on our own. Just as God "restores sight to the blind,"[19] so too we can and must emulate the Divine by helping others to see what they cannot but what is in their benefit to see and understand in order to protect themselves and add dignity to their lives. It is not only others that have gaps in their understanding but each of us and surely we also want loving support that might prevent us from dangerous stumbles. May we build compassionate networks of support to help one another see and catch ourselves.

---

18. *Babylonian Talmud*, Avodah Zarah 62b

19. Psalms 146

#27

Shemirat HaTeva, Guarding the Earth

WHAT IS SACRED? ONLY a house of worship and an object with God's Name written upon it? Or are there different types of sanctity? Might God's natural world created billions of years ago have a type of sanctity for us to honor and preserve?

When God created the world, we, human beings are put in charge.

> God said "let me make humankind in my image. . . Let them have dominion over the fish of the see, the fowl of the heavens, animals of all the earth, and all crawling things that crawl about on the earth. God created humankind in God's image. In the image of God, God created them. . . God blessed them, saying "Bear fruit and be many and fill the earth and subdue it. Have power over the fish of the sea, the birds of the sky, and all living things that crawl about on the earth."[1]

We are charged here to leverage our power to care for the rest of creation. Then, in the next chapter, we are tasked with working and guarding the land:

> At the time that God made the earth and heaven, no bush of the field was yet on earth, no plant of the field had yet sprung up, for God had not made it rain upon the earth and there was no human (adam) to till the ground (adamah). . . and God formed the human (adam) from the dust of the soil (adamah). . . God planted the Garden of Eden. . . God took the human and set him in the Garden of Eden to work it and to guard it.[2]

1. Genesis 1:26–28
2. Genesis 2:1–15

So does this mean that humans are necessarily the top priority of all creation? Perhaps, but the Talmudic rabbis share that if a person exploits their privileges, they are lowered:

> If man is worthy, they (the heavenly hosts) say to him: You preceded the ministering angels. And if not, they say to him: a fly preceded you, a mosquito preceded you, this worm preceded you.[3]

But this will not prove to be a simple task to rise to such a challenge. The Rabbis, in a famous midrash from the 5th century taught of what's at stake:

> When God created Adam, God took Adam and led him around all the trees of the Garden. And God said to Adam "Look at my creations! How beautiful and amazing they are! And everything I made, I created for you. Be careful that you don't spoil or destroy my world—because if you do, there is nobody after you to fix it."[4]

One of the most pressing needs for our contemporary moment is controlling climate change and mitigating the looming disaster if humanity chooses to do nothing. If there is no Earth to live on, there is no way to express our faith traditions, offer kindness to one another, or even survive at all.

Though modern societies as a whole have, in many ways, rejected the call of religion to heal significant global problems, there is much wisdom to be found within religious traditions that can address this most-critical moment.

It is for this reason, among many, that I was moved by how the Pope talked about the work to combat climate change. In 2015, Pope Francis addressed the ecological crisis in *Laudato Si': On Care for Our Common Home.* In his address, Pope Francis connected the inner spiritual lives of human beings with the planet's health. He noted that to address the climate change crisis, we need a new mode of spirituality where the virtues of humility, gratitude, and sobriety overcome the vices of greed and overconsumption due to a fear of scarcity. A statement from the United States Conference of Bishops in 2014 presages the Pope's encyclical: "At its core, global climate change is not about economic theory or political platforms, nor about partisan advantage or interest group pressures. It is about the future of God's creation and the one human family."

3. *Midrash Rabbah*, Genesis 8:1
4. *Kohelet Rabbah* 7:13

Similarly, the Vietnamese Buddhist thinker Thich Nhat Hanh writes:

> Our way of walking on the Earth has a great influence on animals and plants. We have killed so many animals and plants and destroyed their environments. Many are now extinct. In turn, our environment is now harming us. The future of all life, including our own, depends on our mindful steps.

The factory farming industry, more than any other industry on the planet, destroys our land, our water, our animals, and our bodies. We have seen the practices that treated living creatures, divinely created beings, as nothing more than a product subject to abuse. By being a voice against brutal and inhumane practices, we can join the interfaith and international struggle to push society away from needless cruelty while also promoting the health of the body and soul for all people.

Let us consider some theological proposals that all of us, regardless of our faith, might come to agree upon, to different degrees:

1. God created the earth, water, air, fire, and sky—these elements have inherent purity and sanctity.

2. God owns the land and we merely borrow that land while here on earth.

3. Because of the sacred task of stewardship, we are responsible to hand over the Earth to the next generation the same way that we received it from the generations before us.

4. To preserve the environment, we will cultivate character traits such as modesty, gratitude, equanimity (and more).

5. While we will not be punished by the courts of our time for destroying the land, air, or water when our actions comply with secular law, we are indeed religiously culpable for such damage.

Sir David Attenborough, the noted naturalist, commented:

> Right now, we are facing a man-made disaster of global scale, our greatest threat in thousands of years: climate change. If we don't take action, the collapse of our civilizations and the extinction of much of the natural world is on the horizon.

If we do nothing, if we stay in our corners, then we do so at *our own peril.*

There are so many more approaches that could be taken to increase meaningful dialogue. We could offer different articulations of these points as well. But this must be more than just virtue signaling and sermonizing. We must ask ourselves, as faith leaders, how we will model the following:

1. More sustainable communal practices

2. More modesty in how we publicly waste

3. A reduction of consumption of animal products (moving toward veganism or at least vegetarianism)

4. Advocating for environmental policy changes in addition to our parochial self-concerned political issues

5. Develop theological language, beyond our own communal articulations, for how we universally can collaborate

As we approach the difficult—but ultimately rewarding—work to improve ourselves and the world around us, there are countless avenues where we find opportunities to collaborate in both an intra- and inter-religious setting. In fact, cross-religious dialogue is one of the most dynamic paths towards reconciliation and hope. We are able to seek teachers from across the faith spectrum and look beyond leaders within our own faiths.

As we work to create opportunities to collaborate, we engender the ability to plant real seeds of change among the great religious traditions. Our world needs this change urgently. Spiritual leaders need to do more to facilitate inter-religious dialogue. This cross-cultural, intra-communal, and broadly human project is urgent, given how rapidly humans pollute the air and sea, destroy and exploit the earth's natural resources, and the rapid growth of natural disasters and pandemics. The ability to have spaces for true inter-religious dialogue will, hopefully, one day save humanity from its worst impulses.

Nothing less than the future of the world is at stake.

The Talmud tells us of a man named Honi. One day, as Honi walked along a road, he saw a man planting a carob tree. Honi asked of the man, "How long will it take for this tree to bear fruit?" "Seventy years," the man replied. Honi then asked, "Are you so healthy that you expect to live that length of time and eat its fruit?" The man answered, "I found a fruitful world because my ancestors planted it for me. Likewise, I am planting for my children."[5]

There are countless Jewish legal and theological models for engagement:

- *L'ovdah ul'shomrah*—the Divinely mandated work to protect creation[6]

- *Piku'ach nefesh*—the Torah command to save life[7]

---

5. *Babylonian Talmud*, Ta'anit 23a

6. Genesis 2:15

7. *Babylonian Talmud*, Shabbat 150a

- *Bal tashchit*—the Torah prohibition against waste[8]
- *Avodah b'gashmiut*—making interactions with materialism spiritually deep[9]
- *Anivut* (humility)—not engaging in over-consumption; not being *ba'alei ga'avah* (filled with arrogance and self-consumption)[10]
- *Hakarat hatov* (gratitude)—channeling gratitude for our blessings toward responsibility[11]
- *V'halakhta b'drachav* (*imitatio Dei*)—God is merciful and thus we cultivate our characters in emulation of the Divine[12]

It is obvious that Jewish practices teach us to be more mindful, modest, and open to meaningful, transformational experiences. What is less obvious is how we can create sustainable behavioral change. Leadership scholars teach that we should not operate from fear and past models when attempting to "weather the storm."

> The danger in the current economic situation is that people in positions of authority will hunker down. They will try to solve the problem with short-term fixes... They'll default to what they know how to do in order to reduce frustration... Their primary mode will be drawing on familiar expertise to help their organization weather the storm.[13]

Indeed, so much fast paced change occurring today, many will rely on the short term fixes they know rather than thinking collaboratively, adaptively, and boldly.

8. Deuteronomy 20:19–20

9. For example, using natural resources for the service of God (i.e., the *mitzvot* of the four species) and for sharing with others.
For more on this, see Joseph Dan, *The Teachings of the Hasidim* (Millburn, NJ: Behrman House, 1983), p. 24.

10. See Norman Lamm, *Seventy Faces: Articles of Faith, Vol. 2* (Hoboken, NJ: Ktav Publishing House, Inc., 2002), p. 110.

11. See Harold M. Schulweis, *In God's Mirror: Reflections and Essays* (Hoboken, NJ: Ktav Publishing House, Inc., 2003), p. 64.

12. See Dov Schwartz, *From Phenomenology to Existentialism: The Philosophy of Rabbi Joseph B. Soloveitchik, Volume 2* (Boston: Brill, 2013), p. 116.

13. Ronald Heifetz, et al., *Leadership in a (Permanent) Crisis,* Harvard Business Review, Harvard Business Publishing, 4 Apr. 2020; hbr.org/2009/07/leadership-in-a-permanent-crisis. Harvard

In all we do, we need to cultivate consistency; this is where ritual commitment helps us. If we live with religious discipline, this concept can carry over into the discipline of environmental protection and stewardship.

And though the task feels daunting, history is filled with stories of leaders who adapted to change and those who refused and were engulfed by history. Joseph interpreted Pharaoh's dreams to mean that seven years of abundance would be followed by seven years of famine, and so the grain surplus was stored during the years of abundance and helped save Egypt during the succeeding famine.[14] Joseph could have become acquiescent. However, he understood that—eventually—there would come a time of scarcity and acted accordingly (and proactively). On the other hand, the last king of Babylon, Belshazzar, ignored the literal "writing on the wall"[15] at his peril and decided to celebrate what he thought would be a long, secure reign. In reality, a large force of Persians and Medes were about to overthrow him.

This world has been entrusted to humanity to watch over it, and that means we are to relate with care and dignity to all. Rabbi Shimshon Raphael Hirsch taught:

> "Do not destroy anything"[16] is the first and most general call of God, which comes to you, Man, when you realize yourself as master of the earth . . . If you should indulge in senseless rage, wishing to destroy that which you should only use, wishing to exterminate that which you should only exploit, if you should regard the beings beneath you as objects without rights, not perceiving God Who created them, and therefore desire that they feel the might of your presumptuous mood, instead of using them only as the means of wise human activity—then God's call proclaims to you, "Do not destroy anything!" Be a mentsch! Only if you use the things around you for wise human purposes, . . . only then are you a mentsch and have the right over them.
>
> However, if you destroy, if you ruin, at that moment you are not a human but an animal and have no right to the things around you. I lent them to you for wise use only; never forget that I lent them to you. As soon as you use them unwisely. . . you commit treachery against My world, you commit murder and robbery against My property, you transgress against Me!"
>
> In truth, there is no one nearer to idolatry than one who can disregard the fact that things are the creatures and property

14. Genesis 41:25–30

15. Daniel 5:25–28

16. Deuteronomy 20:19–20

of God, and who presumes also to have the right. . . to destroy
them according to a presumptuous act of will. Yes, that one
is already serving the most powerful idols—anger, pride, and
above all ego, which in its passion regards itself as the master
of things.[17]

Nature is to be sustained not only because it sustains us but also because it is a pathway to the Divine. The numerology for one of the names of
God, Elokim, is the same as the Hebrew word for nature, *teva*.

Furthermore, we can study all of nature and realize that God created
everything with a purpose. The Talmud teaches:

Rabbi Yehuda said in the name of Rav: Of all that the Holy One
be blessed, created in God's world, God did not create a single
thing without purpose.[18]

Another midrash shares:

Our Rabbis said: Even those things that you may regard as
completely superfluous to Creation—such as flies, fleas and
mosquitoes—even they were included in Creation; and God's
purpose is carried through everything, even through a snake, a
mosquito, a frog.[19]

Yehoshua Lieberman, a contemporary writer, shares that various Talmudic tractates can also inform us on these matters:

In face of the observation that in modern economic literature
the issue of social responsibility and environmental protection
does not emerge extensively before the 1960s, it is particularly striking to find a fully developed framework for treating
these issues in sources as early as the *Mishnah*. As a matter of
fact, a whole chapter in the tractate of *Bava Batra* is devoted
to environmental protection. . . The chapter of *Lo Yachpor* in
Bava Batra is actually a systematic collection of environmental
protection regulations aimed at restricting activities motivated
by private economic incentives that tend to disregard social responsibility considerations. Examples include: a requirement of
minimum distance between planted trees and city limits (to prevent insects, allergies, etc.), [and] a requirement of minimum

17. Hirsch, *Horeb*, chapter 56
18. *Babylonian Talmud*, Shabbat 77b
19. *Bereishit Rabbah* 10:7

height between a stove in a lower story and the floor of a flat in an upper story (to avoid excessive heat).[20]

As we discussed above, we are not given the right to simply do whatever we please in our personal lives without concern for the welfare of our surroundings. We are all together on one planet. The rabbis taught:

> Chizkiya said: "Israel is a dispersed lamb.[21]" Israel is compared to a lamb because just as in the case of a lamb, when one of its limbs is hurt, all of its limbs feel [the pain], so, too, Israel, "If one man will sin [and, yet, you will become angry at the entire congregation?][22]"[23][24]

Rabbi Jonathan Sacks put it well when he wrote:

> There seems to be little doubt that much biblical legislation is concerned with what we would nowadays call sustainability. This is particularly true of the three great commands ordaining periodic rest: the Sabbath, the sabbatical year, and the jubilee year. On the Sabbath all agricultural work is forbidden. . . . We become conscious of being creatures, not creators. What the Sabbath does for human beings and animals, the sabbatical and Jubilee years do for the land. . .[25]

Rabbi Joseph Soloveitchik taught about the deep relationship between *adam* (a person) and *adamah* (the earth).

> The *mitzvah* of burial indicates the validity of the demand that earth makes of man. She insists upon the return of part of her own self. As soon as the *ruach elokim* (godly spirit) departs man, his inanimate body must be delivered to its rightful owner. . .[26] We are duty bound to act gently towards the earth, not as "an

---

20. Liebermann, *Responsibility of the Firm to the Environment*, The Orthodox Forum: Jewish Business Ethics, ed. Aaron Levine and Moses Pava, New Jersey: Jason Aronson Inc., 1999

21. Jeremiah 50:17

22. Numbers 16:22

23. This statement was made by Moses and Aaron as they challenged God for wanting to destroy the Jewish People because of the sin of one man, Korach, and his cohort. Clearly, in this interpretation, God wished to make the point that all are affected, and potentially influenced, by the behavior of a few.

24. Midrash Rabbah, Leviticus 4:6

25. Rabbi Jonathan Sacks, *The Dignity of Difference*, p. 167

26. Rabbi Joseph Soloveitchik, *The Emergence of Ethical Man*, p. 52

alien autocrat over a people subjugated by force," but as a "loving father over his son."[27]

I have found that the most helpful and sustainable way to carve out time for environmental activism, while there are so many other demands in life, is to make very small but consistent changes in one's daily habits. Though difficult, we can try to remind ourselves of how much we love our children and how badly we want the world to be inhabitable for them.

We cannot wait for change. *We must be the change.*

We must change the world from the inside out; we have to change our behavior to allow self-transformation. Such a method will then, hopefully, lead to an outward change. This pedagogical technique should not be misunderstood to mean that we must first perfect ourselves before we can work for social change, since that, of course, will never happen. The work we do to transform ourselves and the universe around us is never complete; this fact makes life challenging yet so exciting.

To everyone, whether you're a believer or non-believer, a neophyte or an expert, or someone simply invested in the notion that a single person can make an enormous difference, we are all responsible to hand over the Earth to the next generation the same way that we received it from the generations before us. Let us take care of and transform our world, not only for ourselves, but for our descendants for years to come.

27. Ibid., p. 60

#28

Chemlah L'Ba'alei Chayim, Displaying Compassion for Animals

BEING COMPASSIONATE TO ANIMALS ought to be the easiest and most obvious form of kindness. Young children often show empathy toward their pet before their sibling. Few want to act cruelly to their dog or cat. Many enjoy riding and brushing horses. We see an animal's vulnerability and we naturally want to protect it. We also know so well that our ecosystem is complex and how all life is interdependent. Indeed, it seems most probable that an act of cruelty toward animals, found in China's wet market, was what kicked off the covid pandemic.

There are countless sources that teach us to be compassionate towards animals. The Torah instructs us: "Do not muzzle your ox when it is treading."[1] On this verse, Rabbi Aaron of Barcelona[2] teaches that this mitzvah is about kindness to animals.

> One may not prevent an animal from eating that upon which they are working at the time of their work . . . The root of this precept is to teach ourselves to develop beautiful souls, to choose fairness and adhere to it, and to pursue loving-kindness and mercy.[3] By accustoming ourselves to being compassionate even to animals which are really only created for our usage. . . our soul becomes habituated to treat human beings well, and to

---

1. Deuteronomy 25:4

2. Rabbi Aaron of Barcelona is assumed by many to be the author of the anonymous work *Sefer Hachinuch*.

3. We will see below that Rambam shares this view.

protect them . . . to compensate them for any good that they do and to satisfy them with whatever they desire.[4]

While this moral point is quite important, we can still challenge the assumption he makes that animals "are really only created for our usage." Are humans the pinnacle of all existence and all other life merely here for our use, seemingly including not only our appetites, but also our fun or desires?

Another Torah verse teaches: "If you see your enemy's donkey overburdened with a heavy load, and you might hesitate to help, instead you shall certainly help him unload."[5] Some interpret this verse to be about helping our enemy. But others suggest that the focus is that it's so important to help an animal even when it's the animal of our enemy.

The Talmudic rabbis suggest that the prohibition to cause pain to animals is d'oraita (of biblical origin) and they debate which of many verses is the primary verse in which to root the imperative. For Rashi,[6] it is this verse just quoted that is the basis for the biblical prohibition. Rambam (Maimonides), however, cites the story of Balaam whipping his donkey[7] as the basis for the Biblical prohibition.[8]

It is instructive to note that the rabbis did allow killing animals when it is for tzorech adam (human need). At the same time, we are all familiar with the great sensitivity that must be taken regarding how an animal is to be slaughtered. Furthermore, the Shulchan Aruch goes as far as taking an animal's mental state into account when discussing what constitutes a tereifah (an animal that would have died of its own accord due to illness or disease). He teaches:

> If the animal has become scared by a person to the point that its lungs have completely constricted, for example, it witnessed another animal being slaughtered or something similar, the animal is a tereifah. . .[9]

It is perhaps remarkable to note that Rav Yosef Karo[10] understood that an animal being scared can lead to its lungs being constricted to the point that it's physical well-being, even its life, is at stake.

4. *Sefer Hachinuch* 596
5. Exodus 23:5
6. Rashi's commentary on Babylonian Talmud, Shabbat 128b
7. Numbers 22:21–32
8. *Guide for the Perplexed*, Vol. III, Ch. 17
9. *Shulchan Aruch*, Yoreh Deah 36:14
10. Rav Yosef Karo was the author of the *Shulchan Aruch*.

Similarly, the Pitchei Teshuvah[11] writes:

> ...The practice of people with chickens in hand, standing around the butcher while he is slaughtering, so that they can be the next in line, is not correct. This is especially true Erev (the eve of) Yom Kippur, when the butcher is slaughtering the chickens of *kapparot* (an atonement ritual with mystical significance). This [holding the chickens in a way that they can see the others being slaughtered] is not right, since it constitutes *tza'ar baalei chayim* (cruelty to animals).[12]

Regarding the *minhag* (custom) of *kapparot*, many contemporary rabbis and community leaders have spoken out against the practice itself, and several resolutions have been written banning it, as it often involves *tza'ar ba'alei chayim*.

For Rambam, the Torah's prohibitions are here to improve our character:

> This law comes to perfect us in that we should not behave cruelly and that we should not cause unjustified senseless pain ... slaughtering should not be done cruelly, nor is hunting [for sport] permitted.[13]

The concern for the welfare of animals is not only about limiting suffering but also about proactively showing kindness. The Talmud teaches that we should feed our animals before ourselves:

> ... Rav Yehudah said in the name of Rav, "It is forbidden for a person to eat before they give food to their animals. This is learned from the order of the verse found in the Shema: 'And I will give grass in your fields for your animals,' and only then the verse goes on to say, 'and you will eat and be satisfied.'"[14]

It is interesting to note that the above applies to eating, but when it comes to merely drinking, one may indeed drink before giving drink to one's animals. This is deduced from the fact that Rebecca poured water for Eliezer before his camels.[15]

---

11. *Pitchei Teshuvah*, a commentary on the *Shulchan Aruch*, was authored by Rabbi Avraham Tzvi Hirsch Eisenstadt (19th-century, Kovno).

12. *Pitchei Teshuvah*, Yoreh Deah 36:14

13. *Guide for the Perplexed*, Vol. III, Ch. 17

14. Babylonian Talmud, Berachot 40a

15. Genesis 24:17–20

Ramban (Nachmanides) teaches that the reason humans were not permitted to eat meat until after the flood was because of how similar we, as humans, are to animals.

> Meat was not permitted for human consumption until [the time of] the children of Noah, as our Sages have explained. And this goes according to the plain meaning of the Torah's text. The reason for it is that mobile creatures have a certain spiritual attribute which in this respect makes them similar to those who possess intellect (i.e., people); they are capable of looking after their welfare and their food—and they flee from pain and death. As the verse says, "Who knows that the spirit of the children of men is that which ascends on high, and the spirit of the beast is that which descends below to the earth?"[16]

> Yet when the animals sinned and "all flesh had perverted its way on the earth,"[17] it was decreed upon them that they die in the flood. But when, on account of Noah, they were saved in order to maintain their species, mankind was given permission to slaughter and consume animals—since, after all, the animal kingdom owed their existence to them.

> Nevertheless, mankind was not given reign over the [animals'] soul, for it was still forbidden to eat a limb off of a live animal... [and] to consume blood, for it is blood that maintains life... All that was permitted was the flesh of the animal after it has died, but not the animal's soul itself.

Rav Kook taught:[18]

> There is no doubt in the mind of any enlightened thinker that the "dominion" spoken of in the Torah—"They [humans] shall have dominion over the fish of the sea and the birds of the sky and over every living being that moves on the earth"—cannot refer to the dominion of a tyrannical ruler who treats both subjects and servants cruelly in order to satisfy his personal, arbitrary desires. It is unthinkable that there should be an institution of servitude as ugly as this, stamped with an eternal seal in the world of a God who is good to all, whose compassion extends to all creatures...

16. Ecclesiastes 3:21

17. Genesis 6:12

18. Rabbi Avraham Yitzhak HaKohen Kook, "*A Vision of Vegetarianism and Peace*"

Picking up on the point about the consumption of meat being banned at the creation of humanity, Rav Kook continues to teach that this will be our destiny in the time to come as well:

> Is it possible to conceive that a highly valued moral virtue, which had already existed as a part of the human legacy, should be lost forever? It was already established. . .that the very same permission to eat meat, granted after the flood, was not intended to be the actual practice for all time. For how is it possible for a lofty and enlightened moral condition, once instituted, to vanish (as though it had never been)?
>
> When humanity arrives at its goal of happiness and complete freedom, when it reaches that high peak of wholeness which is the pure knowledge of God and the sanctification of life fulfilled according to its nature. . .then human beings will recognize their relationship with all the animals, who are their companions in creation, and how they should properly be able, from the standpoint of pure morality, to combine the standard of mercy with the standard of justice in particular relation to [the animals], and they will no longer be in need of extenuating concessions. . .
>
> Thus, will humanity expand the limits of righteous behavior. Once the gates of righteousness are opened, the light will continue to spread. . .until within the parameters of human righteousness the demand will arise, valid and enduring, to take counsel in seeking ways to improve the lot of these animals, who exist at a lowly and humble level of creation in terms of their material and moral status. Then the "dominion" of which the Torah speaks will be established according to its purpose and its value, as it was intended to be understood.
>
> And certainly, when this noble vision is fulfilled. . .then humanity will no longer be able to in any way brandish its sword over [animal] life, but they will dwell in safety together, and savor the splendor of life.[19]

While Rav Kook was mostly a vegetarian,[20] he did believe that the prohibition of eating meat does not apply to all until the messianic era. However, I would argue that shortly after the passing of Rav Kook, with the massive scale-up for capitalism and its influence upon factory farming, that we've entered a new era. Meat may not blanketly prohibited today, but the rabbis never could have imagined the levels of suffering involved in

---

19. Ibid.
20. Rav Kook reportedly ate a portion of meat (or fowl) on the Shabbat and holidays.

the factory farming industry (experienced in kosher factory farms as well). They also never could have imagined that we'd have as many scientific studies as we do today that point to the detrimental impact on one's health that eating meat can have, nor could they have imagined all the alternative food sources we have access to today to better fulfill our human nutritious needs.

It is easy to be kind to one's dog or cat. It is much harder, it turns out, to be compassionate to cows, chickens, and fish when we do not see them and when we have become accustomed to eating them. Whether we are vegan, vegetarian, or a reducetarian (one who seeks to reduce their animal product intake), we can all advocate for better legislation that protects the most vulnerable among us. Indeed, on a qualitative and qualitative level, animals suffer the most on the planet today. The United Nations' Food and Agriculture Organization estimates that about 80 billion land animals are slaughtered each year for food (which does not include the roughly 51–160 billion farmed fish).

Each of us must do all we can to ensure that animals are treated more humanely. We must do our part to reduce their suffering. The Torah expects nothing less of us. Treating animals with compassion is perhaps the ultimate measure of one's attribute of *chesed*. And ultimately, as we have seen, it can in turn lead to improving our character.

Let us live up to God's mandate of treating all God's creations and creatures with respect and compassion.

#29

Anavah, Walking Humbly

PERHAPS HUMILITY, MORE THAN any other virtue, could be identified with the "religious" personality. Sadly, today, often being more "religious" is instead associated with being more certain, more rigid. The one who is most fervent and adamant might be deemed the master of faith. But a different approach might be that the one with the most humility about themselves and about their knowledge is the master of faith. Acting humbly can be a great kindness, because it gives space to others.

We will explore and examine two forms of humility. The first is the most commonly thought of approach: lowering oneself. In the second, we will explore alternative models of humility.

The Torah teaches us that our greatest model here is Moses. "Now the man Moses was very humble, more so than any man on the face of the earth."[1] Rashi here explains that humble means "low and a patient (or tolerant) person."[2] Ramban (Nahmanides) explains:

> Now the man Moses was very humble: This [is stated] to tell us that God was zealous for Moshe's sake on account of his [great] humility, since he [himself] would never answer the injustice [meted out to him] even if he knew about it. . .
>
> The *midrash* states, "Rabbi Nathan says: They (Miriam and Aaron) spoke against Moshe even in his presence, as it is said, 'And the Eternal heard it. Now the man Moshe was very humble,' and he restrained himself about the matter." [Scripture therefore] mentions Moshe's humility in that he endured [their

1. Numbers 12:3
2. Rashi's commentary on Numbers 12:3

insult] and did not answer them back, and that God was [there-fore] zealous for his sake.[3]

Here the model for us to emulate is to not be so easily offended and that we are to restrain our judgement and lashing out when insulted or otherwise offended. Rather, we should allow ourselves to be pushed around a little bit. One can of course manifest this type of humility by simply not lording themselves over others, by viewing themselves as no greater than the other. This type of humility, the diametric opposite of arrogance, can indeed even be good for us and allow us to experience greater respect and admiration! We need not worry about what others think of us because indeed they are actually likely thinking very little about us.

A friend shared with me that while learning in an esteemed yeshiva in Israel, whenever the *rosh yeshiva* (spiritual dean) would enter the *beit midrash* (study hall), and the hundreds of students would automatically rise for him, he would always motion for them to sit down. When asked, the *rosh yeshiva* explained that, just because he holds that position doesn't make him any greater than anyone else in the room. This same *rosh yeshiva*[4] would often be seen sitting engaged in conversation with a student on a step, quite literally lowering himself to the level of his students.

Rabbi Bahya ibn Pekuda, a great medieval teacher of *musar*, doubts if he is important enough, and his ideas worthy enough, to put out in the world.

> When I planned to execute my decision to write this book, I saw that one like me is unworthy of writing a book such as this. I surmised that my ability would not suffice to analyze all the necessary aspects, owing to the difficulty which I perceived, and to my wisdom being insufficient, and my mind being too weak to grasp all of the issues, and that I am not fluent in the Arabic language in which I wrote it. I feared that I would toil at something that would evidence my inability, and that it would be a presumptuous undertaking, so that I considered changing my mind and abandoning my previous decision.
>
> But when I designed to remove this laborious burden from myself and desist from composing the work, I reconsidered and became suspicious of myself for having chosen to rest and to dwell in the abode of laziness in peace and tranquility, and I feared that it was the desire of the [evil] passion which was placing this thought [within me]. . .and I know that many minds

3. Ramban's commentary on Numbers 12:3
4. Rav Meir Schlesinger of Yeshivat Sha'alvim

have been lost out of apprehension, and many losses have been caused by fear. . .if all those involved in good causes. . .were to remain silent and still until they could completely attain their ideal, no man would ever say a word after the Prophets. . .who were chosen by God. . .[5]

Ibn Pekuda ultimately concludes that we must speak truth even if we don't feel ourselves worthy. How many of us have lacked the confidence or held a form of humility that prevented us from doing what's right and necessary. "Who am I do to do this or say this," we might ask ourselves.

We may, sometimes correctly so, think of ourselves as strong or rich or beautiful. But those are nothing to be proud of; rather, they are to fill us with responsibility. The *Mesilat Yesharim* teaches:

One who is wealthy may rejoice in their lot, but at the same time they must help those in need. If one is strong, they must assist the weak and rescue the oppressed. The situation is analogous to that of a household where there are different servants assigned to different tasks, and where each servant must fulfill their appointed task if the affairs and requirements of the household are all to be attended to. In truth, there is no place for pride here.

Similarly, the Talmud teaches us a Divine model that we are to emulate: "God upholds the cause of the orphan and widow, and loves the stranger, giving them food and clothing."[6] We sit low in a hospital because the Divine presence is above the bed. Just as God is present with the sick, so too do we lower ourselves before the vulnerable. So too, the rabbis teach us not to seek honor but to honor others. Indeed, honoring others will be the greatest honor to ourselves. Ben Zoma taught: "Who is honored? One who honors others."[7]

It is not only that humility is a virtue and good for others, but that it's good for ourselves as well. With arrogance, we are weak. The Talmud records: "Rabbi Alexandri said, 'Whoever has arrogance, the slightest breeze will shake them.' "[8]

Furthermore, people detect arrogance and distance themselves from it. Rabbi Yisrael Salanter[9] used to say, "When I see an arrogant person, I

5. Rabbi Bahya Ibn Pekuda, in his introduction to *Hovot HaLevavot* (*Duties of the Heart*)

6. Babylonian Talmud, Megillah 31a

7. Pirkei Avot 4:1

8. Babylonian Talmud, Sotah 5a

9. Rabbi Yisrael Salanter, a famed Lithuanian Talmudist and scholar, is considered to be the founder of the *musar* movement.

feel such a revulsion that I almost vomit."[10] Don't most of us want to cultivate meaningful relationships that can be sustained? Rabbi Salanter further teaches that we can lose ourselves in this if we're not careful.

> Do not be surprised how it could be that a person with all their faults and smallness of stature nevertheless considers themself greater than their contemporaries. For the more a person loves being praised and admired, the more will their desire for praise grow and cover up their deficiencies, to the point that they no longer sense them. And as the desire to feel that they are better than others grows, their self-admiration heightens the sense of other people's shortcomings. By virtue of their arrogance, they will no longer sense other people's virtues and will eventually only be able to sense their own virtues and other people's deficiencies. And so, arrogance will come to fill their entire soul without their even sensing it.[11]

Additionally, one's arrogance can show that they have a low self-esteem. Rabbi Shlomo Wolbe wrote:

> One who craves attention from others has not yet found themself. They are unaware of their true worth. Lacking self-esteem, they depend on the opinions of others. They hunger for their praise, for without their appreciation, they feel worthless. When people fail to applaud them, they become hostile and angry.[12]

And so one pathway toward humility is to consider how small the value of our own life is. Consider the following:

> Akavya ben Mahalalel said, "Know where you have come from—a putrid drop; and where you are going—to a place of dust, vermin and worms; and before Whom you are destined to give an accounting and reckoning—the King of kings, the Holy One be Blessed.[13]

A similar but slightly different approach is to understand that our responsiveness to God should be born out of humility. The arrogant person puts themselves first, but a humble one submits to God. Rashi teaches this model in his commentary on the *akeidah* story. God calls for Abraham, and he replies, "*hineini*" ("here I am"). Rashi writes:

10. Rabbi Yisrael Salanter, *Tenuat HaMussar*, vol.1, p.303
11. Rabbi Yisrael Salanter, *Ohr Yisrael*, Letter 30
12. Rabbi Shlomo Wolbe, *Alei Shur*, volume 1, p. 43
13. Pirkei Avot 3:1

Here I am/*hineini*: This is the response of the pious. This [*hineini*] implies *anavah* (humility and alacrity).[14]

One of the important lessons of religion is the idea that the job of God is taken. It cannot be us. Psalms teaches: "The arrogant cannot stand in Your presence, You hate all who do wrong."[15] To stand before God, we must be filled with awe and humility. And another psalm states: "For You delight not in sacrifice, else would I give it; You have no pleasure in burnt offerings. The sacrifices of God are a broken spirit; a broken and a contrite heart, O God, You will not despise."[16]

An alternative approach to humility is not that it means to lower ourselves and think lowly of ourselves, but the opposite: to see our beauty. Rav Kook teaches about how one should find their inner perfection:

> To the extent that inner perfection is lacking, nature will strive for exterior perfection. The drive for self-glorification before others will only awaken from a state of baseness of spirit, whether in what the spirit really has or in what it doesn't have. Therefore, a person must increase the impression of their inner perfection, and then their words, when speaking of themself before others, will always be properly balanced.[17]

Rav Kook shares in a different work: "When humility effects depression, it is defective; when it is genuine, it inspires joy, courage and inner dignity."[18] In other words, for Rav Kook, we must know our self-worth and strive to have a positive self-esteem. Only then can we achieve true humility before others.

Rav Kook lived this truth as is told in one of countless relevant stories. One of Rav Kook's detractors, who hated him for being too modern and open minded, used to scream slanders at him and pour garbage upon Rav Kook when he would see him. One day the daughter of this detractor became very sick and he heard that Rav Kook was the only one to have a connection to the leading specialist in Europe that was needed to heal his daughter. He sent Rabbi Aryeh Levine to talk to Rav Kook since he obviously couldn't go himself. Rav Kook immediately wrote a letter to the doctor pleading for his help and describing his detractor only in positive terms. Then Rav Kook also made sure to ensure financial support for the family.

14. Rashi's commentary on Genesis 22:1

15. Psalms 5:6

16. Psalms 51:18–19

17. Rav Kook, *Midot HaRe'iya*, Kavod 4

18. Rav Kook, *The Moral Letters*

Rav Kook wasn't concerned with how he was treated. Rather he stayed true to his principles.

There is a famous image of footprints and a person realizing after their life that there was only one set of footprints when they knew they weren't alone because they were being carried. Indeed, so much of what we achieve, and even the fact that we're alive, is due to someone else carrying us. There is a Jewish teaching that we should speak "b'shem omro," quoting others for their ideas rather than taking credit for them and that this will bring moshiach. When we see ourselves in a perspective of gratitude and giving credit, we bring a piece of redemption to the world.

We can learn to carry both our light and our darkness, our greatness and our smallness. We need not think low of ourselves. Humility divides confidence from arrogance. If we are entitled, we are self-focused but when we are humble, we are other-focused ready to serve. There is just less self present in all interactions. We hold self-awareness alongside a deep other-consciousness. We can embrace self-celebration but not for ourselves as the ends but because we value ourselves and bring others into the celebration of ourself and of them.

We can help young people today by modeling this balance of self-awareness with other consciousness. But also, we can support them by praising them not for what they do but for their very being. What gives people worth is not their accomplishments but their very being. The human value is intrinsic and not to be proven.

The type of humility we wish to cultivate is not one rooted in low self-worth but in high self-worth. At the same time, it is to be rooted in submission and subjugation to the will of God. Such a sense of self, based a deep sense of intrinsic value, will lead one away from needing to prove their external value, and will ultimately lead to healthy humility.

#30

Meni'at Ka'as, Restraining Anger

EVERYONE HAS A BIT of anger in them. We have all been wronged and hurt. Reacting to anger is human and natural, and each of us will react to that anger, when triggered, in very different ways. Nonetheless, the Jewish ethical tradition wants us to do everything possible to contain or squash or limit the control that anger has over us.

At the outset, it is important to distinguish between simply *being* angry and *acting on* that anger. *Being angry*, if kept in check and unmanifest, is not necessarily inherently destructive. However, it is extremely difficult, and often an exercise in futility, to not give voice to that anger. Acting on anger, then, becomes almost inevitable, and it is for this reason that simply being angry is frowned upon and viewed negatively as well.

Anger, unchecked, will not only harm others but will harm ourselves. The Talmud warns: "An angry person is left with nothing but anger."[1] Anger overtakes us, and can result in our losing our senses and throwing us off balance. Another statement in the Talmud takes anger to the extreme: "One who is angry does not even consider the Divine Presence important."[2] Furthermore, the Talmud explains that anger causes one to lose their most cherished abilities: "Anyone who is angry, if they are wise, their wisdom flees

1. Babylonian Talmud, Kiddushin 41a
2. Babylonian Talmud, Nedarim 22b
Perhaps the intent of this harsh statement is that when one is angry, they lose all perspective, even to the extent of casting aside what they otherwise know God expects of us. Furthermore, acting on anger so often leads to transgressing a plethora of other negative commands, thereby equivalent to "not even considering the Divine presence important."

from them. If they are a prophet, their prophecy flees from them."[3] Finally, how we control our anger tells others who we are and what we're about. It is taught: "A person is recognizable through three things: their pocket, their cup, and their anger."[4]

Eckart Tolle, a new age religious thinker, writes:

> ... For example, anger and resentment strengthen the ego enormously by increasing the sense of separateness, emphasizing the otherness of others and creating a seemingly unassailable fortresslike mental position of "rightness." If you were able to observe the physiological changes that take place inside your body when possessed by such negative states, how they adversely affect the functioning of the heart, the digestive and immune systems, and countless other bodily functions, it would become abundantly clear that such states are indeed pathological, are forms of suffering and not pleasure.[5]

And just as character traits and physiological makeup are interconnected, as we see above, so too are character traits interrelated, and that applies here too.

One *musar* teacher taught:

> If a person wants to discern his or her level of humility, look at how you behave when someone speaks ill of you and insults you. If you become angry, know that you are arrogant, because the humble person does not become angry. Even though anger and arrogance are two separate character traits, anger is impossible without arrogance. One who comes to anger is often because he or she is more arrogant.[6]

One might feel righteous and/or justified in their rage, but King Solomon teaches otherwise: "Be not hasty in your spirit to be angry, for anger rests in the laps of fools."[7]

---

3. Babylonian Talmud, Pesachim 66b

4. Babylonian Talmud, Eruvin 65a

The general understanding of this dictum is that one is recognized by how they spend their money, how they behave when drinking or by how much they imbibe, and how they display their anger. The original Hebrew statement is written alliteratively (as all three words begin with the same letter), making it easy to remember: "kiso (his pocket), koso (his cup), and ka'aso (his anger).

5. Eckhart Tolle, *A New Earth: Awakening to Your Life's Purpose*, p. 111

6. Rabbi Yerucham Levovitz, *Da'at Torah*, Bamidbar, p.94.

7. Ecclesiastes 7:9

If one wants a quality of life, merely out of self-interest, diminishing anger becomes imperative. Rambam teaches:

> Those who frequently become angry have no quality of life; therefore, [the Sages] instructed us to distance ourselves from anger to the farthest degree, until a person acts as though they do not sense even those things that would justifiably anger a person.[8]

We cannot reach truth if we are angry. In fact, the *musar* work Orchot Tzadikim, of anonymous authorship, records that all traits, even negative ones, have their time and place, with anger being the only exception.

> Anger causes a person to be stubborn, and because of their anger a person will not make concessions, and they will not admit the truth.[9]

Similarly, Rambam normally recommends the golden mean, following a path of moderation. But not with anger:

> There are certain character traits that one must distance oneself from in the extreme. In fact, it is forbidden to take [the standard approach of] the "middle path" regarding these character traits. . . Anger is an extremely negative character trait, and it is fitting for a person to distance themself from it to the opposite extreme. One should train oneself never to become angry, even regarding things for which anger might be justified.[10]

Even worse, the rabbis go to the extent of saying that, in a state of anger, we are like idolaters.

> A person who tears their clothes in anger, or breaks their possessions, or scatters their money in rage, is considered as though they worship idols . . . What is the verse that alludes to this? "There shall not be a foreign god among [literally, inside] you, nor shall you bow down before an alien god."[11] What is the "alien god" that is present inside a person? This is the *yeitzer hara* (the self-destructive evil inclination[12]).[13]

---

8. *Mishneh Torah*, Hilchot Dei'ot 2:3

9. *Orchot Tzaddikim*, Gate 12

10. *Mishneh Torah*, Hilchot Dei'ot 2:3

11. Psalms 81:10

12. The idea being expressed here is that when a person is angry, he is a servant of the *yeitzer hara* within him.

13. Babylonian Talmud, Shabbat 105b

But we can't just wish anger away. It takes hard work and determination. The famed 20th-century *musar* teacher Rabbi Shlomo Wolbe teaches that we need to set time aside each day to work at it:

> We will train ourselves to be patient: we will fix a specific amount of time every day—for example, approximately fifteen minutes—in which we will strive to bear with patience all that we see and hear, even when things may be upsetting to us, and even if they are hurtful to us, without losing our composure at all. In cases where it is necessary or obligatory to react, we will do so with measured, calm words, without becoming overly emotional.[14]
>
> Rabbi Simcha Zissel Ziv (19th-century, Kelm, Poland) cultivated his own strategy to avoid losing his temper. He had a special jacket that he had set aside to wear when he was angry. He said, "When I feel anger coming on, I know that I have to get my special jacket. But, by the time I do, I am no longer angry."[15]

Contemporary writers on self-compassion offer us some deep guidance:

> When anger is no longer helpful to us, the most compassionate thing we can do is change our relationship to it, especially by applying the resources of mind-fulness and self-compassion.
>
> How? The first step is to identify the soft feelings behind the hard feelings of anger. Often anger is protecting more tender, sensitive emotions, such as feeling hurt, scared, unloved, alone, or vulnerable. When we peel back the outer layer of anger to see what is underneath, we are often surprised by the fullness and complexity of our feelings. Hard feelings are difficult to work with directly because they are typically defensive and outward focused. When we identify our soft feelings, however, we turn inward and can begin the transformation process.
>
> To truly heal, however, we need to peel back the layers even further and discover the unmet needs that are giving rise to our soft feelings. Unmet needs are universal human needs. . . Some examples are the need to be safe, connected, validated, heard, included, autonomous, and respected. And our deepest need as human beings is the need to be loved.[16]

---

14. Rabbi Shlomo Wolbe, *Alei Shur*, Vol. II, p. 215

15. Alan Morinis, *Every Day, Holy Day*, p. 90

16. Kristen Neff PhD & Christopher Germer, PhD, *The Mindful Self Compassion Workbook, Self-Compassion and Anger in Relationships*, Page 145

We have to learn to be patient and tolerant and not allow a rush of impulsive anger to overtake us. Another connected trait we need to focus on is humility.[17] Rabbi Yeshayahu Horowitz (16th- 17th-century, Prague and Cracow, Poland)[18] writes:

> "Words of the wise, spoken gently, are accepted."[19] Somebody who has acquired this trait will never come to anger. The meaning of "spoken gently" is that they are not spoken with arrogance. For a person who clings to the attribute of humility will never come to anger, for they are patient and ignore those who deride them.[20]

The Talmud suggests that even God, as it were, struggles to overcome anger.

> . . .From this we learn that the Holy One prays. What does God pray? Rav Zutra bar Tuvia taught in the name of Rav: "May it be My will that My compassion overcome My anger, that My mercy overflow My other attributes and that I act toward My children with the quality of mercy . . ."[21]

And so, if the Perfect Being can experience anger, perhaps it's not, in its essence, completely bad. Of course, we must cultivate our capacity for outrage at injustice. Rabbi Abraham Joshua Heschel writes:

> The prophets never thought that God's anger is something that cannot be accounted for, unpredictable, irrational. It is never a spontaneous outburst, but a reaction occasioned by the conduct of man. Indeed, it is the major task of the prophet to set forth the facts that account for it, to insist that the anger of God is not a blind explosive force, operating without reference to the behavior of man, but rather voluntary and purposeful, motivated by concern for right and wrong.[22]

To be sure, there are times where it only makes sense that one would be angry: "Every person has their hour, and everything its place."[23]

17. Humility being the diametric opposite of arrogance mentioned earlier in this chapter.

18. Rabbi Yeshayahu Horowitz is better known as the Shelah HaKadosh, so named for his work Shenei Luchot HaBrit (for which Shelah is an acronym).

19. Ecclesiastes 9:17

20. *Shelah HaKadosh*, letter 200:19

21. Babylonian Talmud, Brachot 7a

22. Heschel, *The Prophets*, 282

23. Pirkei Avot 4:3

Toni Morrison writes: "Anger is better. There is a sense of being in anger. A reality and presence. An awareness of worth. It is a lovely surging." How can we, when warranted, not be upset? Ma Jaya Sati Bhagavati[24] writes:

> It is easy for a spiritual teacher to say, "give up anger." There is reason for anger if we look at the plight of the world's children— and I don't just mean the babies, I mean all of Earth's children who are caught in war, hunger, disease, injustice. Sometimes it looks as if there's no justice anywhere in the world.

But there is a big difference between contained righteous indignation and a pervasive uncontrolled cultural phenomenon of anger. It is the latter that is the primary focus of this topic and that we must shy away from. Rav Kook writes:

> We must hate anger with all the depth of our being. . . [for it] jumbles the mind and invalidates all the advantages of being human, individual and collective. When we see any group always expressing itself in anger, it's a sign that it has no understanding, no content with which to fill its emptiness, that in truth it's angry with itself, but that egoism comes and forces it to deposit the venom of its anger on others. The higher sages, who have reached the height of justice and kindness, are full of will, and kindness and truth garland them all the day.[25]

On this point, Professor Michael Walzer teaches:

> The members of oppressed groups have been encouraged— mistakenly, I think—to believe themselves injured above all by the disrespect of the dominant others and to seek the signs of proper regard. But a permanent state of suspicion about the demeaning or malicious things that are about to be said or done is self-defeating. It leads too often to a dead-end politics of anger and resentment.[26]

President Obama learned about his own maturity to decide that if one wants to be a leader, righteous indignation is not enough.

> I wanted to be neither a supplicant, always on the periphery of power and seeking favor from liberal benefactors, nor a

---

24. Ma Jaya Sati Bhagavati, 1940–2012, was the founder of the Kashi Ashram in Sebastian, Florida, and an activist involved in hunger alleviation among other causes.

25. *Shemoneh Kevatzim* 3: 134; *Orot HaKodesh* 3:244

26.. Michael Walzer, *Politics and Passion*, 37.

permanent protester, full of righteous anger as we waited for white America to expiate its guilt. Both paths were well trodden; both, at a fundamental level, born of despair.[27]

Lama Rod Owens, a black gay Buddhist teacher explains how, even when anger may be morally justifiable, it is not going to be productive.

> In activist communities, our relationship to anger is immature, ill-informed, and overly romanticized. We manipulate anger as a false source of energy and inspiration. Many of us have no idea how to really use anger to see the changes we need to see in our communities. Our relationship to anger is reactive and compulsory one. We feel the anger and respond. When I am asked to illustrate this point, I talk about finding yourself in a burning room and reacting to the danger by jumping out of a window to escape. You didn't have time to think about how far up you were or what you would land on. You just react to the fire and split.[28]

Our tradition, thankfully, is not only morally robust, but also gentle with us mortals. We will struggle with, and sometimes fail at, controlling our anger, and so we should be grateful that it is indeed a mitigating factor. The Midrash teaches:

> "And they said to them, 'May the Lord look upon you and judge'"[29] From this we see that a person is not held responsible [for what they say] in their moment of anger, for [what they say] is not considered to be a sin in such a situation.[30]

And so God is compassionate with us for our sins done in rage. Indeed, it is a mitigating factor when done as a passion crime. So too, we can be gentle with others when they slip and act in a state of anger. It can also remind us of our own soul curriculum.

If we wish to live with kindness, we need others to feel safe around us. Being volatile can break down trust and make it more difficult to create safe, compassionate spaces. Let us strive to control both our internal and expressed anger, thereby making this world a better place. Indeed, not acting angry is an act of kindness toward all around us.

---

27. Barack Obama, *A Promised Land*, p. 118
28. Lama Rod Owens, *The Path of Liberation through Anger*, p. 22
29. Exodus 5:21
30. Midrash Lekach Tov, quoted in *Torah Sheleimah* on Shemot Ch. 5, source 78

#31

Hafchatat De'agah, Reducing Worry

THERE IS AN OLD Jewish joke that someone received a telegram: "Start worrying, details to follow." It's a reminder of how much anxiety is built into Jewish culture and Jewish memory.

We all worry. Some of us may just have occasional and relatively minor occurrences of worrying while others may suffer from severe anxiety attacks. Bracketing these extreme cases, do we need to be concerned with reducing our worrying? If so, how might each of us, on a spiritual level, go about doing so? And what does this have anything to do with kindness?

To start, we may realize that the more we worry, the less equipped we may be to live joyfully and fulfill the moral goals in our lives. Yes, a little bit of worry can be normal and healthy, but when it inhibits our quality of life and our ability to perform, it becomes, in a sense, a negative force. To serve others, we need to reduce our worry, or at very least we need to not appear worried, so that we bring positive, joyful energy in our service rather than anxious energy. As Proverbs teaches: "If worry is in a person's heart, it weighs it down."[1]

One way to decrease worry, as it relates to the materialistic dimensions in our lives, is to find contentment with what we have rather than to constantly immerse ourselves in consumerism. The Talmudic rabbis famously taught: "One who increases possessions, increases worry."[2] A larger home, not to mention a second home, may bring us pleasure, but it also brings a

1. Proverbs 12:25
2. Pirkei Avot 2:7

lot more worry. Owning a business rather than working for one can significantly increase stress. Owning more means more worrying about what we own.[3]

We may feel that because we live in America (or other equally developed and advanced countries) in the 21st century and thus have access to technologies no one could have dreamed of just twenty years ago, we ought to be more healthy people. Sadly, this is hardly the case. Rabbi Jonathan Sacks writes:

> Some of the most affluent societies in the world are way down the list of happiest populations, Britain at fifteenth, the United States at eighteenth. To quote Richard Wilkson and Kate Pickett in *The Spirit Level*, their book on market economics: "It is a remarkable paradox that, at the pinnacle of human material and technical achievement, we find ourselves anxiety-ridden, prone to depression, worried about how others see us, unsure of our friendships, driven to consume and with little or no community life." How could this have happened?[4]

Another area about which we tend to worry is the future, for ourselves, for our kids, for the Jewish people, for humanity. The rabbis teach: "It is not yours to complete the task, but neither are you relieved of the obligation to begin."[5] This profound wisdom reminds us that we can neither be like the cynic who neither takes initiative nor participates in already existing endeavors since we cannot solve all of the world's problems; nor can we be down on ourselves for not being able to completely solve all the problems we address. We must engage and do what we can, but not worry beyond that.

The Hebrew term for the trait necessary to cut off that worry is *bitachon* (trust). And the Hebrew word for worry is *de'agah*, which is comprised of four of the first five letters of the alef-bet (dalet, alef, gimel, and hei). The one missing letter is bet, which can be understood homiletically in this context as representing *bitachon*. In other words, when we worry, what we're lacking is trust.[6] The great *musar* teacher Rabbi Eliyahu Dessler taught:

---

3. This is not to say that one should not own a second home, for example, or own a business. But we do need to realize that there is a direct correlation between more materialism and increased worry. Just being aware of this reality can help one reduce their worry or to at least deal with it in a healthier fashion.

4 Rabbi Jonathan Sacks, *Morality: Restoring the Common Good in Divided Times*, p. 103

5. Pirkei Avot 2:12

6. I heard this idea at a Mussar Institute learning session.

The true source of constant worry is that we have no *bitachon* of attaining the external things that we desire. This desire for "possession," and "taking," its realization always depends on others and external circumstances. *Bitachon* flourishes when we desire internal things—the desire "to be," because in that we are not dependent on others. Therefore, one who desires material possessions feels deep within one's heart that the desire is futile, and is not up to him or her. This is the root of worry.[7]

How might we root our trust? Some of us may trust in God, some in scientific experts, while others in their own subjective reasoning or conscience. We can all make choices regarding the foundation of our trust, but what we dare not choose to have no trust at all. To make such a choice leaves one in a sea of worry without anyone or anything to rely on to navigate storms.

The noted psychiatrist Rabbi Abraham J. Twerski relates the following:

> It is difficult to be happy if one is subject to fear and anxiety.
>
> There are people who experience "morbid expectations." For no apparent reason, they anticipate [that] something terrible is going to happen. A telephone ring precipitates anxiety.
>
> I know, because I was one of them.
>
> My secretary knew that when I was in session with a client, I was not to be interrupted unless it was an emergency. When the telephone rang in my office during a session, and my secretary said, "It's your daughter-in-law," I froze. When my daughter-in-law got through, she said, "Mazal Tov!" and informed me that I had another grandchild.
>
> I decided that this had gone far enough. The call was wonderful news, yet I had expected the worst. I had to do something, but what?
>
> I came across the verse in Psalms[8], "Of evil tidings one will have no fear; one's heart is firm, confident in God."
>
> I decided to say this chapter every day, praying for God to strengthen my trust in the Lord.
>
> It has worked wonders, and I strongly urge people to pray for trust in God. We pray for all our other needs; *bitachon* is no less a vital need.[9]

---

7. *Michtav Me'Eliyahu* volume 5, page 90

8. Psalms 112:7

9. This story appears in the online website JewishMOM.com
https://jewishmom.com/2013/03/10/a-tip-to-overcoming-anxiety-by-rabbi-dr-abraham-j-twerski/

The Talmud teaches further: "A person's livelihood is as difficult as the splitting the Sea."[10] Indeed, when each of us works as hard as we can, with integrity, to tirelessly and faithfully support our families, and contribute to the welfare of society at large, we are miraculously emulating the redemptive splitting of the sea. When each of us advocates for economic justice to ensure that workers can actually live off their wages, we are, in holy covenantal partnership, emulating Divine liberation.

How can we shift from a mindset of scarcity to a mindset of abundance. If we live with a sense of fear and scarcity, how can we not be overcome with worry? Similarly, if we are constantly mindlessly listening to the news and scrolling through social media feeds, we allow everything to hit us. We need more filters to decide what has the right to take up real estate in our minds and hearts.

I recall a few years ago, sitting in the middle of the diverse heartland of Israel (between Tel Aviv and Jerusalem), with such a complex electoral landscape, and feeling the incredibly tense emotional spirit on that monumental election day. Rightfully so, folks In Israel knew how much was at stake with such major decisions: at stake for their daily lives as citizens, for the Jewish people around the world, and for global stability.

But there was also an optimism in the air. A positive solidarity that within this democracy, anything is possible, and that united around a common purpose of building this state (albeit with many vastly conflicting visions), we are together in the *medinah baderech* (state in the making).

I approached such a moment with pride as being an insider here at home, however temporarily, and also with the humility of being an outsider who can't vote and lacks the privileges and responsibilities of citizenship. I also approached such a moment with a deep sense of responsibility, as one serving in Jewish communal leadership, to help protect global Jewry from rapidly growing anti-Semitism and a growing global dissatisfaction with Israeli state policies; and a responsibility to help ensure that our global Jewish leadership is guided not by narrow self-interest but by our most cherished, timeless, and exalted Jewish values. How can we reject Jewish exceptionalism while simultaneously striving to be morally and ethically exceptional?

It is a time for us to cultivate an elevated spiritual consciousness of worry-alleviating empathy and solidarity, that includes but also transcends our personal ideologies as we seek to embrace multiple interpretations of reality, an expansive phenomenological state that fervently avoids embarking down a path either of fundamentalism or relativism, of zealotry or apathetic cynicism, which can in turn lead to kulturkampf.

10. Babylonian Talmud, Pesachim 118a

Part of the goal here is to remember how uncharitable and unfair it would be to suggest that everyone on the right is a fascist and racist OR that everyone on the left either doesn't respect Judaism or is naïve and/or apathetic about security and peace. The integrity of our discourse really matters and is formative. It would be completely myopic to not understand the merits of the concerns and priorities of each unique faction, given the complex, sundry cultural contexts.

At such historically formative moments, it is a time for *hishtadlut* (striving & struggling for justice) but also for *bitachon* (letting go and trusting a process that is far beyond each of us individually and factionally). It is also a crucial time to remember that, as important as authority roles can be, some of the most important work that changes the deepest realities on the ground happens on a grassroots level.

We are all empowered to participate in this holy enterprise, both in the holy land and in the diaspora. Our faith and activism must go beyond the political dimension. We can bring compassion and connectedness where others look to spread division, distrust, and fear of the other.

The hasidic thinker Rabbi Sholom Noach Berezovsky[11] explains that there are two types of trust. The first we learn from *yetzi'at Mitzrayim* (the Exodus from Egypt): how to relinquish control and be patient and wait; the second we learn from *keri'at Yam Suf* (the splitting of the Red Sea): rising up and acting in situations of uncertainty.

Sometimes, our trust-based challenge is to give up control and cultivate the trust to calmly keep walking on the same righteous path as we spiritually wait for change. At other times, our trust-based challenge is to proactively alter the course and remain confident as we strive to take control of the situation and create change.

Each day, we might ask ourselves: In what area of my life do I need to just stay the course, let go of control, and stop wasting so much of my physical and spiritual energy in anxiety, worrying about that which I cannot control. We might also ask: In what area of my life do I need to rise up, become more active, take control, and create change.

We need the wisdom to find this spiritual clarity and to then strengthen our trust (I refer here to a three-fold trust: 1. Trusting in the conclusion that the highest good will ultimately prevail; 2. Trusting that the ontological foundation of all being, of all existence, is itself good; and 3. Trusting in the process itself that walking the righteous path is good in itself) as we walk, at times passively and at times actively, from darkness to light, from

11. Rabbi Berezovsky, more commonly known as the Netivot Shalom, the title of his famed work, was the Slonimer rebbe for the last twenty years of his life.

uncertainty to clarity, as each of us leaves our own personal Mitzrayim, our own personal narrow place[12] each day to cross through a new sea. The uncertainty itself can be holy, since it deepens the light of trust in us, and thus our sense of the holy interdependence and spiritual interconnection of all. May this deep trust reinvigorate and renew us.

This is true not only of our work regarding Israel, as I described above, but equally true of our work here in America. We need to do the hard work of building our society but also have some level of trust and of letting go of control. We have to commit, but we also must embrace the inevitability of our death, the ultimate loss of ego and of letting go. The contemporary philosopher Ryuu Shinohara writes:

> . . . Instead, practice detachment. Make your choice and then relax and know that forces greater than you or I can comprehend are in motion. You're being taken toward your destination, whether you know it or not. Thus, become an observer instead of being a passenger to your ego. Trust that the universe is taking care of everything and that you will also be taken care of.[13]

The moral concern here, however, is not just about worrying less so we can be stable and giving for others. It is also about being a positive response to others' worries. We live in a society plagued by worry. We can help others worry less and feel less isolated. Many worry because they don't have anyone or anything to trust. How can we become people that others can trust, that others can rely on, that enables others to feel less alone in the world because of our very existence and willingness to help?

Our best teachers are the ones very closely aligned with our values and in whose moral boundaries we can trust. Their views are in line enough with our own so that we do not slowly kill off our moral intuition. But they also diverge enough from our own approach and even startle us enough that they are not nearly projections of our own will.

To be sure, we can and should also learn from folks who see the world just like us and articulate our position very well, as well as from folks who see the world completely differently than us. But a mentor, teacher, or adviser is something else altogether, as they can help us ensure that we are always growing by being challenged by new ways of thinking, not pushed too hard or too far, but rather softly and consistently.

---

12. The Hebrew spelling of Mitzrayim shares the same letters as the word *meitzarim*, meaning narrow spaces or straits. Much has been written about the correlation and connection between the two.

13. Ryuu Shinohara, *The Magic of Manifesting*, p. 57

We live in an era of simplistic clichés like "just trust your gut." While that cliché may at times be appropriate, as we do indeed need to believe in and trust ourselves, it also can and does lead to a breakdown of dialogue, of mentorship, and of learning. It is therefore equally important, if not more important, to have others we can trust to guide and help us. And for those of us in a position to do so, to be that someone whom others can turn to for trust and encouragement. We can reduce our own anxiety and worrying. At the same time, we must, each of us in whatever way we are able, be engaged in reducing the worry and anxiety of others.

#32

Simchah, Emanating Joy

PERHAPS THE MOST OBVIOUS proposal for how to live a life of kindness to others is that we live emanating joy. But it is far from obvious how cultivating our own joy will actually trickle over to others in ways that are helpful, meaningful, and healing for them.

Let's start with understanding perspectives, from Jewish thought, on *simchah* (joy). We know that we cannot live in a constant state of joy but rather that joy is often fleeting. King David taught: "In the evening one lies down weeping, but with dawn--a cry of joy!"[1] Even further, "They who sow in tears will reap in joy."[2]

Anyone who has experienced a sudden family tragedy understands what it means to suddenly shift from joy to sorrow. At times, one is even forced to deal with both emotions simultaneously, such as one who is in mourning for a relative during the *shalosh regalim* (the three pilgrimage festivals of Pesach, Shavuot, and Sukkot), about which the Torah mandates "*V'samachta b'chagecha*," ("You are to rejoice in your holiday").[3]

Rabbi Joseph B. Soloveitchik reflected on the complexity of emotional life for a religious person:

> In the first place, the dialectical character of our existence and our total experience manifests itself in the halakhic principle of the totality of the emotional life. Judaism has insisted upon the integrity and wholeness of the table of emotions, leading like a spectrum from joy, sympathy, and humility (the conjunctive

1. Psalms 30:6
2. Psalms 126:5
3. Deuteronomy 16:14

feelings) to anger, sadness and anguish (the disjunctive emotions). Absolutization of one feeling at the expense of others,
or the granting of unconditioned centrality to certain emotions while denoting others to a peripheral status, may have
damaging complications for the religious development of the
personality."[4]

So part of the life journey seems to be about embracing the fullness
of emotional life. Ecclesiastes famously teaches that there is a time for
everything:

Everything has its season, and there is a time for everything
under the heaven.
A time to be born and a time to die.
A time to plant and a time to uproot the planted.
A time to kill and a time to heal.
A time to wreck and a time to build.
A time to weep and a time to laugh.
A time to wail and a time to dance.
A time to scatter stones and a time to gather stones.
A time to embrace and a time to shun embraces.
A time to seek and a time to lose.
A time to keep and a time to discard.
A time to rend and a time to mend.
A time to be silent and a time to speak.
A time to love and a time to hate.
A time for war and a time for peace.[5]

Similarly, William Blake expressed beautifully:

He who binds himself to a joy
Does the winged life destroy;
But he who kisses the joy as it flies,
Lives in Eternity's sunrise.[6]

We are to embrace conflicting emotions so much that the Talmud
imagines that even one type of joy competing with another type of joy
would be little personified voices of heresy.

From where was this derived (that we blow the trumpet during
the *simchat beit hashoeivah*)?[7] Rav Eina said: From the verse:

4. Rabbi Joseph Soloveitchik, *Out of the Whirlwind: A Theory of Emotions*, p. 179
5. Ecclesiastes 3:2–8
6. William Blake, *Eternity*
7. *Simchat beit hashoeivah* literally means "the rejoicing over the drawing of

'*U'she'avtem mayim b'sason*' ('And you shall draw water while rejoicing').[8]

There were these two heretics, one was named Sason and one was named Simchah. Sason said to Simchah, 'I am better than you,' for it is written: 'They shall attain *sason* and *simchah* (rejoicing and gladness)'.[9] Simchah replied to Sason, 'I am better than you, since it is written: 'The Jews had *simchah v'sason* (gladness and rejoicing)'. . . .'[10]

Perhaps the rabbis are teaching us that God doesn't want positive toxicity or for us to pretend that everything is joyful in life. Rather, as we stated above, we are to embrace the reality and the fullness of existence. The two emotions that are on the same end of the spectrum are "heretics," perhaps because they can't see the other end of the spectrum. They pick a fight not with sadness but with other joy.

On the other hand, there is a real value to cultivating *simchah* in one's life. I don't mean a type of happiness found in vanity. Rather, a deep sense of purpose, connection, and meaning, which in turn bring us true joy and contentment. If we don't, we will miss out on so much. Rabbi Chaim Vital[11] taught:

> Sadness prevents a person from serving God and fulfilling the commandments; it prevents studying Torah and concentrating while praying. It negates one's good intentions to serve God. It is the beginning of the evil impulse's enticement, even of a righteous person, by showing them that they have no benefit from serving God because troubles come upon them, and so on. And it [*the yetzer hara*, one's evil inclination] also comes upon a person in the form of piety, saying to them: 'How can you possibly think that a lump of earth, maggots, and worms can come close and sanctify themself with the Holiness of the King of the

---

water," and refers to an annual grand event which took place in the *beit hamikdash* (Temple) in celebration of water being drawn up to Jerusalem. As Jerusalem is situated on a hilltop, it was necessary for water to be drawn from below, and the drawing of water was therefore reason for great celebration.

8. Isaiah 12:3

9. Isaiah 35:10
The reasoning here is that *sason* is mentioned prior to *simchah* in the quoted verse.

10. Babylonian Talmud, Sukkah 48b

11. Rabbi Chaim Vital was a 16th- 17th-century Safed kabbalist and was considered the foremost disciple of Rabbi Isaac Luria.

Universe?' [As] Rabbi Elazar said:[12] "The Divine Presence does not dwell in the midst of sadness."[13]

Rabbi Yehudah HaLevi,[14] in his philosophical work *The Kuzari*, similarly teaches:

> The general principle is this: Our holy Torah is divided into awe, love, and joy. Each of these can bring you closer to God. Your submission to God on fast days is not dearer to Him than your joy on Shabbat and festivals. . . You should rejoice in a *mitzvah* because of your love of it. You should realize the good God has bestowed on you. It is as if you were invited to the King's table to partake of the King's bounty. You will then be grateful both inwardly and outwardly. If your joy moves you to sing and dance—this is an act of Divine service and of holding close to God.[15]

Rabbi Nachman of Bratzlav said that we should even tell ourselves jokes in order to achieve a more positive mental state:

> Here are a few ways to make yourself feel happy at all times. . . Generally speaking, you can make yourself feel happy by uttering nonsensical words that make you laugh and by telling jokes to yourself. . .because depression and sadness can overcome a person more than anything else. It is hard to overcome this sadness, which can be very harmful to you.[16]

The Talmudic rabbis also expressed great admiration for joke tellers:

> While [they were conversing], two men passed by, whereupon he [Elijah] remarked, "These two have a share in the world to come." R. Beroka then approached and asked them, "What is your occupation?" They replied, "We are jesters; when we see men depressed, we cheer them up."[17]

It seems that bringing joy to others is a great *mitzvah*. Further, we cannot seek joy for ourselves in the first place without extending it to others

12. Babylonian Talmud, Shabbat 30b

13. Rabbi Chaim Vital, *Shaarei Kedushah* (part 2, chapter 4)

14. Rabbi Yehudah HaLevi was an 11th- 12th- century philosopher, physician and poet. Beyond his magnum opus *The Kuzari*, he is best known for his many poems expressing his yearning for The Land of Israel. Towards the end of his life, he embarked on his journey to Israel, only to die on the way or shortly after his arrival.

15. *The Kuzari* 2:50

16. Rebbe Nachman, *Hayei Moharan*, p. 85

17. Babylonian Talmud, Ta'anit 22a

as well. Consider Rambam's (Maimonides') teaching about the *mitzvah* of *simchat yom tov* (cultivating joy on the holidays):

> Men should eat meat and drink wine, for there is no happiness without partaking of meat, nor is there happiness without partaking of wine. When a person eats and drinks [in celebration of a holiday], he is obligated to feed converts, orphans, widows, and others who are destitute and poor. In contrast, a person who locks the gates of his courtyard and eats and drinks with his children and his wife, without feeding the poor and the embittered, is [not indulging in] rejoicing associated with a *mitzvah*, but rather the rejoicing of his gut. And with regard to such a person [this verse] is applied: "Their sacrifices will be like the bread of mourners; all that partake thereof shall become impure, for they [kept] their bread for themselves alone."[18] This happiness is a disgrace for them, as [it is written]:[19] "I will spread dung on your faces, the dung of your festival celebrations."[20]

There are some forms of *simchah* that may be simple, such as merely having a seat at the table with community, accompanied by delicious food. This seems like a basic and eternal truth about human needs. But there is another form of *simchah* that is more complex. Rabbi Shlomo Wolbe[21] taught: "*Simchah* results from the unification of opposing elements."[22] Indeed, we want not only the fullness and totality of experience, as noted above, but we also want integration and harmonization rather than living in a world of binaries and polarities.

Rabbi Isaac Arama[23] taught that the sound of one shofar blast (the *teruah*) is the sound of fear and trembling. The sound of another shofar blast (the *tekiah*) is the sound of joy, hope, and faith in a redemption to come. Indeed, Rosh Hashanah seeks to instill in us both fear and joy, and not simply as two distinct emotions, but rather a harmony and synchronization of the two. It prepares us to live meaningfully in society today where we must carry both a serious and heavy commitment to addressing dark injustices and oppression while also living and leading with joy and with the optimism that there is light at the end of the tunnel.

---

18. Hosea 9:4
19. Malachi 2:3
20. Rambam, *Mishneh Torah*, Laws of Yom Tov 6:18
21. Rabbi Shlomo Wolbe was a famed 20th-century *musar* teacher.
22. Rabbi Shlomo Wolbe, *Alei Shur* II, p. 325
23. Rabbi Isaac Arama was a 15th-century Spanish scholar and author.

Cultivating joy and creating spaces for others to cultivate joy is a crucial part of our kindness practice. The contemporary scholar Rabbi David Jaffe shares:

> Rabbi Nachman refers to these [aforementioned] emotions as *lev shavur* (broken-heartedness) and *tza'ar* (pain). *Simchah* is a key tool for change makers. Despair is a partner of oppression. . . Someone in despair is not going to put up much of a fight against oppression.[24]

There is a sad word in German, *schadenfreude*, which means finding pleasure in the experience of another's misfortune. But there is a less well-known opposite joyful word in German as well: *freudenfreude*, which means finding joy in another's good fortune. On this note, Pirkei Avot (Ethics of Our Fathers) famously teaches: 'Who is rich? One who is content with what they have.'[25] The simple read of this rabbinic teaching is that we can learn to be satiated with what we have and not always wanting more. But there is another reading that lines up with *freudenfreude*: 'Who is rich? One who is content with what *they* have (i.e., not what he/she him/herself has, but with what he/she, the other, has).' We can, and must, find joy not only in our own gains but in the gains of others.

In addition to finding joy in our personal lives and in that of others, we can find it in our ancestors. We can experience the joy of learning Torah and history and tapping into the spiritual realities and emotions of our great forebears. The contemporary author and activist Lama Rod Owens has his own way of expressing tapping into the emotions of ancestors.

> When I experience rage, I understand that I am experiencing the rage of all my ancestors. When I experience love, I am also experiencing the love of all my ancestors. It is the transhistorical love that is often felt as resilience that keeps me and many of us alive; and when we fall deeply into the love that we are being gifted, then we begin to thrive, and it is that thriving that begins to disrupt the systems of violence that were only created to annihilate us. We disrupt these systems because we survive the system, summon our joy, and dance into our thriving. . . I am my ancestors' wildest dreams because I thrive.[26]

Sometimes joy is complicated and multi-faceted. Other times, joy can be quite simple. Consider a deeply joyful encounter with nature. Part of the

---

24. Rabbi David Jaffe, *Changing the World from the Inside Out*, p. 69

25. *Pirkei Avot* 4:1

26. Lama Rod Owens, *Love and Rage: The Path of Liberation through Anger*, p. 244

joy is enabled by getting beyond the self and immersing one's consciousness into the forest, into the waves, or into the stars.

Other times, the goal of joy is not to get to a 10 out of 10 but, if one is in a really low state, perhaps to get from a 1 out of 10 to a 2 or 3 out of 10. We can just sit with someone suffering not with the goal of them being in a state of joy but with the goal of them suffering a little less.

There are so many places and ways to cultivate joy and to share joy with others. It is a spiritual project, a Jewish enterprise –and indeed at the center of our work—to build a kinder world, a world which revolves around *chesed*. Let us do our utmost to spread joy throughout the world.

#33

Meni'at Atzlanut, Avoiding Laziness

ARE HUMANS HARDWIRED TO primarily seek meaning? To seek pleasure? To avoid pain? What is at our core? It is hard to say what is most fundamental to the human being, and perhaps there is no "one size fits all" answer, but any student of history or contemporary psychology can easily see the common desire of avoiding effort. Today, if one can get someone else to do things for them (mow their lawn, clean their pool, deliver their groceries, etc.) then it's viewed as desirable. Is there anything that's still worth doing ourselves?

Laziness, as discussed here, can be understood as a lack of discipline to enact our kindness commitments. Why do I throw my newspaper in the garbage when there is no recycling bin present rather than carrying it with me home to my own recycling bin? Is it anything other than laziness? Sometimes we have to set habits to commit to and then figure out how to balance *kavanah* (intention) with *kevah* (habit).

Perhaps the biggest culprit in our laziness and unwillingness to exert ourselves can be found in the psychological tools of excuse making. *Orchot Tzadikim*[1] explains how the traps of laziness affect one's learning:

> If people say to a lazy person: "Your teacher is in a nearby city, go and learn Torah from them," they respond: "I fear a lion on the highway." If they say: "Your teacher is in your own city," they respond: "I fear a lion in the streets." If they say: "Your teacher is near your home," they respond: "I am afraid a lion is outside." And if they say: "Your teacher is in a room inside your home," they respond: "I am afraid that if I rise from the bed the door

---

1. *Orchot Tzadikim* is a well-known *musar* work of anonymous authorship.

will be locked." And if they say: "But the door is open," they respond: "I need a little more sleep."[2]

How many of us just want a little more self-care and relaxation! We may know that there is no viable excuse for anyone of us to not be addressing others' suffering for at least a few minutes each week, yet we manage to find twenty excuses while maintaining the memory of our soup-kitchen volunteer experience from three months earlier as our justification to comfort ourselves from facing our entrapment in sloth. The great *musar* teacher R. Chaim Luzzato paints the picture well:

> We see with our own eyes, on numerous occasions, how a person who is already cognizant of their duty and who already knows what is appropriate for the salvation of their soul and what their obligation is to their Creator, can nonetheless neglect their duty, though not because of a lack of awareness of their obligation or for any other reason. Rather, their lethargic indolence dominates them. And this is what it says (to them): "I'll eat a bit," or "I'll sleep a bit," or "It's hard for me to get out of the house," or "I took off my shirt; how can I put it back on?" or "It's very hot outside," "It's very chilly," or "rainy," and all such other pretexts and excuses that the mouths of the indolent are filled with.[3]

Indeed, none other than King David himself fell prey to laziness. The biblical text[4] informs us that he was strolling on his rooftop after rising from his bed in the evening when he took notice of Bathsheba and subsequently summoned her. The 19th-century commentator Malbim explains:

> This means to say that even in his home he was not busy with the needs of the people, for he rose from his bed in the evening. And our sages said that [after] David ate a regular meal he would sleep until the ninth hour, and if he ate a meal fit for kings he would sleep until the evening. . .and even after that he didn't deal with the needs of the people, and because of this he came to sin and did not prevent his eyes from seeing a woman bathing. . ."[5]

It is, of course, not only the privileged and powerful who struggle with energizing themselves to transform the world. The oppressed are also

---

2. *Orchot Tzadikim* 16:5
3. *Mesilat Yesharim* 6:18
4. II Samuel, 11:2–3
5. Malbim's commentary, ad loc.

plagued with this complex problem. The great Brazilian educator and author Paulo Freire wrote:

> The oppressed, having internalized the image of the oppressor and adapted his guidelines, are fearful of freedom. Freedom would require them to eject this image and replace it with autonomy and responsibility. Freedom is acquired by conquest, not by gift. It must be pursued constantly and responsibly. Freedom is not an ideal located outside of man; nor is it an idea which becomes myth. It is rather the indispensable condition for the quest for human completion.[6]

Now, this is certainly not sloth but rather a different example of one of the many inhibitors placed in our minds and souls that prevent liberation. German philosopher Georg Hegel called it our subordination to the consciousness of the master.

Christian philosopher Thomas Aquinas argued[7] that sloth can be sinful in two situations: when one is in despair to perform what is spiritually good, and when one is so regretful about their wrongdoings that it becomes preventative for them. We can think of a number of other psychological reasons outside of the "sin" category, and perhaps our framework for not falling into the trap of laziness can therefore be more positive, focusing on alacrity and motivation rather than on our sinfulness and sloth itself.

Consider the following: A yeshiva, particularly one with out-of-town students living in a dormitory, typically requires its students to attend the morning *minyan*. One such yeshiva had a reputation for penalizing students who slept in and failed to attend. While perhaps the impending fine served as an incentive for some students, others were turned off to the very idea of *davening* as a result. On the other hand, a *rosh yeshiva* of another institution took a radically different approach. He would speak to students who overslept lovingly and with a smile, reminding them of the expectation to attend *minyan*, and then add, "But if you're going to sleep late, at least sleep well."

Psychologists have found that life satisfaction is twenty-two percent more likely for those with consistent, ongoing minor accomplishments than for those who express interest only in massive accomplishments.[8] Laziness, too, is not conquered by being major life goal, but incrementally, every moment of our existence. We must seek little victories. The research shows that this can lead to a more meaningful and happy life.

---

6. Paulo Freire, *Pedagogy of the Oppressed* 31
7. *Summa Theologica*, chapter 35, article 1
8. Orlick, 1998

To this effect, the Vilna Gaon[9] found it meaningful to argue that the reward for doing *mitzvot* is so much greater than the effort expended.

> How difficult it is to leave this world. In this world, for a few kopecks a person can purchase *tzitzit*, and as a reward for that simple *mitzvah* merit to experience the Divine Presence in the World to Come. But in the Upper World, one can no longer earn anything, even if they exert all their energies.[10]

Laziness is a great force in our modern age, but it doesn't have to be a dominating one. Every day, countless people wake up to face the day with the ability to combat the forces inside them that tempt them to lay in bed for five minutes more. Those five minutes turn into ten minutes, and then suddenly an hour has gone by. Two hours. Twelve hours. A whole day wasted. Laziness is easy, which makes it an appealing trait. But we know intellectually that laziness breeds apathy, and apathy leads to destruction: of mind, of environment, and, at the most extreme levels, of other people.

Our laziness is not only found in the realm of action but also in the realm of thought. Sometimes we don't want to exert the effort to think more critically, so we fall back on old ways of knowing, all too simple ways of thinking, and biases. Lama Rod Owens writes:

> I don't believe in evil people. Nor do I believe in crazy people. I think evil and crazy are things we label people when we are too lazy to deal with their complexity or our own complexity. When we fail to relate to our own complexity, we fail to see the complexity of other people, especially the ones who cause a lot of harm. To step into the middle. . .is to step away from the extremes of black and white into the discomfort of the many shades of gray. . .where we head to the edge of our practice where our hearts break and we are forced to sit with both the love and the rage.[11]

The Torah teaches *naaseh v'nishmah* (that sometimes we should move ourselves to act and do what we know is right before we fully understand). This is an approach to avoiding the intellectual trappings that can lead toward laziness. It's not always easy or comfortable because it can be more desirable to believe a pretty lie than to face an ugly truth. It can be easier to

9. The term *gaon* means genius. The Vilna Gaon, Rabbi Eliyahu of Vilna (Vilnius), is also known by his acronym, Gr"a. He was a great halakhist, largely responsible for much of the *nusach tefillah* (liturgical nuances) in use in Ashkenazi circles today, particularly in Israel.

10. Story in full as quoted in Rabbi Soloveitchik's *Halachic Man*, pp. 30–31.

11. Lama Rod Owens, *Love and Rage: The Path of Liberation Through Anger*, p. 171

believe what the crowd tells us than to have to think on our own. How can we make meaning of our discomfort?

We have to be careful though to hold ourselves accountable to not be lazy but be very careful not to judge others. For too long, kids have been deemed lazy and thus we should give them more homework to avoid them from choosing their own inclinations lead them toward which will only be vanity, due to their laziness. There is also a bias where sometimes minorities have been deemed lazy by the more powerful and privileged. "Laziness" can be politicized in furthering biases.

We should also think about, with new technologies available to us, how we don't choose the lazy path but the responsible path. In regards to re- lationships, when does a certain message warrant a call over a text or mail- ing a letter over an email or meeting in-person rather than over zoom? In regards to our search for truth, how do we engage in proper research rather than just read the first thing that google pushes toward us?

Perhaps a helpful pathway toward overcoming laziness can best be found in zooming out of the immediate present toward our long-term life purpose.

> Professor of psychology and education Sol Schimmel posits[12] that sloth or religious laziness consists in our submission to the natural human tendency to avoid our obligations when they demand effort and sacrifice. The failure often occurs not because we are evil, but because we take a narrow view of life. If we could fully appreciate the long-term positive consequences of benevolent behavior for ourselves and for society, we would overcome the annoyance we feel when in acting charitably we forgo immediate pleasures.[13]

Merely hiding behind our religious denominations and convictions or our political parties is lazy and deadens the soul. Far more important than choosing what denomination or party we'll affiliate with is deciding whether we'll live each day as an indifferent Jew or journeying as a passion- ate Jew, vigorously seeking wisdom and virtue. We must loosen our grip on our conformist affiliations and embrace others. We can't afford to lose them. Yes, we need to build communities that have shared assumptions and values, but we can't rely so heavily on them that we stop thinking about those who do not conform to our beliefs.

---

12. Sol Schimmel, *The Seven Deadly Sins: Jewish, Christian, and Classical Reflec- tions on Human Nature)*, 202–203

13. Dr. Erica Brown, *Spiritual Boredom: Rediscovering the Wonder of Judaism*, pp. 21–22

If we wish to live lives infused with kindness, we'll need to be prepared to jump at the opportunity. When we're about to jump, many doubts will emerge. Some of those doubts may be helpful and productive to listen to. But other times, it may be the voice of laziness telling us that staying put comfortably is what feels most right.

We need balance in our life. We can't always be running a marathon, but we also know that living a meaningful life means some things are worth fighting for, and worth going out of our comfort zone for. May we all be blessed with the passion, motivation, and will to conquer the inner force demanding complacency, conformity, and ease of existence.

#34

Tikvah/Dechiyat Yei'ush, Being Hopeful/Rejecting Despair

WE DO TAKE MITIGATING factors seriously in law and understand that social barriers are real for people. Not everyone is totally free at every moment to do whatever they please. We do not cruelly tell those in poverty: "Work harder, no excuses!" We must learn what is in our control and what is not. We can leverage our freedom to enable more freedom for ourselves and for others. We don't just preach that another should be hopeful; rather, we help them find a pathway. We don't preach to someone to have faith but rather we be kind to them. By helping address others' needs, we can help them find hope.

Rebbe Nachman of Bratzlav was known for teaching a meta-*mitzvah* that one should never despair. It was told by his students that he would scream, "*Ein yei'ush ba'olam klal!*" (There is to be no despair in the world!)

In a world of high anxiety, it is harder and harder for many of us to stay positive, focus on all that is good, and live with gratitude. Here with a call to live with hope means to remain positive despite evidence that leads us to be negative. We have an opportunity to live with *emunah* (faith*), bitachon* (trust), and hope (tikvah).

Emily Dickinson wrote:

> "Hope" is the thing with feathers—
> That perches in the soul—
> And sings the tunes without the words—
> And never stops—at all—[1]

---

1. Emily Dickinson, "*'Hope' is the Thing with Feathers*" (written c. 1861, published 1891)

Living with a lack of hope means that our actions don't matter, our lives don't matter. But having hope that our lives and actions in fact *do* matter is not a leap into the absurd. Hope can be factually grounded from the meta-view of the broad sweep of history. It is factually true that things generally get better.[2] Consider history without democracy, vaccinations, medical technology, airplanes, etc. Harvard Professor Steven Pinker has argued that the world has become less violent. We can thus be both optimistic and realistic at the same time.

The talmudic rabbis understood that we, as humanity, are interconnected.

> A certain non-Jew asked Rabbi Yehoshua: "You have festivals, and we have festivals. We do not rejoice when you do, and you do not rejoice when we do. When do we both rejoice together?" [Rabbi Yehoshua answered:] "When the rain falls!"[3]

Now, more than ever before, we know that our earth, air, and water (and our souls too) are interconnected. We can find hope in this interconnectivity that we are all on this planet together as we are more and more aware of it.

We can also find hope not only in universalism but also in particularism.

Consider, how even with all the despair in Egypt for the Israelite slaves, how many lived with hope. Consider how Yocheved, Moshe's mother, puts Moshe in the basket believing in a better future for him. And consider how Miriam, Moshe's sister, watches out for him. Consider, too, how Miriam brought instruments from Egypt with the hope that that time will come for music![4] It is also instructive to note that Pharaoh's daughter Bityah[5] named the baby Moshe (using the active verb form, meaning "one who draws others out"), rather than Mashui (using the passive verb form, meaning "he was drawn out"). This would prove to be Moshe's strength, to facilitate the drawing out of others, in the form of freedom from slavery in Egypt and the subsequent exodus. Seforno[6] says this was Bityah's mandate to Moshe: "Just like you were drawn out, you will draw others out." This was the hope she transmitted to Moshe.

Consider how Anne Frank wrote about her experience in solitude and fear:

2. Of course, there are exceptions, both globally and individually.

3. Genesis Rabbah 13:6

4. Miriam was proven correct, as she and the other women played instruments and sang as they crossed the Red Sea.

5. Although often pronounced Batyah, Divrei HaYamim makes clear her name is pronounced Bityah

6. Rabbi Ovadiah Seforno was a 15th-century Italian commentator and philosopher.

> I keep my ideals, because in spite of everything I still believe that people are really good at heart. How wonderful it is that nobody need wait a single moment before starting to improve the world. Think of all the beauty still left around you and be happy. Whoever is happy will make others happy too. I don't think of all the misery, but of the beauty that still remains. No one has ever become poor by giving. We all live with the objective of being happy; our lives are all different and yet the same.[7]

On Tisha B'Av, a day of immense sadness, we read the book of Eichah (Lamentations). Here is how Jeremiah (the author of Eichah) depicts that 'city that sits alone.'[8]

> Let him [man] sit alone and keep silence, because God has laid it upon him. Let him put his mouth in the dust; if so, there may be hope. Let him offer his cheek to the smiter; let him be surfeited with mockery.[9]

Eichah seems to imply that forced isolation and degradation was actually a foundation of hope for us!

Let's also reconsider the story of Rabbi Akiva and his colleagues on the Temple Mount post-destruction. They all see the same destruction, yet he sees a rebuilt future:

> Another time, they were going up to Jerusalem. When they reached Mount Scopus, they tore their clothes. When they reached the Temple Mount, they saw a jackal come out of the Holy of Holies. They began to cry, and Rabbi Akiva to laugh. They said to him: "Why do you laugh?" He said to them: "Why do you cry?" They said to him: "Jackals now walk upon the place of which it is written 'And the stranger that comes near shall be put to death.'[10] Shall we not cry?" He said to them: "That is why I laugh. For it is written 'And I took unto me faithful witnesses to record, Uriah the priest, and Zachariah the son of Jeberechiah.'[11] What has Uriah to do with Zechariah? Uriah [lived at the time] of the First Temple, and Zechariah [at the time] of the second Temple! Rather, the verse linked the prophecy of Zechariah to the prophecy of Uriah. Regarding Uriah it is written 'Therefore

---

7. Anne Frank, *The Diary of a Young Girl*

8. Eichah opens with the words, "How it sits alone, the city that once was heavily populated, has become like a widow."

9. Lamentations 3:28–30

10. Numbers 1:51

11. Isaiah 8:2

shall Zion, because of you, be plowed as a field.'[12] Regarding
Zechariah, it is written 'There shall yet old men and old women
dwell in the streets of Jerusalem.'[13] Until the prophecy of Uriah
was fulfilled, I feared that the prophecy of Zechariah would not
come to be. Now that the prophecy of Uriah has come to be,
it is known that the prophecy of Zechariah will come to be."
They said to him in these words: "Akiva, you have comforted us;
Akiva, you have comforted us."[14]

Jews (and the roughly 4,000-year-old project of Judaism) are pretty
meshugana (crazy)! We believe in the most radical way that everything we
do matters, that we must have hope, and that we can and must change the
world! Even though there are only about 13 million of us, we believe that every one of us matters in our national and global commitments to transform
the world. Should we really be so radically hopeful?

Edgar Allan Poe once wrote, "Men have called me mad; but the question is not yet settled, whether madness is or is not the loftiest intelligence—
whether much that is glorious– whether all that is profound– does not
spring from disease of thought– from moods of mind exalted at the expense
of the general intellect."[15]

We, as a people, are ambitious, and we strive to excel beyond the norm.

Albert Einstein said, "Great spirits have always encountered violent
opposition from mediocre minds." We are a people with a bold task and the
rigorous ethical and religious demands of the Torah. And we believe that
we are free and capable of changing the world. Animosity from small minds
will always assail us, and others may remain aloof.

Sometimes we may also be challenged by our own lack of personal
autonomy and sense of responsibility. Do you recall the infamous case of
Kitty Genovese, who in 1964 was raped and murdered in New York City
as dozens of people watched from their windows and did nothing? Social
psychologists have showed that the larger the number of bystanders, the less
likely we are to intervene to help one another. Perhaps we see that others are
not helping so we need not help. Or perhaps we feel that someone else has
probably responded or may be better equipped to help, so we need not help.
We are social beings, and at times social conformity can have disastrous
results. Rather than live with the bold goal of actualizing our individual
responsibility and giving others hope, too often we live with the goal of

12. Micah 3:12

13. Zechariah 8:4

14. Babylonian Talmud, Makkot 24b

15. Edgar Allan Poe, *Complete Tales and Poems*

avoiding shame, avoiding taking risks or doing anything new or different than what is done all around us.

The shortest question in the Torah is, remarkably, G-d's first question in the Torah. It is a question asked in Genesis 3:9. Adam and Eve had just eaten some fruit from the forbidden tree and, sensing God's presence in the Garden of Eden, they hid among the trees. While they were hiding, G-d asked Adam a one-word question: *Ayeka*? "Where are you?"

This is a question only those with courage ask themselves each year: "Where am I? Am I just getting by? Eating, sleeping, working? Seeking instant gratification? Or am I driven by a greater purpose? Am I aware every day that what I do with my life truly matters?"

There is indeed an urgency to find ourselves. When we arise each day from bed, we are to say, as did Avraham,[16] "*hineini*," ("here I am"). We know that we cannot resolve all of the problems of the world, but we also know that we can and must try our best. As the rabbis teach: "It is not upon you to complete the task, but neither are you free to desist from it."[17]

One of the great sicknesses thriving today in the 21st century is cynicism. Ever seen it? Someone who thinks that nothing is important and nothing matters and nothing needs to change. Things are really just fine as they are, or maybe terrible but beyond hope, not worth improving. This is perhaps the most un-Jewish approach to life and the most uninspired way to live. It is a sickness that spreads to all others around us, where everything becomes a joke rather than a holy opportunity to engage.

Rambam (Maimonides) teaches[18] that we should view our lives as if our next action will determine whether the world is redeemed or destroyed. Now, how many of us really believe that our next action will have this impact? And even if one does not believe this to be literally true, Rambam is nevertheless instructing us that this is a way to see the world and live our lives. We are to live as though everything matters. We live with hope and faith and possibility.

I think of my friend and teacher Oscar in Guatemala. Oscar lost all of his family in war. His friends, all around him, gave up. There was no more meaning, no more hope, no more purpose. Somehow, Oscar found the courage and inspiration to protest this mentality. Today, Oscar travels from poor village to poor village around his country helping the leadership to build their communities. Oscar saw the bait to deny hope and to be stuck in the past. He resisted, and he is a faith hero!

---

16. Genesis 22:1

17. Pirkei Avot (Ethics of Our Fathers) 2:21

18. Maimonides, *Mishneh Torah*, Laws of Teshuvah (Repentance) 3:8

The hasidic master Rabbi Hayim of Krosno, Poland, a close student of the Baal Shem Tov, used to love to watch a certain rope dancer with awe and attentiveness. One day, his students asked him why he spent so much free time watching the man dancing high upon a rope. He responded that this person, while risking his life, could not be thinking for even a moment about the one hundred coins that he was going to earn, because then he would fall. And that this is how we should view our lives—we are all walking on a very thin rope. . .at any moment, it could all be over for us. If we remember this, then we'll always have to be focused on the big things that really matter. Our lives are deeply sacred!

Rabbi Shlomo of Karlin, the second Karliner rebbe, once explained that the greatest invitation to the *yeitzer hara* (inclination to do evil) is that we forget that we are the children of the King. We are not without value or purpose. We are here because God brought us into being with love and gave us work to do, saying in a quiet voice, "Bring a fragment of My presence into other lives."

We are free to respond "*hineini*" with deep integrity as we answer the question "*ayeka*." We have the ability and freedom to choose our lives. After all, the absolute foundation of Jewish philosophical commitment is that we are free.

This message is not always clear, because unfortunately, the three great advocates of determinism, Karl Marx, Baruch Spinoza, and Sigmund Freud, were Jews. Karl Marx argued that our behavior is determined by structures of power in society, among them the ownership of property. This is called economic determinism. Baruch Spinoza argued that human conduct is given by the instincts we acquire at birth. This is called genetic determinism. Sigmund Freud argued that we are shaped by early experiences in childhood. This is called psychological determinism.

But determinism leads to excuses and a sense of despair. We know that we are affected by our culture, by the economy, by our upbringing, by our genes, etc. But Judaism comes to tell the world that there are no excuses! We are free! We have choice! We are responsible! We can transcend our reality! And we can answer the call with "*hineini!*" Adam's first response is the denial of freedom: "The woman gave it to me."[19] And Eve's first response also denies freedom: "The serpent duped me."[20] The Torah is warning us at the outset that at the core of human nature is the need to give excuses and to deny our freedom for how we choose to live.

19. Genesis 3:12
20. Genesis 3:13

We are charged to live with hope. It is, after all, hope, and refusing to succumb to despair, that brought about the creation of the State of Israel. It's not for naught that Israel's national anthem focuses on, and is even titled, HaTikvah (The Hope). And it is that very hope that keeps so many Jews alive and thriving today. So many post-Holocaust refugees lived with hope. They were our heroes who experienced unimaginable cruelty and yet heroically had so many achievements through their resiliency and hope for a brighter day.

Hope is based on what we know whereas faith is based on what we don't know. There can be a value to both. There is bad-hope too. This is where one passively says that environmental destruction and climate change will simply work itself out. This is where one hopes that other people they disagree with will just disappear from the planet. Hope for the wrong things, and passive hope can be irresponsible and destructive. Hope can be politicized not only by the far-right but by the far-left as well where some try to sell that there is no hope and that everything is a mess of oppression and brokenness that is irredeemable.

Yes, ours is an active-hope, not a passive-hope, where we do all we can to improve ourselves, our family, our community, and our world. And alongside that effort, we never let go of the dream, the hope, the promise that we can bring light to darkness, that things can get better, that we will collectively heal.

#35

Yirah, Living with Awe

THE TALMUD TEACHES: "EVERYTHING is in the hands of heaven except for the fear of heaven."[1] The Hebrew term used for "fear" in this dictum is *yirah*, which can actually be translated as both "fear" and "awe." An alternative reading, then, is "everything is in the hands of heaven except for awe of heaven." All of this is to say that *yirah*, in both senses, is completely within our control.

Let's explore this further. There are two primary forms of *yirah* that we discuss in Judaism. The first is that we should fear God, fear the heavens, a notion not so attractive for many modern people. Modern people typically describe this approach as being unmeaningful and outdated.[2] The second form of *yirah* is about living with awe, being blown away by the awesomeness of our outer world, by our inner world, and by God's involvement in the world.

We'll begin with *yirat shamayim* in the classical sense. We are to fear God because God is our creator and our judge. The story is told:

> A disciple of the Kotzker [Rebbe] complained to his master that he was unable to worship God without becoming aware of his pride. "Is there a way of praying that prevents the self from intruding?" he asked. "Have you ever met a wolf while walking alone in the forest?" returned the Kotzker. "I have," he answered. "What was on your mind at that moment?" "Fear. Nothing but

1. Babylonian Talmud, Berachot 33b

2. The term *yirah* in the sense of fear can alternatively be translated as reverence. The word "reverence" can thus be substituted for every usage of the word "fear" throughout this chapter, and is more attuned to the sensitivities and attitudes of many today. We will further explore *yirah* as reverence later in this essay.

fear, the need to escape." "You see," replied the Kotzker, "at that moment you were afraid without being self-conscious or aware of your fear. It is in this way that we must worship God."[3]

Here, the Kotzker Rebbe is teaching that you can't fully love someone if you're always aware of the love and never overwhelmed by it. So too, one can't fear the greatness of God if one is never overwhelmed by it. We might ask ourselves what experiences we cultivate that humble us so greatly to even allow the possibility of feeling this. For some, perhaps, it's a really frightening diagnosis from the doctor. For others, it might be a financial crisis. It's often moments such as these that make us feel more vulnerable, and thus more in fear of God, than we could ever imagine.

We recite in the second blessing before the Shema of Shacharit:

> And enlighten our eyes in Your Torah, and cause our hearts to hold fast to Your commandments. Make us single-hearted to love and fear Your name.

Further, The Torah states in Deuteronomy 10:12:

> And now, O Israel, what does the Lord your God demand of you? Only this: to fear (l'yirah) the Lord your God, to walk in God's paths, to love God, and to serve the Lord your God with all your heart and soul.[4]

For the rabbis, this idea is expanded from fear of God and God's name to also fearing sin.

One Mishnah teaches:

> There were two chambers in the Temple, one the chamber of secret gifts and the other the chamber of vessels. The chamber of secret gifts: *Yirei cheit* (sin-fearing persons) used to put their gifts there in secret, and the poor who were descended of the virtuous were secretly supported from them. The chamber of vessels: Whoever offered a vessel as a gift would throw it in, and once in thirty days the treasurers opened it. Any vessel they found in it that was of use for the repair of the temple they left there; the others were sold and their price went to the chamber of the repair of the temple.[5]

Another Mishnah teaches:

---

3. Rabbi Abraham Joshua Heschel, *A Passion for Truth*, 95
4. This verse is the source for the talmudic dictum with which we began this essay.
5. Mishnah, Shekalim 5:6

> When Rabbi Meir died, the composers of fables ceased.
> When Ben Azzai died, the diligent students [of Torah] ceased.
> When Ben Zoma died, the expounders ceased.
> When Rabbi Joshua died, goodness ceased from the world.
> When Rabbi Akiva died, the glory of the Torah ceased. . .
> When Rabbi [Yehudah HaNasi] died, humility and fear of sin ceased.[6]

And most famously in the Mishnah, we learn:

> Rabbi Hanina ben Dosa said: Anyone whose fear of sin precedes their wisdom, their wisdom is enduring, but anyone whose wisdom precedes their fear of sin, their wisdom is not enduring.[7]

Furthermore, the Torah teaches that we should fear God, paradoxically, in order that we not be afraid of what lies before us:[8]

> Moses answered the people, "Be not afraid; for God has come only in order to test you, and in order that the fear of God may be upon your faces, so that you do not sin."[9]

The Midrash interprets:

> "And so that God's *yirah* (fear) be upon your faces:" Fear (here) is shame-facedness (boshet). Shame-facedness is a good sign in a person, "so that you do not sin." We are hereby apprised that shame-facedness leads to fear of sin.[10]

Perhaps the key to understanding this is found in yet another *Mishnah*:

> It is stated: "And it shall be, when you draw near to the battle, that the priest shall approach and speak to the people."[11] The priest identified in the verse is the priest anointed for war, the priest who is inaugurated specifically to serve this function. . . The Torah[12] dictates the priest's address: "And he shall say to them: 'Hear Israel, you draw near today to battle against your enemies; let not your heart faint; fear not, nor be alarmed, and do not be terrified of them'. . . And the officers shall speak further to the

6. Mishnah, Sotah 9:15. Also see Mishnah, Eduyot 5:6.

7. Pirkei Avot 3:9

8. The verse quoted here refers to the Israelites' fear upon witnessing the thunder, torches, and sound of the shofar at Mount Sinai.

9. Exodus 20:17

10. Mechilta d'R. Ishmael, Exodus 20:17

11. Deuteronomy 20:2

12. Ibid.

people, and they shall say: 'What person is there that is fearful and fainthearted? Let them go and return to their home.' Rabbi Akiva says, "fearful and fainthearted" is to be understood as it indicates: that the person is unable to stand in the battle ranks and to see a drawn sword because it will terrify them. Rabbi Yossi HaGelili says, "That is fearful and fainthearted" is one who is afraid because of the sins that they have.[13]

This notion of *yirah* as fear is carried over to one's teacher as well. Pirkei Avot teaches:

Rabbi Elazar ben Shammua said, "Let the honor of your student be as dear to you as your own, and the honor of your colleague as the fear of your teacher, and the fear of your teacher as the fear of heaven.[14]

So here we see a crucial shift in our understanding of *yirah* from one of fear (of punishment, perhaps) to one of honor or reverence. One might think that such a *yirah* is about quieting one's own moral reasoning and moral intuition and just submitting to others. But we must consider this profound teaching from Rav Avraham Yitzchak Kook on natural morality:

A person's fear of God should not displace natural moral-ity, since then it ceases to be a pure fear of God. The sign of pure *yirat shamayim* is when it aids natural morality, which arises from the human being's upright nature, to attain an even higher level, higher than it could attain alone. However, if fear of God is depicted as hindering the person's effectiveness and capacity to perform beneficial actions for the individual and the community, and as causing fewer activities to be undertaken, then that fear of God is invalid."[15]

A religious fear, for Rav Kook, does not quiet one's moral conscience but enlivens it. Such a sentiment expands us rather than limits us. Indeed, if one feels truly accountable for their life and responsible for their choices, and that they'd ultimately be accountable for their choices, the stakes are raised.

But let's now move from *yirah* as fear and reverence, a *yirah* of judg-ment, toward the phenomenological *yirah* experience of awe.

13. Mishnah, Sotah 8:1, 5

14. Pirkei Avot 4:12

15. Rabbi Abraham Isaac Kook, *Orot Ha-kodesh* 3:11. Also see his *Midot Harayah* on Love, Section 11, p. 27.

Tehillim (Psalms) teaches us that *yirah* is the basis of human wisdom: *"Reishit chochmah yirat Hashem"*— *"The beginning of wisdom is the awe of God."*[16]

Reishit chochmah yirat Hashem! Here, God's name is rendered as *yud-hei-vav-hei*, used when honoring the sacred, ineffable nature of God. When God is revealed before Moses at the Burning Bush, the "name" that is given is *"ehyeh asher ehyeh"* ("I will be what I will be")[17]. This is to say that our awe of "God" can also be understood as our awe of the Divine capacity for evolving, growing, and becoming. Through wisdom, we invite ourselves to take the slightest glimpse into the Divine corelative of the human mind—the mind-like essence of the Infinite Creator of the Universe. Through wisdom, we stand on the edges of the universe looking for clarity into life's greatest mysteries. And through wisdom, we are able to taste awe, at the same time realizing that the human mind is a speck compared to the wisdom-center of God.

Anticipating that one might choose to embrace this type of radical, spiritual consciousness, Rabbi Kook explains in more detail the process of what might happen:

> In the flow of the holy spirit, one feels the divine life force coursing the pathways of existence, through all desires, all worlds, all thoughts, all nations, all creatures."[18]

Rabbi Abraham Joshua Heschel writes:

> Among the many things that religious tradition holds in store for us is a legacy of wonder. Wonder goes beyond knowledge. Wonder is a state of mind in which we do not look at reality through the perspective of our memorized knowledge; in which nothing is taken for granted. . . ..
>
> As civilization advances, the sense of wonder almost necessarily declines. Such decline is an alarming symptom of our state of mind. . . What we lack is not a will to believe but a will to wonder. . .
>
> Wonder. . .is the root of all knowledge. There is no answer in the world to radical amazement.[19]

---

16. Psalms 111:10

17. Exodus 3:14

18. Rabbi Abraham Isaac Kook, *Orot Ha-Kodesh* (Jerusalem: Mossad Harav Kook, 5724 [1963/1964]), vol. 1, p. 269

19. Abraham Joshua Heschel, *Man Is Not Alone*

A person of faith, we might suggest, is not someone who believes in something but someone who is full of wonder about it.

The Jerusalem Talmud[20] teaches:

> Rabbi Yossi bar Chanina would pray with the rising and the setting of the sun so that the awe of Heaven would be upon him all day."[21]

We can be full of awe for nature, for God, and also for humans (the dignity of humans and for the human capacity for resiliency). After all, are humans entirely predictable or do human actions fill us with wonder and intrigue? Social media may, at times, deaden our capacity for awe as the outrageous gets normalized, but engaging directly with humans can return us to awe for human uniqueness.

When one is filled with awe for the greatness of our universe, it can truly be transformative for how we live each day. Indeed, if we are committed to a life of *chesed*, we might ask ourselves how our sense of *yirah*, our awe of God and the world, can contribute to that. How can a sense of radical amazement contribute to our humility, our gratitude, and our need to give back?

20. Generally speaking, when one mentions "the Talmud" they are referring to the Babylonian Talmud. The Jerusalem Talmud is an entirely different work. While both use the Mishnah as their starting point, their styles radically differ as well. (The Jerusalem Talmud is much more succinct and almost exclusively *halachah*-oriented, whereas the Babylonian Talmud is replete with *aggadah* (stories) in addition to *halachah*.

21. Jerusalem Talmud, Berachot 4:1

#36

Emunah u'Bitachon, Holding Faith and Trust

WE OFTEN SEPARATE THE ritual from the ethical, the dogmatic from the moral. *Mitzvot bein adam laMakom* (between people and God) are considered different from *mitzvot bein adam lachaveiro* (between people). But, is there a relationship between the two? More specifically, how might *emunah* (holding faith) and *bitachon* (trust) in a higher Being have an impact upon our ability to live with and engage in acts of kindness?[1] Conversely, how might engaging in kindness impact our relationship with the Divine?[2] It goes without saying that one can have no faith or trust and still live with kindness. Being kind is not something exclusively for the "religious." But, can ancient Jewish wisdom around the power of *emunah* and *bitachon* fuel us with a greater potential to have a positive impact on the world?

Judaism places an extremely high importance upon working on our character traits each day. The Chazon Ish, in his work on faith and trust, wrote about how our faith and commitment to Torah can enhance this work:

> If the Torah corrects character traits by virtue of its toil and by the acquisition of its wisdom, as the laws of the spirit dictate, there is a further aspect of the Torah, a light beyond human cognition whose revelation in the Torah cleanses a person's soul, and sensitizes them to taste the subtleties of wisdom and the

1. Later in this essay we will address the issue of faith in one another as well.

2. It is instructive to remember, and to constantly remind ourselves, that the Ten Commandments consist of two tablets, the first devoted to *mitzvot bein adam laMakom* and the second devoted to *bein adam lachaveiro*. Clearly, God wants and expects of us to place equal emphasis on both.

pleasantness of light. They therefore love humility by nature, and, conversely, hate haughtiness; they love kindness and hate cruelty; love patience and hate anger. For the entire being and desire of a wise person is to correct their character traits, and they are greatly distressed by their bad inclinations. A wise person feels no greater pain than when they stumble in a base character trait, and feel no greater joy than the joy of correcting their character traits.[3]

Rabbi Eliyahu of Vilna[4] taught:

It says in the Talmud,[5] "Chabakuk came and established the entire Torah on one principle: 'The righteous person lives through their faith.'"[6] This refers to the quality of being satisfied with what one has.[7]

To be sure, to live with faith in a Jewish context should not be misunderstood as turning off the mind and making a leap into the absurd. Rabbi Jonathan Sacks writes:

In Judaism, to be without questions is not a sign of faith, but a lack of depth. To ask is to believe that somewhere there is an answer. The fact that throughout history people have devoted their lives to extending the frontiers of knowledge is a compelling testimony to the restlessness of the human spirit and its constant desire to go further, higher, deeper. Far from faith excluding questions, questions testify to faith—that history is not random, that the universe is not impervious to our understanding, that what happens to us is not blind chance. We ask, not because we doubt, but because we believe.[8]

Rabbi Sacks also writes about the importance of building and maintaining "communities of faith":

The more friendship I share, the more I have. The more love I give, the more I possess. The best way to learn something is to

---

3. Chazon Ish, *Emunah U'Bitachon* (*Faith and Trust*), Ch. 4

4. Rabbi Eliyahu of Vilna is also known as the Vilna Gaon due to his great scholarship (*gaon* means scholar), as well as by the acronym Gra (which conforms to Gaon Rabbi Eliyahu in Hebrew).

5. Babylonian Talmud, Makkot 24

6. Chabakuk 2

7. Rabbi Eliyahu of Vilna, *Aggadot of Chazal*, commentary to Babylonian Talmud, Bechorot 8b

8. Rabbi Jonathan Sacks, *The Chief Rabbi's Haggadah*, (Essays) p. 106

teach it to others. The best way to have influence is to share it as widely as possible. These are the things that operate by the logic of multiplication [and] not division, and they are precisely what is created and distributed in communities of faith: friendship, love, learning and moral influence, along with those many other things which only exist by virtue of being shared[9]....Communities of faith are where we preserve the values and institutions that protect our humanity[10]. . .. A community of faith. . . cuts across boundaries. It brings together what other institutions keep apart.[11]

But how fundamental is trust to how our society can function beyond our parochial communities? Rabbi Sacks continues:

I believe faith is part of what makes us human. It is a basic attitude of trust that always goes beyond the available evidence, but without which we would do nothing great. Without faith in one another we could not risk the vulnerability of love. Without faith in the future, we would not choose to have a child. Without faith in the intelligibility of the Universe we would not do science. Without faith in our fellow citizens, we would not have a free society.[12]

But here Rabbi Sacks gives us the greatest challenge of all:

The test of faith is whether I can make space for difference.[13] Can I recognize God's image in someone who is not in my image, whose language, faith, ideal[s], are different from mine? *If I cannot, then I have made God in my image instead of allowing him to remake me in his.*[14]

As we mentioned above, in addition to faith in God, we can talk about faith in people. Rav Avraham Yitzchak HaCohen Kook wrote about his faith in others who have fallen from their spiritual potential.

The fallen souls with whom I associate give me strength. I sympathize with them, I desire their rectification, their wellbeing, their light, their salvation, and they feel revivified and peace of

9. Rabbi Jonathan Sacks, *Celebrating Life*, p. 54

10. Ibid., p. 60

11. Ibid., p. 144

12. Rabbi Jonathan Sacks, *The Power of Ideas*, p. 127

13. Italics are added by the author for emphasis.

14. Rabbi Jonathan Sacks, *The Dignity of Difference: How to Avoid the Clash of Civilizations*

mind. The essence of their depression stems from a thirst for the light of God and God's goodness, and they rejoice, for there is someone who can speak to their inherent goodness. For I know how very deep the light of God burns in these fallen [souls]; a spirit from on high blows within them: how deeply in their souls do they want to walk in the pathways of light, in the ways of goodness and dignity. I am certain that in the end, God's aid will come to them. . .[15]

Further, believing in the possibility of *teshuvah* (one's return to their core goodness) means believing in others and their potential for transformation. In a similar fashion, one should have faith in oneself as well. We can have faith in ourselves in our times of greatest clarity. We can't always be immersed in the most introspective aspects of our lives but we can trust ourselves in the past that when we made major life decisions that we were operating from clarity. Rav Kook continues:

The righteous person must have faith in their life. They must believe in their lives and that they go in the righteous path from the foundation of their soul, that they are good and righteous. . . But one's constant status needs to be having confidence in oneself.[16]

Elsewhere, Rav Kook writes:

It is an evil sickness when moral sensitivities weaken too much until not only does one hold back from acting [out of fear] of doing wrong, but one is always terrified that they might engage in sin in thought or action. The exaggerated fear of all sin causes one to lose the good within themselves and turns one into a lowly depressed creature that does nothing except lie around and tremble. A person must believe in both their physical and moral capabilities. Faith unites it all together like love. Faith in our lives is [a] blessing from God, just as lacking faith is a terrible curse.[17]

Rav Kook charges us here to believe in ourselves. It is easy to lose confidence in oneself and forget one's own dignity and light. This too requires a form of faith.

---

15. *Shemonah Kevatzim* 6:86
16. Rav Kook, *Orot HaTorah*, 11:2
17. Rav Kook, *The Lights of Faith*, Introduction

Consider two different types of righteous people as described by Rabbi Levi Yitzchak of Berditchev[18] in his work the Kedushat Levi:[19]

> There are two types of *tzaddikim*)righteous individuals (who serve the Creator: There is the *tzaddik* who serves the Creator and has no other desire than to do so. This one believes that his or her power can influence the uppermost realms, as our Sages taught. . . 'The Holy Blessed One decrees and the tzaddik transmutes the decree into goodness.' But there is another type of *tzaddik* who serves the Holy Creator. This one is exceedingly humble in their own eyes and thinks to themself, 'Who am I that I should pray to cancel a divine decree?' And so, they don't . . . This is, as Rashi commented, 'Noah was of little faith.'[20] That is to say, Noah was little in his own eyes—he did not have faith in himself that he was a *tzaddik* who could cancel a decree, for he did not think anything of himself at all.[21]

In addition to two types of tzaddik, we are fortunate to have two archetypes of great people in Judaism: the tzaddik and the chassid. The chassid is the pious one while the tzaddik is the moral exemplar. Ideally one is spiritual and moral but one can also choose their priority at different stages of life.

So, how do we cultivate faith? The opportunities are actually all around us. We can rekindle our faith in people by following more righteous people and observing their ways. We can reawaken our faith in the Divine by watching a baby being born or by sitting at the edge of the sea. And we can look up on a starry night.

> The Sefat Emet argued that a lunar calendar is a sign of faith. The new month is declared when the moon is at its ebb. When the night is darkest, wrote the Sefat Emet, we declare belief in the month to come. "One who sees the new moon is as one who sees God's presence." Having waited out the days of darkness, there is again light.[22]

When we recite *kiddush levanah* (prayers sanctifying the new moon), we can be reminded of this message of hope and resilience. When we hope,

---

18. Rabbi Levi Yitzchak of Berditchev was an 18th-century Hasidic leader and scholar.

19. *Kedushat Levi*, Noach 2

20. Rashi on Genesis 7:7

21. Translation from Rabbi Josh Feigelson, *Eternal Questions: Reflections, Conversations, and Jewish Mindfulness Practices for the Weekly Torah Portion*, p. 7

22. Rabbi David Wolpe, *Making Loss Matter: Creating Meaning in Difficult Times*,178

we wish for what we want to be but when we have faith, we go further and believe in it.

Faith can add so much to our quality of life.

> Love itself is an act of faith. Our mistake is to believe that it is an act of faith in the beloved. Surely faith in the beloved is part of it, but deeper is faith in the world, and in the presiding Spirit of the world. When we love, we have faith that this universe will be kind to love, believes in it with us, will enable it to grow. Through faith, love is granted its measure of immortality. Fragile creatures cling to one another. . . Faith crosses the bridge of longing, the gulf of loss.[23]

We will need to have faith to allow ourselves to love because love can hurt. But "it is better to have loved and lost and then never have loved at all." To love is to be human. We can have faith in what we don't know but we can also have faith in what we know by committing to live it. We know love is beautiful but it may require faith to have the courage to live with love.

But in talking about faith, let's not only talk about good faith but also bad faith. Rabbi Abraham Joshua Heschel taught:

> Religion declined not because it was refuted but because it became irrelevant, dull, oppressive, insipid. When faith is completely replaced by habit, when the crisis of today is ignored because of the splendor of the past, when faith becomes an heirloom rather than a living fountain, when religion speaks only in the name of authority rather than with the voice of compassion, its message becomes meaningless.[24]

I once had the privilege to speak at a film festival about a wonderfully complex film. After my remarks, the first question was of someone felicitously taking issue with my critique of religious fundamentalism. The inane suggestion was that a non-violent fundamentalist is actually good or at least okay. To her dismay, I adamantly disagreed and argued for my working definition of a fundamentalist: "One who is willing to do something evil (or even justify it) because one believes that G-d, in some non-rational form of faith, obligates them to."

I suggest that even one who justifies irrational religious principles above basic ethics when they clash is, in a sense, guilty of a type of violence. We all have ethical fundamentals we agree with. Religious fundamentalism,

---

23. Rabbi David Wolpe quoted in Twelve Jewish Steps to Recovery (2nd Edition): A Personal Guide to Turning from Alcoholism and Other Addictions, page 22

24. Rabbi Abraham Joshua Heschel, *The Insecurity of Freedom*, 1–2.

on the other hand, is about embracing an entire closed system with blind faith regardless of the ethical consequences. One key facet of fundamentalism is a rejection of pluralism (that there are multiple approaches): "There is only one truth and I have it!" And there are different kind of "violence." There is, of course, the physically abusive kind, but there is also intellectual/spiritual/emotional violence. For example, when Christians pushed Native Americans to be Christians, that was a violent act. Then there is emotional violence. This is why the talmudic rabbis taught that to shame another is akin to killing them.[25]

Faith can sustain us in a messy, uncertain world. Rudolf Otto called faith "the *mysterium tremendum*," a feeling of smallness encountering the Infinite. It can inspire us to be connected to more beyond ourselves and to be connected to one another.

My son's biggest fear is that the "bad guys" might be stronger than the super heroes. Indeed, that's my biggest fear too: that the forces of evil (and the complicit bystanders) are stronger than the forces of love and justice. I don't know where I'd be without faith. Faith in G-d. Faith in good people. Faith in faith. It sustains me.

Rabbi Harold Kushner wrote: "To have a child is more than a biological event. It is a statement of faith in the future, a way of saying that you want there to be a future."[26]

If we are rooted in the faith that the Highest Power wants us to courageously live our unique purpose in our short lives, then we should not be concerned about what others think when we live our truth and speak our truth. Rather, we can and indeed must allow our faith in one another and in the future to drive us towards *chesed* towards one another.

Let's pledge to break from the conformist herd mentality and reconnect with our deepest purpose of connecting with one another, thereby ensuring a bright future for those who follow us on this beautiful earth.

---

25. Babylonian Talmud, Bava Metzia 58b
26. Rabbi Harold Kushner, *Conquering Fear*, p. 86

#37

Menuchat HaNefesh, Achieving Equanimity

IN OUR COMPLEX WORLD, we often feel overwhelmed and anxious. The cost of living is high, our moral responsibilities are great, the demands on our time are substantial, the spiritual challenges are heavy, and relationships are complex. Within that race, however, we strive for happiness and peace. At times it seems like one can either choose complexity and anxiety, or simplicity and happiness. But, must that be so? Can one choose a path of actualizing one's unique potential and living with joy and inner calm? Can one find balance in the disarray of modern living?

The Jewish tradition contains within it a rich literature that provides inspiration about tackling the complexities of life's challenges. As a people concerned with the minutiae and exactitude of wisdom for its own sake, it makes sense as well that Jewish ethics evolved in tandem with a sense of creating opportunities that allow us to transcend mundane tasks by pairing them with a Divine purpose. Such is the case that we will follow in these succeeding pages.

How can we enable ourselves to face both the challenges of contemporary American life and the ancient challenge of living an ethical life of Torah? How can we make physical and emotional space for both?

For me, a first step to answering these questions is to recognize one's own limitations, and to be vulnerable even at the most trying of times. If one has not addressed the messiness of one's inner life, one will have limited capacity to address the messiness of one's outer life. Therefore, it is crucial to first achieve emotional health and spiritual clarity on one's life mission.

King David writes in Tehillim (Psalms): "*Yehi shalom b'cheileich, shal-vah b'armenotayich*" ("May there be peace within your walls, serenity within your palaces.")[1] While generally understood to be a wish, there is another way to read this verse: "If you would like there to be peace within your walls, there must be serenity within your palaces." That is to say, "peace begins in the home." The idea that I presented above, then, that one must address one's inner life before one's outer life, is perhaps implied in the words of the Psalmist.

The *middah* (character trait) required to obtain this balance is *menuchat hanefesh* (equanimity). Cultivating equanimity is the crucial ingredient to living a meaningful, passionate, purposeful life, in joy, peace, and inner calm.

How can we deal with our worries? Traditional thinkers tell us to cultivate the *middot* of *bitachon* and *emunah* (trust and faith). We need not worry too much, they suggest, since ultimately God is in control, and not we. Everything happens for a reason. We therefore need not get too worked up in worry, fear, and anxiety.

Indeed, as the Israelites sense that they are trapped, with the Sea in front of them and the Egyptian army behind them, Moses cries out to God. God's response is swift and straightforward: "Why are you crying out to Me? Tell the Israelites to travel forward!"[2] God seized this teaching moment: When faced with all-but-certain doom, the only viable option is to take initiative, to transcend our limitations. At the same time, Moses tells the Israelites: "God will fight for you."[3] The message is clear: If we advance forward, if we rise up when called upon, then God will indeed fight for us and be there for us.

Worry can be holy when it is about something profound and warranted. It can be channeled, refined, and even appreciated. But worry also allows us to push our bodies and our minds to be their best. If we are worried about a college placement test, or an interview for a dream job, or if someone wants to be our partner in marriage, then the reward when seeing such goals achieved is all the sweeter and consequential to our identity in this life.

But how can we recognize our own limitations? While we must do all we can to strive forward, we must also remember, with humility, that we are limited beings. The rabbis taught: "You are not obligated to complete the

1. Psalms 122:7
2. Exodus 14:15
3. Exodus 14:14

work, but neither are you free to desist from it."[4] We are not angels, perfectly prepared to fulfill God's will. No. We are human beings, profoundly imperfect and limited. This sensibility should not lower our self-esteem, but give us a healthy sense of balance and perspective.

Rabbi Avraham Isaac HaCohen Kook taught that we must repent for being overly obsessed with details and for missing the big picture:

> When a great person involves themself too much with details, whether by studying them or by anxiety about them, they are diminished and their stature is lessened; they must return and repent with love, with greatness of soul, and bind the contents of their spiritual life with great and sublime ideas. Certainly, they must not slight any detail, and always expand force and holiness in their deeds as well.[5]

Laws and ethics are complex. It is easy to get lost within the minutiae of the rules and fail to zoom out to the broader principles guiding our moral lives. To be clear, Rabbi Kook deeply valued details. Furthermore, there are too many today who are clearly not concerned enough about facts and the process of truthful inquiry. However, Rav Kook was aware that one often easily begins to worship details in a way that is paralyzing for one's broader spiritual vision and for actualizing our most cherished values in the world.

The rabbis teach: "Three things sap a person's strength: anxiety, travel, and sin."[6] To be a Jew means to think critically and openly about life, to seek and find a proper balance in everything. No matter how strongly we are pulled in one direction, we must always pause and ask ourselves if this is indeed the direction in which we should be going. The path that we follow determines so much in our life.

How can we create change, one step and one *mitzvah* at a time? For me, creating change is based on Jewish spirituality. Jewish spirituality is not a one-time-a-day act. We do not simply meditate or pray in the morning and declare ourselves done. Rather, Jewish spirituality is about carrying a spiritual consciousness throughout our day. Our child is screaming in the middle of the night, and we center ourselves. Our colleague at work is being obnoxious and triggering us, and we reground ourselves. We want to scream and complain to our life-partners, but we internally calm ourselves rather than externalize our aggravations. We see a multitude of options ahead of us, and we take the time to inquire which of them might be the path guided by the *mitzvot*. Rather than being ruled by outer stimuli, we

4. Pirkei Avot 2:21

5. Rabbi Avraham Isaac Kook, *Orot HaKodesh*, volume 3, p. 259

6. Babylonian Talmud, Gittin 70a

contain them. There is a quiet inner stillness that helps us steer through the messiest storms around us.

Menuchat hanefesh provides us with spiritual direction. As we journey from darkness to light, from uncertainty to clarity, from the oppression of Egypt to the freedom of the Promised Land, each of us will need to take some time to discern between the urgent and the unimportant. May our sacred values help us to achieve the inner calm, the equanimity that we need for this task. With cool-headedness, we can cultivate the empathy to see beyond ourselves to others, and the wisdom to determine our next steps on our paths.

The Torah teaches that "Moses ascended the mountain, and the cloud covered the mountain."[7] The Kotzker Rebbe shares that it was easy for the masses to stand afar and tremble at the sight but Moses entered the dark cloud, knowing that the deepest spiritual treasures are not found in seemingly perfect certainties, but rather in humble places that are often times quite blurry and uncertain. And so, we should prepare ourselves—our hearts and our souls—for a life on earth, and in the midst of the clouds.

Ever feel like at every moment you're urgently called above toward spirituality and below toward pressing human pursuits? Ever feel overwhelmed by it all? The great 20th-century Israeli poet Yehuda Amichai articulates this challenge well:

> Taxis below
> And angels above
> Are impatient.
> At one and the same time
> They call me
> With a terrible voice.
> I'm coming, I am
> Coming,
> I'm coming down,
> I'm coming up!

For those of us deeply troubled by Jewish suffering and universalistic suffering of all humans, we might find it strange how calm some can be.

> Walking along Kelm's main road, which had been paved by the king's prisoners sentenced to slave labor, R' Simcha Zissel would think of their suffering. "How can people walk calmly through this place," he wondered, "where people suffered so much and invested their blood and sweat?"[8]

7. Exodus 24:15

8. Rabbi Chaim Ephraim Zaitchik, *Sparks of Mussar: A Treasury of the Words and*

On the other hand, working toward *menuchat hanefesh* doesn't mean letting go of our concern for justice and our protest against oppression. Rev. Dr. William J. Barber II[9] is one of the many amazing people that I've had the great privilege to march with. He is a fierce advocate for racial and economic justice. Watching him up close, I could see his humble and bold leadership in action. In an act of civil disobedience, we collaborated on, outside a senator's office, I saw how painfully slow-moving he was with his cane and yet how much moral conviction and faith was carried in each step of conscience. He marches with *menuchat hanefesh*.

We learn from the Midrash that Moshe approached Pharoah with a great sense of conviction and calm. How could anyone, representing slaves, approach the most powerful person on the planet with such calmness? Perhaps he knew that God was with him. Or perhaps he knew that no man could hurt him. The night before Dr. Martin Luther King Jr. was shot and killed, he said, "I'm happy tonight. I'm not worried about anything. I'm not fearing any man." Indeed, there is a liberation in coming to only fear God but not any man. One walks with *menuchat hanefesh*.

The Torah instructs us: "You shall not fear [or be intimidated by] any man, for judgment is God's."[10] "Be Strong and of Good Courage," Joshua instructs[11]. Rabbi Joseph Telushkin explains:

> Based on this verse, the Talmud rules[12] that prior to hearing a case, a judge may tell the litigants who seek him out, "I don't want to take your case." A judge is also permitted to do so if he knows that one of the litigants is a harsh person whom the judge fears will harass him if he rules against him. However, once a judge has heard litigants present their arguments and has reached a conclusion as to who is the guilty party, he cannot withdraw and say, "I don't want to get involved in your dispute, for [to do so would violate the command of the Torah that] . . . 'You shall not fear any man.' "[13]

Deeds of the Mussar Greats, 82

9. Rev. Barber is the co-chair of the Poor People's Campaign: A National Call for Moral Revival, a campaign that takes its name from the original 1968 Poor People's Campaign, which was an effort to gain economic justice for poor people in the United States, organized by Dr. Martin Luther King, Jr. and the Southern Christian Leadership Conference.

10. Deuteronomy 1:17

11. Joshua 1:9

12. Babylonian Talmud, Sanhedrin 6b

13. Rabbi Joseph Telushkin, *A Code of Jewish Ethics*: Volume 2, page 412

To live by Jewish values means to do what's right over what's popular. It means putting oneself at risk by breaking from social conformity and a desire for social acceptance, instead living by an elevated spiritual consciousness rooted in connection and empathy. To do so requires one to find the right balance of giving of oneself while living with equanimity. We can learn to manage our triggers and be responsive rather than reactive. May we be blessed with the ability to attain *menuchat hanefesh* as we engage in bettering the world we are blessed to inhabit.

#38

Ometz, Striving for Courage

COURAGE, AT ITS HEART, is in a sense the *middah* (character trait) that underlies every other. Now, this may seem counterintuitive. If one were to look at the classical, most normative, or even noble *middot*, courage is not listed among them. Courage, for example, does not necessarily impart *anivut* (humility), it may be only tangentially related to *simchah* (joy), and it may actually be counterproductive to inculcating *savlanut* (patience). But, without courage, would we be able to go out into the world and fulfill our soul's potential? Without the spark that illuminates the challenging path called experience, would we be able to satiate the desire to learn and grow? Maya Angelou wrote:

> Without courage we cannot practice any other virtue with consistency. We can›t be kind, true, merciful, generous, or honest.[1]

Courage is not reserved for the likes of Martin Luther King, Nelson Mandela, Rosa Parks, or David Ben-Gurion. Rather, each of us has opportunities for courage every day. Nor does it require putting one's life at risk. We do not need to have the temerity of someone like Nachshon ben Aminadav who, according to a *midrash*, walks into the water hoping that God intervenes and creates a miracle. There is no virtue in taking senseless risks that put our lives or our family's financial or emotional well-being in jeopardy.[2]

---

1. See Lindsay Deutsch, "13 of Maya Angelou's Best Quotes," USA Today, May 28, 2014. Accessed April 30, 2018. https://www.usatoday.com/story/news/nation-now /2014/05/28/maya-angelou-quotes/9663257/.

2. Nachshon ben Aminadav felt that he had no choice in the matter, as the Israelites were trapped by the Red Sea in front of them and the Egyptian army behind them.

In this chapter, we will explore eight variations of the *middah* of courage that are necessary to excel at all other character traits. The following is by no means a comprehensive or definitive summation of Judaism's ethical view towards courage. Rather, the classifications here are based on my personal experiences and anecdotal meditations on the subject. In truth, the inherent definition of courage on display here will play with many facets of the term in a loose, de-constructionist manner. These 8 characterizations will work in concert with each other and clash against each other; such is the nature of courage. Thus, this piece acts as a stepping stone, a primer if you will, to place courage in the broader epistemological context of Jewish ethics.

Courage of Being

The first level of courage is understanding that each of us is unique. And inherent in that uniqueness is the mandate to do extraordinary feats that will, in some way, change the world. While one of the great mysteries of existence is to unlock our innermost strengths, we never achieve these strengths if we don't possess self-value.

Peer pressure and the desire to fit in and be loved are powerful emotions. But they are also crippling. Somewhere in the world, someone will always despise you. It could be for your skin color, your religious beliefs, your favorite sports team; this litany of petty excuses to hate a fellow person is, sadly, staggering. In the end, this is only noise, static in the ether. So, courage here means to have the courage to strive to be our authentic self.

But how do we achieve this seemingly straightforward imperative? Firstly, we have to realize that it takes enormous courage to hold ourselves accountable to our potential. Rabbi Abraham Joshua Heschel breaks down the essence of this potential in a beautiful Biblical metaphor:

> We are all Pharaohs or slaves of Pharaohs. It is sad to be a slave of a Pharaoh. It is horrible to be a Pharaoh. Daily we should take account and ask: What have I done today to alleviate the anguish, to mitigate the evil, to prevent humiliation? Let there be a grain of prophet in every man![3]

Staying true to one's forthright convictions is an apt contemporary embodiment of the prophet's purpose. Of course, the vision for our lives

---

3. Abraham Joshua Heschel, "The Religious Basis of Equality of Opportunity: The Segregation of God" in *The Insecurity of Freedom: Essays on Human Existence* (New York: Farrar, Straus & Giroux, 1967 ed.) p. 98.

need not be steeped in the purely righteous. Courage means setting a goal for yourself—modest or grand—and having the perspicacity to see it made manifest. Even Steve Jobs, the late founder of Apple Inc., whose life was marked with as many failures as triumphs, remarked, pithily, that we should go out and pursue the dreams that will further our lives:

> . . .[H]ave the courage to follow your heart and intuition. They somehow already know what you truly want to become. Everything else is secondary.[4]

Courage of being means asking hard questions; it's an introspective pursuit. This is quiet courage, a courage that radiates from deep within the recesses of our essence yearning to break free.

Courage of Will

Mark Twain is attributed as saying: "It's not the size of the dog in the fight, it's the size of the fight in the dog."[5] In all we do, we must cultivate a sense of bravery, an intractable perseverance, and the capacity to have resilience. With the balanced mix of an indomitable persistence of grit and a reservoir of spiritual inspiration, we become better equipped to get through challenges.

This was the essence of courage for the talmudic rabbis. In a moving talmudic passage, they posit the following inquiry: "Who is courageous?" There are manifold possible paths that the rabbis could have pursued here: The person with the most faith in God; One who adheres loyally to the letter of the law; One who can be victorious in battle. But instead, what do they say? "One who can control their own inner drives," that one is the most courageous.[6]

Indeed, before we approach any type of action, our vigorous inner life must align with our outer life. At the center of this quest for enthusiastic earnestness is *ratzon* (will). We must have the *will* to be courageous; otherwise, we can't *be* courageous. This is no mere tautology. We must desire to cultivate a burning passion and a lasting energy to overcome internal and external obstacles. We must desire to overcome our fear of pain, of failure, and of loss.

4.. Stanford University Commencement, June 2005. A full transcript of the speech is archived at https://news.stanford.edu/2005/06/14/jobs-061505/.

5. While Twain was a great creator of homespun quips, the above quoted phrase is most likely apocryphal. The sentiment remains the same.

6. *Pirkei Avot* 4:1

Courage of Speech

Humanity was blessed with the gift of speech. And when our minds and souls coalesce around an action, a passion, or a cause, it takes the human ingenuity of speech to convey the importance of said pursuits. A crucial element of spiritual courage is being able to speak up even when it is terrifying to do so. At times it's a *mitzvah* to do so. The Torah teaches:

> You shall not hate your brother in your heart; you shall reprove
> your fellow and do not bear a sin because of him.[7]

The late social activist Maggie Kuhn (1905–1995), who spoke out passionately for protections for senior citizens in America, said powerfully: "Speak your mind, even if your voice shakes!" Indeed, we must give feedback, otherwise we will "bear a sin" and be culpable of complicity as a bystander. In those moments, we will come to "hate our brother." We must never allow this type of moral timidity to invade our souls. Still, as the Talmud instructs, we must choose our words carefully and speak in a manner in which our words will be received and not have a negative effect.

Courage of Action

"Always do what you are afraid to do."—Ralph Waldo Emerson[8]

To be sure, courage does not always require leadership but, at times, requires a modicum of followership. Some either prefer to lead or be cynical. But this middle space of participating yet not being in control can require enormous courage too.

At momentous points during our lives, we must be willing to take critical risks. Not life- threatening or impulsive risks, but measured considerations about how we intend to live our brief moment in this universe. For many, leadership is a constituent piece of their desire to see tangible change. Yet, inevitably, when one takes the difficult step to rise up and lead, the critiques not only begin, but may become incessant. These responses often stymie others who would love to lead but cannot take the negativity and constant second-guessing. To overcome this mindset, it takes a healthy

---

7. Leviticus 19:17

Alternatively, the last clause of this verse can be translated as "and do not cause him to sin." It is this translation that leads to the rabbis offering the following talmudic explanation.

8. Ralph Waldo Emerson, *Essays*, 262.

amount of courage to maintain conviction and propel action. Nelson Mandela, whose life story is the stuff of courage, wrote:

> I learned that courage was not the absence of fear, but the triumph over it. The brave man is not he who does not feel afraid, but he who conquers that fear.

Courage of Restraint

For every notion about courage being an outward display of character, having the foresight to restrain oneself is an underexplored avenue of courageous behavior. Courage is not only about acting publicly or about speaking up, but also about being silent when the times call for it. Not every situation requires our voice, not every pursuit needs our opinion. Knowing when to back off is as important, maybe even more so, than to stand up. To be sure, as we mentioned above, the Talmud teaches us that there is a *mitzvah* to give constructive feedback to our peers, to reprove or rebuke them when called for. But there is also a *mitzvah* not to speak up when it will not be heard, or when our actions or speech make situations worse:

> Just as there is a *mitzvah* for a person to say words [of rebuke] that will be accepted, so too there is a *mitzvah* for a person not to say words [of rebuke] that will not be accepted. Rabi Abba said: [It is not merely a *mitzvah*, rather] it's an obligation. As it says, 'Do not rebuke a scoffer, lest they hate you; rebuke a wise person, and they will love you' (Proverbs 9:8).[9]

To be sure, others suggest that we should still speak up even when it won't be heard.

> R. Zeira said to R. Shimon: Our master should reprove these [officials] of the House of the Exilarch. [R. Shimon] said to him: They do not accept [words of reproof] from me. [R. Zeira] said to him: Even though they do not accept it, our master should nonetheless reprove them.[10]

Another form of restraint is taking the initiative to step back and create space for others to shine. Lao Tzu, the philosophical progenitor of Daoism, teaches: "From caring comes courage."[11] Indeed, when we begin our ac-

9. Babylonian Talmud, Yevamot 65b
10. Babylonian Talmud, Shabbat 55a
11. Lao Tzu, *Tao Te Ching*, chap. 67

tions from a compassionate conviction of love, and not from the ego-filled position to be a hero, then we step back when we need to.

Courage of Mind

It is, without a doubt, an immense challenge to exist in a world suffused with ambiguity. Indeed, most people struggle deeply with living within a gray zone rather than the easy binary of black and white. Some need to run toward certainty and clarity rather than orient their inner struggle with uncertainty. This is understandable. American author and educator Parker Palmer writes:

> There is a name for the endurance we must practice until a larger love arrives: it is called suffering. We will not be able to teach in the power of paradox until we are willing to suffer the tension of opposites, until we understand that such suffering is neither to be avoided nor merely to be survived but must be actively embraced for the way it expands our own hearts.[12]

Not everyone can live up to the pressure of living in an un-bifurcated world. However, one type of courage is about continuing to live mentally within the discomfort of uncertainty, continuing to grapple with questions before jumping to answers, and continuing to seek truth beyond ideological comfort.

Courage of Spirit

To cultivate courage on the spiritual level is to learn how to transcend self-interest, to transcend one's own body, and perhaps even transcend one's own consciousness. The late Lithuanian *mussar* teacher Rabbi Chaim Shmulevitz explains how people are capable of much more than they may imagine, even during a trying moment of existential crisis:

> Our strengths are greater than we realize. A person has the ability to reach much more than their natural [physical] strengths. . . It appears that this is the explanation of our sages on the verse, 'The daughter of Pharaoh stretched forth her arm and took the basket [that Moses was in].'[13] The rabbis explain that her arm

---

12. Parker J. Palmer, *The Courage to Teach: Exploring the Inner Landscape of a Teacher's Life*, 88.

13. Exodus 2:5

extended many *amot* (cubits).[14] It's not intended to be understood that her arm physically got longer. . . Rather, through
her will to save this child, . . .it was in her ability to [retrieve
the basket] even though it was far way. There is no measure to
the strength of someone when they arm themselves with *ometz*
(courage). . . If they do it's in their hand to reach much more
than their natural strengths would dictate.[15]

To imbibe meaning from the constant renewal of our spiritual work
should not only comfort us but also challenge us in the best way. Rabbi
Abraham Joshua Heschel suggests that prayer can become a vehicle for the
cultivation of courage in the soul. He writes:

> Prayer is meaningless unless it is subversive, unless it seeks to
> overthrow and to ruin the pyramids of callousness, hatred, op-
> portunism, falsehoods. The liturgical movement must become a
> revolutionary movement, seeking to overthrow the forces that
> continue to destroy the promise, the hope, the vision.[16]

Courage of Heart

Finally, and perhaps most importantly, courage is a product of the heart. To
be sure, we must learn to be comfortable with honest vulnerability. Brené
Brown, a professor at the University of Houston and an expert on the diverse dimensions of courage, writes on the inner nature of courage and its
effect on her life:

> [A]s I look back on my life. . . I can honestly say that nothing is
> as uncomfortable, dangerous, and hurtful as believing that I'm
> standing on the outside of my life looking in and wondering
> what it would have been like if I had the courage to show up and
> let myself be seen.[17]

14. The Hebrew biblical phrase used here for arm is *amah*, which means both
maidservant and arm. The rabbinic commentary referred to here is assuming the "arm"
meaning, and then coupling that with a play on the word *amah*, which is additionally
the Hebrew word for cubit.

15. Rabbi Chaim Shmulevitz, *Selections from Sichot Mussar*

16. Abraham Joshua Heschel (Susannah Heschel, ed.), "On Prayer" in *Moral Grandeur and Spiritual Audacity*, 257–267.

17. Brené Brown, *Daring Greatly: How the Courage to Be Vulnerable Transforms the
Way We Live, Love, Parent, and Lead* (New York: Gotham Books, 2012), p. 249.

Such a prospect can be terrifying. We all feel vulnerable at some point in our lives. To not do so is to not experience the full expression of our humanity. Yet, being vulnerable is not equivalent to being weak or cowardly. On the contrary, vulnerability is an element of greater courage. As C.S. Lewis wrote:

> To love at all is to be vulnerable. Love anything and your heart will be wrung and possibly broken. . . Wrap it carefully round with hobbies and little luxuries; avoid all entanglements. Lock it up safe in the casket or coffin of your selfishness. But in that casket, safe, dark, motionless, airless, it will change. It will not be broken; it will become unbreakable, impenetrable, irredeemable.[18]

Conclusion

One might think that acting courageously is antithetical to humility. This is not the case. Consider how Rabbi Abraham Isaac HaKohen Kook explains this point:

> We need to make a careful distinction. . .[between] a *regesh hapasul* (insincere feeling) that distances a person from consciousness of one's Maker, and a *regesh adin* (delicate feeling) that expands a person's consciousness and reminds one of one's full spiritual existence. Often, a person's heart will feel full of strength. At first glance, this feeling will seem similar to a feeling of arrogance. But. . .the reality is that one's heart is filled with courage from the Divine light that shines in one's soul.[19]

How does Rav Kook suggest we achieve such an end goal? He continues:

> A person. . .must rise up at once and mobilize the *middah* (trait) of holy arrogance. They must look at themself very favorably and find the good aspects of their shortcomings and weaknesses. For as one sets one's mind to seek out the good, immediately all of their weaknesses transform into strengths. It is possible for a person to find within themself much good, and to be very happy with their goodness. Day by day such a person will increase their positive activities with a pure heart and full of compassionate hope.[20]

18. C.S. Lewis, *The Four Loves*, 121.

19. *Midot HaRayah*, p. 25, translated by Rabbi David Jaffe.

20. *ibid.* p. 26

One final note: We must learn to listen in order to know what opportunities and moments are crucial for us to cultivate courage. Rabbi Lord Jonathan Sacks writes about the imperative of listening to these voices, of being *here*:

> There is no life without a task; no person without a talent; no place without a fragment of God's light waiting to be discovered and redeemed; no situation without its possibility of sanctification; no moment without its call. It may take a lifetime to learn how to find these things, but once we learn, we realize in retrospect that all it ever took was the ability to listen. When God calls, He does not do so by way of universal imperatives. Instead, He whispers our name—and the greatest reply, the reply of Abraham, is simply *hineni*: 'Here I am,' ready to heed your call, to mend a fragment of Your all-too-broken world.[21]

Every day, we should awake with "*hineni*" inscribed on our hearts and animated within our souls. Only in this way do we ensure that the grand experiment of humanity continues fresh and anew with every obstacle that the universe presents before us. Fortunately for the human spirit, we aren't ill-equipped for such a challenge. We have courage. But as is true with all virtues, cultivating that courage takes practice and patience. We must come out of our comfort zone to grow. We must learn the art of when to listen and when to speak, when to act and when to hold back, when to paddle to ride a wave, and when to sit back to enjoy the calm waters.

Rabbi Yisrael Salanter, the founder of the *mussar* movement, leaves us with a final message of hope. For Rabbi Salanter, every person must hold on to and keep precious three qualities in order to lead and live a life with courage: not to despair, not to get angry, and not to expect to finish the task. Courage does not mean one makes an appearance and then hurries out the door. No, courage must be cultivated daily. It must be cultivated for years before it's even given the chance to blossom. Courage comes from realizing that our role in the universe is unique but at the same time limited. Yet, it's this limitation that allows us to excel beyond our wildest dreams. It allows us to pursue our destiny. And whether we know it or not, courage is the engine that allows us to move forward perpetually, with intentionality, with compassion, and with the knowledge that meaning is found through navigating the tribulations of living a full, active life.

---

21. Jonathan Sacks, *To Heal a Fractured World: The Ethics of Responsibility*, 262.

#39

Hitlamdut, Constantly Learning

> *Hitlamdut* is a new and wonderful way of life, not just in the
> study of Torah but in all areas of life—Rabbi Shlomo Wolbe[1]

In Pirkei Avot (Ethics of Our Fathers), we are taught:

> Ben Zoma says: Who is wise? One who learns from every per-
> son, as it says,[2] 'From all my students I gained wisdom.'[3]

Indeed, at the core of Judaism is a commitment to lifelong learning. It
seems Benjamin Franklin was inspired by this *Mishnah*'s teaching:

> Who is wise? He that learns from everyone. Who is powerful?
> He that governs his passions. Who is rich? He that is content.
> Who is that? Nobody.[4]

Commenting on this *Mishnah* from Pirkei Avot, Rabbi Ovadia mi-
Bartenura[5] teaches:

> 'He who learns from every person:' Even though [that person that
> he learns from] is lesser than he. Since he is not concerned about

---

1. Rabbi Shlomo Wolbe, *Alei Shur*, vol. 2, sel. 172–174
2. Psalms 119:99
3. Pirkei Avot 4:1
4. Benjamin Franklin, *Poor Richard's Almanac*. Franklin quotes the entire *Mishnah* referenced here; only the closing words ("Who is that? Nobody") are his own.
5. Rabbi Ovadiah miBartenura, 15th-century Italian rabbi and scholar, is most widely known for his commentary to the Mishnah.

his honor and learns from the lesser ones, [it shows] that his wisdom is for the sake of Heaven and not to boast and revel in.[6]

Rabbi Simhah Zissel Ziv, founder of the Kelm Yeshiva,[7] writes:

Every person that has a special feeling for a certain endeavor will be extremely sensitive when she sees any little thing having to do with it. For example, when a tailor meets someone, he will immediately look at his clothes; the shoemaker—at the shoes; the milliner—at the hat. Similarly, a businessperson will be sensitive to any words or actions that have an impact on his business. Another type of person would not see or hear any of these things because her heart is not given to inquire and investigate anything from these matters. . .if one is not engaged in such activities, one will not notice them when performed by others. If this is the case, "one who learns from every person," behold— THIS is a great "businessperson"—they trade in everything and thus they understand the necessity to learn from the other and thus they are called "wise."

R Simhah Zissel continues:

[If,] in all my actions, I am "only" learning, then I always see a place for improvement and great wholeness. Anyone who wants to "work on themselves" needs to understand well the depth of these things. . ."

This can also be true for allyship. That sometimes we're only sensitive to the forms of marginalization that we've personally experienced. But to be in relationship with other individuals and groups means that we gain a sensitivity for their marginalization, that is foreign to our personal experience, as well.

Our learning can be informed by watching others, even animals. The Rabbis instruct us:

Rabbi Yohanan said: If the Torah had not been given, we could learn modesty from a cat, not stealing from ants, fidelity from a pigeon, and proper sexual relations from a rooster who appeases its partner before engaging in sexual behavior.[8]

6. Bartenura's commentary on Pirkei Avot 4:1:3

7. Rabbi Simhah Zissel Ziv, 19th-century Kelm, Lithuania, was a close student of Rabbi Yisrael Salanter and one of the earlier leaders of the *mussar* movement.

8. Babylonian Talmud, Eruvin 100 b

Everything around us can deepen our practice of being lifelong learners. Rabbi Shlomo Wolbe teaches:

> There is no place for arrogance in *hitlamdut*. If I do some action well, behold, I have not done anything to be proud of, because I am only *mitlameid* (practicing)! And when I am *mitlameid*, I recognize that the action was not done perfectly.[9]

Rabbi Wolbe is teaching here that our learning, whether experiential or textual, must be constant. We are forever in a state of 'practicing,' never quite perfecting our knowledge and skill, as there is always room for improvement and to learn more.

Just as there is value to learning *from* others, there is equal value to learning *with* others. The Talmud teaches:[10]

> Rabbi Ḥama, son of Rabbi Ḥanina, said: What is the meaning of that which is written, "Iron sharpens iron, so a person sharpens the countenance of their friend" (Proverbs 27:17)? This verse comes to tell you that just as with iron implements, one sharpens the other when they are rubbed against each other, so too, when Torah scholars study together, they sharpen one another in their legal studies.

Rabbi Abraham Joshua Heschel writes:

> The prophet is not a mouthpiece, but a person; not an instrument, but a partner, an associate of God. Emotional detachment would be understandable only if there were a command which required the suppression of emotion, forbidding one to serve God "with all your heart, with all your soul, with all your might." [But] God, we are told, asks not only for. . .action, but above all for love, awe, and fear.[11]

Learning, then, is not to be viewed as an end in and of itself, but rather a vehicle by which one comes closer to God. By extension, when one learns with another, they have the opportunity to become closer and be in awe of one another. Indeed, *hitlamdut* has the power to transform one into a more loving, caring individual.

Dr. Viktor E. Frankel, a Holocaust survivor and founder of logotherapy, writes: "Between stimulus and response there is a space. In that space is

---

9. Rabbi Shlomo Wolbe, *Alei Shur*, vol. 2
10. Babylonian Talmud, Taanit 7a
11. Rabbi Abraham Joshua Heschel, *The Prophets*

our power to choose our response. In our response lies our growth and our freedom."[12]

I've noticed in my house something unusual about my son's experience in Jewish preschool. Recently, more and more, upon getting home from school, my 4-year-old son, Shay, tells my wife Shoshana and I how much he loved that day's yoga session. Over the years, my kids have been exposed to this kind of practice throughout their preschool experiences, and seeing its impact on my son, on days when he does yoga, and how he seems more centered and more thoughtful, has made me wish this experience were given to kids of all ages throughout the Jewish world and in society at large.

There are so many areas of development in preschool, from letters and numbers to social skills to moral growth. But with all that noise (holy noise!), I want to make the case for just how important it is to learn how to breathe, calm oneself, sit in silence, expand one's consciousness, and increase one's attention span. We know all about how to get our kids ahead in math and science, but what are we doing to help them learn to boost their sense of self-awareness, increase their oxygen circulation, and reduce their stress?

Mindfulness education is necessary for numerous reasons. For an obvious one, we all know of the importance of physical health. Yoga and meditation are helpful not just for the mind, but for our kids' growing bodies.

But also, studies from 2016 to 2019 show[13] that 9.8% of children have ADHD, 9.4% suffer from anxiety, 8.9% have behavior problems, and 4.4% suffer from depression. In a world in which technology has made mental health one of the greatest crises of our time, the need to proactively improve our kids' mental strength and spiritual resiliency cannot be ignored.

"Emerging research studies also suggest that yoga can help children with attention deficit hyperactivity disorder (ADHD) by improving the core symptoms of ADHD, including inattentiveness, hyperactivity, and impulsivity." Certified yoga teacher Dr. Marlynn Wei wrote in Harvard Health Publishing:[14] "It can also boost school performance in children with ADHD."

Yoga, specifically, and mindfulness in general, are catalysts for better learning!

The New York Times reports:[15]

> At this age, mindfulness practice can also help children in school. A recent study found that fourth and fifth graders who took a

12. Dr. Viktor E. Frankel, *Man's Search for Meaning*

13. https://www.cdc.gov/childrensmentalhealth/data.html

14. https://www.health.harvard.edu/blog/more-than-just-a-game-yoga-for-school-age-children-201601299055

15. https://www.nytimes.com/guides/well/mindfulness-for-children

four-month meditation program demonstrated improvements in cognitive control, working memory and math test scores. Other studies have shown that mindfulness can be especially helpful to children with attention deficit hyperactivity disorder, and also reduce children's aggression, anxiety and stress.

Furthermore, mindfulness is indeed crucial for moral development. A quieter and more controlled mind has great potential for expanding the capacity for empathy. It improves one's *middot* (character traits) such as *menuchat hanefesh* (equanimity), *hitlamdut* (learning from everything), and *anivut* (humility or managing the ego).[16] These are but three of many *middot* that can be cultivated through mindfulness.

And beyond a moral and ethical aid, mindfulness can be an explicitly spiritual experience. Yes, our schools often do a great job of teaching Jewish holidays, the Hebrew language, and even Jewish rituals. But they are often not sufficiently teaching children how to search for and feel God's Presence. The starting place of the religious journey should be the realization of the soul, as the search for God is not primarily intellectual, but achieved through the channel of the soul. By training their minds today, our kids will be equipped to have better and more meaningful Jewish prayer as they get older. But a prayer curriculum, as important as it can be, cannot replace a mindfulness one. A mindfulness practice expands the inner container that we call the soul, whereas a prayer practice is an expression emanating from that container. The enterprises, while still separate pedagogically, are in fact linked.

Maybe most importantly, spiritual practices honor our children's innate dignity. Through mindfulness, they learn that they're valuable not only for their academic achievements or soccer goals scored, but also just for being themselves. In school, we're very good at teaching kids about *doing*, but we don't lastingly teach students about *being*. We give them a long *to-do* list but not a space to fulfill a *to-be* list.

In our chaotic world that will only make our kids more anxious as they grow up, it is, in my view, indispensable that we give them a strong foundation not only in pure academic skills, but in healthy breathing and mindfulness. If our children do not go on to live mentally healthy lives, everything else they learn in school will be of diminished benefit.

Instead of letting them be overwhelmed by the world, we should be teaching them how to answer God's great question in Genesis,[17] "Where

16. *Menuchat hanefesh* and *anivut* each have a chapter of their own elsewhere in this book.

17. Genesis 3:9

are you?" As humans, we need to be training ourselves to be able to answer not like Adam, who responds that he was hiding from God because he was afraid, but like Abraham, who boldly proclaims,[18] "Here I am!"

I believe the way we accomplish this should be to have yoga—or other forms of mind-body meditational experiences—offered to 3-year-olds, fourth-graders, summer campers, high-school seniors, adults, and everyone in between. Mindfulness education should be available not only in preschools, but also in day schools, Hebrew schools, camps, and synagogues.

All of us, young children and lifelong learners alike, can think about how to become more present to listen, learn, and make each moment filled with curiosity. Only with practice can we learn to be like the Psalmist, who says,[19] "Return, my soul, to restfulness!"

Hitlamdut, in all of its expressions, including those we explored above and more, serves as a basis and springboard for being there for ourselves and in turn for one another, propelling us toward greater acts of kindness.

How can we heal rifts today when Orthodox Jews and Reform Jews don't read the same books and when liberals watch CNN but conservatives watch Fox News? We can address societal and communal polarization by flipping judgement into curiosity. By taking a learning approach with those we disagree with, we can build bridges.

Reb Zalman Schachter-Shalomi once commented that an ordination may make a person a rabbi but until one approaches the rabbi seeking help in finding God, they are not a rebbe. So too a diploma makes one a doctor and a marriage license makes one married but those documents are the beginning not the end. We need to continue a journey of deep learning to maintain that status of married or being a professional.

This is not only in service to others but also for our health. We know that learning can help prevent dementia. Physical growth stops as young adults but our mental growth should not in our emerging adulthood and later stages of adulthood.

In addition to learning external information, we can learn more about ourselves. Indeed, to know oneself on the deepest level is a pathway toward knowing God. To be lifelong learners we need to break from ideology that blocks learning that doesn't fit neatly into that ideology. We need to learn "lishma" (for its own sake) and not just for social capital.

> Rabbi Yishmael, his son, said: One who learns in order to teach,
> it is granted to them to study and to teach; But one who learns

---

18. Genesis 22:1

19. Psalms 116:7

in order to practice, it is granted to them to learn and to teach
and to practice.[20]

Learning itself is the goal and learning is most deep when lived and
not just abstract. We don't learn to gain the esteem of others but to be of
deeper service toward others. This is a crucial element in living a life infused
with kindness.

20. Pirkei Avot 4:5

#40

Zerizut, Being Quick to Act on What's Right

WE KNOW HOW IMPORTANT it is to infuse *chesed* into our everyday activities. We also know that there are many barriers (physical, financial, psychological, spiritual, etc.) preventing us from this. One of our best tools to overcome those barriers is *zerizut* (alacrity). When we know something is right, we should move fast before something gets in our way. Living with alacrity and diligence will help us to achieve our goals in fostering more acts of kindness in our lives.

The Talmud teaches:

> *Zerizin makdimin l'mitzvot* (The alacritous perfom *mitzvot* as early as possible), as it states,[1] 'Avraham awoke early in the morning.'[2]

The Talmud (ibid.) explains that this is the reason for the *minhag* (custom) of performing a *brit milah* (circumcision) early in the morning. Of course, circumstances, e.g., the *mohel* is not available earlier, may dictate waiting to perform the *brit* until later in the day.

The Talmud further provides an example of *zerizut* as not only a *minhag* but an obligatory *mitzvah*:

> If one's bread was baked, and their animal slaughtered, and their wine diluted, and the father of the groom or the mother of the bride died [before the wedding], one moves the corpse into a

1. Genesis 22:3. This verse is found in the *akeidat Yitzhak* (binding of Isaac) narrative, the understanding being that Avraham was vigilant and at the ready to answer the call of God, even if it entailed sacrificing his son.

2. Babyonian Talmud, Pesahim 4a

room, and the bride and groom [are brought] to the wedding canopy.[3] And [the groom] engages in intercourse of *mitzvah* [with the bride]. . . and the corpse is buried. And [the groom] observes the seven days of the feast, and thereafter he observes the seven days of mourning.[4]

Sometimes when life brings us unexpected curveballs we have to be prepared to adapt and make decisions about moral priorities. Rabbi Moshe Chaim Luzzatto teaches:

> There are two components to promptness, one before the action and one during its performance. Before the action one should make sure not to delay performing a *mitzvah*. Rather, when the time comes, or when the opportunity arises, or the thought crosses one's mind, one should quickly act and one should not allow time to pass . . . Promptness during performance means that once one has begun performance, one should quickly complete it, not for the purpose of removing the burden but out of fear that one may not complete the task.[5]

Now, of course, not everything should be rushed. There is a danger to that. Orchot Tzaddikim teaches:

> Although promptness is very positive, one should make sure not to rush in one's work too much. One who rides [a horse] too quickly is likely to get hurt and one who runs very quickly will fall. One cannot complete a task properly if it is rushed; doing something properly requires patience. This is why our rabbis stated, "be patient in judgment." Promptness is to be awake, alert and ready to act, but never to rush what one is doing. These issues require great wisdom to determine when one should act quickly and when one should act with patience.[6]

Further, there is something to say for gradualism rather than quick change. Consider this verse in the Exodus narrative:

> It happened when Pharoah sent out the people that God did not lead them by way of the land of the Philistines, because it

---

3. In other words, if the wedding preparations are already in place and delaying the wedding would result in hardship, e.g., financial loss, waste of catered food, etc., then the wedding ceremony takes place at the planned time even though the groom is in a state of mourning.

4. Babylonian Talmud, Ketubot 3b-4a

5. *Mesillat Yesharim*, Chapter 7

6. Orchot Tzaddikim is an anonymous 16th-century work of *mussar*.

was near, for God said, 'Perhaps the people will reconsider when they see a war, and they will return to Egypt.'[7]

"Because it was near." Apparently God rejected the quick short path "because it was near." A longer journey was needed. Rambam teaches that this was because the Israelites, having just been freed from Egypt, had a slave mentality, and slaves are not equipped to handle sovereignty.

> For a sudden transition from one opposite to another is impossible. . . It is not in the nature of man that, after having been brought up in slavish service. . . that he should all of a sudden wash his hands of the dirt [of slavery]. . . God used a gracious ruse in causing [the people] to wander perplexedly in the desert until their souls became courageous. . .and until, moreover, people were born who were not accustomed to humiliation and servitude.[8]

Professor Michael Walzer shares that there are two dimensions to the pace of change in the Exodus story.

> Here again is the argument for gradualism. Physically, the escape from Egypt is sudden, glorious, complete; spiritually and politically, it is very slow, a matter of two steps forward, one step back. I want to stress this is a lesson from the Exodus experience again and again.[9]

We can't just expect big miracles and massive paradigm shifting changes in society. Rather, we need to stay focused on the work of today. A well-known powerful *midrash* reminds us of how redemption cannot come if we stop our daily work.

> Rabbi Yochanan ben Zakkai used to say, "If there is a sapling in your hand when they say to you, 'Behold, the Messiah has come!' complete planting the sapling, and then go and welcome the Messiah."[10]

In a similar vein, a rabbi in Chicago[11] writes of his own experience:

> Last night, I was in the midst of delivering an online *shiur* on the subject of Hanukkah and *kiddush Hashem*. I had reached

---

7. Exodus 13:17

8. *Guide for the Perplexed* 3:32

9. Michael Walzer, *Exodus and Revolution*, p. 58

10. Avot d'Rebbe Natan, version B, #31

11. Rabbi Matanky is the rabbi of Congregation KINS in Chicago and the dean of Ida Crown Jewish Academy.

the words of the Rambam in *Hilkhot Yesodei Ha-Torah.* . .when a text message flashed across my computer screen that simply said, "BDE Rabbi Schwartz."

For a split second, I was unsure of what to do—to apologize and cancel the *shiur*; to share the news that our mentor and guide HaRav Schwartz had passed away and then teach, or simply to plow ahead and deliver the *shiur* as planned. I wasn't sure.

But then, just as quickly, I thought of what Rabbi Schwartz would do. And I decided to say nothing, teach the class, and only afterward did I share the terrible news with those who had joined.[12]

Birth happens quickly but it takes a long time to learn to be a parent. Marriage happens quickly but it is an extended journey to learn to be in a long-term committed marital relationship. Receiving a medical degree on stage happens quickly but being on call for decades as a doctor is a demanding comprehensive commitment. Some change occurs quickly but the journey emerging from that change is long. Revolutions fail, in general, because they fail to understand that the desire for immediate change without a comprehensive commitment plan to sustain the new good is unsustainable. Many revolutions violently overthrow the past model without replacing it with a better plan that is sustainable. There are technical changes to make when solving problems and also adaptive changes to make and each has very different demands. Technical solutions (like overthrowing the current dictator) still requires major adaptive changes (new systems, new thinking, etc.) to be sustained.

On the other hand, sometimes we need radical responses to unique opportunities. Consider this crucial moment in Moshe's development, where he quickly and boldly responded to suffering and injustice:

> It happened in those days that Moses grew up and went out to his brethren and observed their burdens; and he saw an Egyptian man striking a fellow Hebrew man. He turned this way and that and saw that there was no man, so he struck down the Egyptian and hid him in the sand.[13]

Moshe apparently would have preferred that someone else intervene here, but when he saw there wasn't anyone who could, he did what needed to be done.

---

12. These words are an excerpt from Rabbi Matanky's eulogy for Rav Gedalia Dov Schwartz o.b.m., the esteemed *Av Beit Din* (Head of the Rabbinical Court) of both the Chicago Rabbinical Council and the Rabbinical Council of America, recorded in the online forum *Lehrhaus.*

13. Exodus 2: 11–12

Rabbi Aharon Lichtenstein[14] reflected on how a student of Talmud could be lacking alacrity in a way that can dull their moral clarity.

> A couple of years after we moved to Yerushalayim, I was once walking with my family in the Beit Yisrael neighborhood, where R. Isser Zalman Meltzer used to live. For the most part, it consists of narrow alleys. We came to a corner, and found a merchant stuck there with his car. The question came up as to how to help him; it was a clear case of *perika u-te'ina* (helping one load or unload his burden). There were some youngsters there from the neighborhood, who judging by their looks were probably ten or eleven years old. They saw that this merchant was not wearing a kippa. So they began a whole *pilpul* (discussion), based on the *gemara* in Pesachim (113b), about whether they should help him or not. They said, 'If he walks about bareheaded, presumably he doesn't separate *terumot u-ma'asrot*, so he is suspect of eating and selling untithed produce. . .'
>
> I wrote R. Soloveitchik a letter at that time, and told him of the incident. I ended with the comment, 'Children of [that] age from our camp would not have known the *gemara*, but they would have helped him.' My feeling then was: Why, Ribbono shel Olam, must this be our choice? Can't we find children who would have helped him and still know the *gemara*? Do we have to choose? I hope not; I believe not. If forced to choose, however, I would have no doubts where my loyalties lie: I prefer that they know less *gemara* but help him.[15]

Now, Rabbi Lichtenstein was a person who invested his life in the *beit midrash*. Nonetheless, he knew that the essence of being a Torah Jew is responding quickly and immediately when the opportunity arises.

It is not always easy, but we can train ourselves to be *zerizim*, so that we may be ready to perform the *mitzvot* with alacrity and to answer the call to help others when called upon to do so. May we, both individually and as a collective, through engaging in this and all acts of *chesed* we have studied in this work, do our share of *tikkun olam*, making this world a better place.

---

14. Rabbi Aharon Lichtenstein was the co-Rosh Yeshiva of Yeshivat Har Etzion and son-in-law of Rav Joseph B. Soloveitchik.

15. Rav Aharon Lichtenstein, *By His Light*, p. 249

Conclusion

IT MAY BE THAT babies are born with tight fists and people die with open hands because when entering this world, humans don't yet know just how much they need others, but when leaving this world, we reach out knowing how dependent we truly are. But, it is also true that right from infancy we seek a deep connection and are capable of enormous empathy.

Brian Goldman writes:

> The word *synchrony* means "a simultaneous action or occurrence." . . . Synchrony is an important topic among developmental psychologists. In 1974, William Condon and Louis Sander published a groundbreaking study in the journal *Science* in which they observed the interaction between newborns and their parents. They found that as early as the first day of life, newborns move in sync with the sound of a parent speaking.
> Later, Andrew Meltzoff from Oxford University and M. Keith Moore from the University of Washington demonstrated that babies as young as three days old imitate the facial expressions of their mothers. Thus, newborns mirror their parents' faces, and their parents mirror theirs. It's one of the earliest examples of what developmental psychologists refer to as *interactional synchrony*, an essential part of the process by which babies become attached to their parents.[1]

Humans are unique in that we have so many layers of depth of understanding and of connection to others. It is undeniable that humans have the most unique potential of all in the animal kingdom. Rabbi Abraham Joshua Heschel writes:

> One thing that sets man apart from animals is a boundless, unpredictable capacity for the development of an inner universe. There is more potentiality in his soul than in any other being

1. Brian Goldman, "A Question of Kindness," p. 10

known to us. Look at the infant and try to imagine the multitude of events it is going to engender. One child named Johann Sebastian Bach was charged with power enough to hold generations of men in his spell. But is there any potentiality to acclaim or any surprise to expect in a calf or a colt? Indeed, the enigma of [the] human being is not in what he is but in what he is able to be.[2]

I'd suggest that Judaism is less interested in the question of "Do you believe in God" than in the question of "Do you believe that God believes in you?" With such a belief, we can unlock our potential. Later, Heschel wrote about how man is separate from both the angels and animals:

> Man is a little lower than the angels and a little higher than the beasts. Like a pendulum he swings to and fro under the combined action of gravity and momentum, of the gravitation of selfishness and the momentum of the divine, of a vision beheld by God in the darkness of flesh and blood.[3]

Humans have free will, and with that we have enormous potential for good and for evil. For good, we have an incredible ability to love others. But it's not enough to really love someone. We need to make sure they truly *feel* how much we love them.

We learn a similar idea in Pirkei Avot (Ethics of The Fathers):[4]

> Beloved is man for he was created in the image [of God]. Especially beloved is he for it was made known to him that he had been created in the image [of God].

God could have just loved us by gifting us with the image of God, but God modeled for us what it means to love another by not just gifting His image to us but by making it known to us what we have received.

This is a role we can play in our kindness endeavors: not just to care about others but to have them truly *feel* cared for.

In this book, we've embarked upon a thorough investigation of Jewish approaches to kindness. The material is broad, deep, and provocative. The difficult part will now be for each of us to construct our own vision, or strategic plan, for a model of kindness that works best for us. No one can do it all, and no two visions will be identical. But without a plan, one can ensure they do little to nothing.

2. Abraham Joshua Heschel, *Who Is Man?* 39

3. Abraham Joshua Heschel, *Man Is Not Alone* (Philadelphia: Jewish Publication Society, 1951), p. 211.

4. Pirkei Avot 3:13

I continue to believe that being rooted in awe of God can enable us to transcend our vices with the help of a higher power and be inspired by the highest ideals. The Be'er Mayim Chaim wrote:

> The Holy Blessed One is not like a human being. . . When we are angry and upset, we are unable to do something joyous and loving. For a human being is inherently limited, and when one emotion fills our body, we cannot enact its opposite. Just as two physical bodies cannot occupy the same space, so, too, two strong emotions cannot fully take up our emotional space. Not so the Holy Blessed One, however, Who is not bounded in this way. When the Creator is angry and in a rage, even so nothing prevents Him from showing love and happiness to those who do His will.[5]

The problem with comparing our kindness with the Divine, though, is that we can feel low on ourselves. Every one of us will fall short in such a comparison. So we need to cultivate a practice of self-compassion.[6] Doing so is emulating Divine compassion but it can also make us more capable of being compassionate to others. Kirsten Neff, PhD and Christopher Germer, PhD write:

> . . . The researchers found that participants who were helped to be self-compassionate about their transgression reported being more motivated to apologize for the harm done, and more committed to not repeating the behavior, than those who were not helped to be self-compassionate.[7] Research shows that self-compassionate people. . .have greater self-confidence.[8]

To embrace Judaism means embracing a path of committing to growth in our compassion each day. This is central to our founding stories. Here is one of them.[9]

> Our Rabbis teach us: Once when our teacher Moshe, peace be upon him, was shepherding Yitro's flocks in the wilderness, a kid ran away from him and he ran after it until it reached a

5. Be'er Mayim Chayim 18:17:1. Translated in *Eternal Questions: Reflections, Conversations, and Jewish Mindfulness Practices for the Weekly Torah Portion*, Rabbi Josh Feigelson, p. 21.

6. It is precisely for this reason that a section on self-improvement is included in this book.

7. Kristen Neff, PhD & Christopher Germer, PhD, *The Mindful Self Compassion Workbook*, p. 153

8. Ibid., p. 79

9. Midrash Shemot Rabbah 2:2

shady spot. When it came to the shady spot there was a water hole and the kid stopped to drink. When Moshe reached the kid, he said, "I did not know that you ran away because you were tired and thirsty." So he put it on his shoulder and walked back. Said the Holy One, blessed is He: "You have compassion in the way that you tend to the flock. So too with the [rest of] your life, you will tend to My flock of Israel." This is the meaning of the words "Moshe was shepherding the flock."[10]

Another *midrash* shares:[11]

"G-d saw the Children of Israel"[12]—What did God see? God saw how they had compassion towards one another. When one of them completed their quota of bricks before their friend, he would come and help his friend. When the Holy One be blessed saw how they had compassion towards one another, God said: "They deserve compassion, for he who shows compassion has compassion shown to him, as it says: 'God will show you compassion, and have compassion on you'"[13]

These noble ideas are wonderful. But how do we get there? Ibn Ezra teaches that our work is both inner and outer. We need to cultivate our character and cultivate our actions, and those two will strengthen each other. "The main purpose of all of the commandments is to straighten the heart."[14] We learn, we act, and then we reflect. We deepen our inner consciousness and we recommit to living that way in all ways in our life. It is not in the intellectual rigorous study halls that we discover the most profound enlightenment, but through our acts of compassion in our everyday interactions with others and in our isolated chambers of hospitals, factories, & orphanages. Jewish enlightenment can be touched in study and prayer, but it is actualized when we are actively in service of others.

Sometimes this requires us to engage in a relatively simple yet heartfelt act, even while going out of our comfort zones. I heard from a colleague that a highly respected pulpit rabbi (who prefers anonymity) would, every year on the Shabbat before Purim, exhort his congregants to not only give *mishlo'ach manot* to their actual friends, but to also give to the family down the block that you think just may be Jewish, and to the person whom you haven't spoken to for decades because you had a falling out and no longer

10. Exodus 3:1
11. Torah Shelemah on Shemot Ch. 2, source 208
12. Exodus 2:25
13. Deuteronomy 13:18
14. Ibn Ezra, commentary on Deuteronomy 5

remember what you were fighting about. Such a simple actualization can lead to even further harmony and unity.

And sometimes acting with kindness asks of us to do nothing more than to choose our words carefully and meaningfully. A dear friend of mine and his wife were going through a rough personal time. The rebbetzin of their synagogue delivered to them a tray of pastries, on which was attached a note that read, "Have as good of a Shabbat as you can right now." She realized that this couple was not in a position to have a truly joyful "good Shabbat," and so she catered a message specifically for them. My friend tells me that he remembers this small act of twenty-five years ago as if it just happened.

May our reflections on kindness inspire us to transcend our perceived limitations and actualize our unique potential to bring joy and healing to the world. May our doing so also lift us up with the happiness of a life filled with meaning and purpose. May our collective joyful dance for kindness, healing, and repair bring about an era where there is no more war, illness, pain, or suffering. May we all do our unique part, each day, to bring about such an era that we all dream of.

> Thus God will judge among the nations
> And arbitrate for the many peoples,
> And they shall beat their swords into plowshares
> And their spears into pruning hooks:
> Nation shall not take up
> Sword against nation;
> They shall never again know war.[15]

---

15. Isaiah 2:4

Bibliography

Alshich, Moshe. *Alshich on Torah.*

Alter, Yehudah Aryeh Leib. *Sfat Emet.*

Aquinas, Thomas. *Summa Theologica.*

Aristotle. *Nicomachean Ethics, Book VIII.*

Avot d'Rebbe Natan.

Avot d'Rebbe Natan, version B.

Baal Shem Tov, Yisroel. *Ba'al Shem Tov Al HaTorah.*

Babylonian Talmud.

Bamidbar Rabba.

Bartenura, Ovadia. *Bartenura on Pirkei Avot.*

Ben Bezalel, Judah Loew, *Maharal's commentary on Pirkei Avot.*

—— *Netivot Olam.*

Ben Eliezer, Tobiah, *Midrash Lekach Tov.* One instance (quoted in *Torah Sheleimah* on Shemot Ch. 5, source 78)

Ben Nachman, Moshe. *Ramban on Torah.*

Ben Yechiel, Asher. *Teshuvot HaRosh.*

Ben Yehiel Michel Wisser, Meir Leibush. *Malbim on Ruth.*

—— *Malbim on Tanakh.*

Bereishit Rabba.

Berkowitz, Dasee. *Becoming a Soulful Parent.*

Berman, Lisa F., and Lester Breslow. *Health and Ways of Living: The Alameda County Study.* New York: Oxford Univ, 1983.

Bible.

Blake, William. "Eternity."

Bornsztain of Sochatchov, Shmuel. *Shem MiShmuel.*

Braunstein, Glenn D. "Caring for Aging Parents Is Labor of Love—With a Cost." https://www.huffpost.com/entry/caregivers-aging-parents_b_3071979.

Brown, Brené. *Daring Greatly: How the Courage to Be Vulnerable Transforms the Way We Live, Love, Parent, and Lead.* New York: Gotham, 2012.

Brown, Erica. *Spiritual Boredom: Rediscovering the Wonder of Judaism.* Woodstock, VT: Jewish Lights, 2009.

Buffet, Warren. "My Philanthropic Pledge." https://www.google.com/url?sa=t&rct=j&q=&esrc=s&source=web&cd=&ved=2ahUKEwi5rfuL4qD_AhXtLUQIHWLKCgcQFnoECAsQAQ&url=https%3A%2F%2Fmoney.cnn.com%2F2010%2F06%2F15%2Fnews%2Fnewsmakers%2FWarren_Buffett_Pledge_Letter.fortune%2Findex.htm&usg=AOvVaw2Ezp_QQVcu7Orqfqu2pho3 .

Campling, Penelope. "Reforming the culture of healthcare: the case for intelligent kindness." *BJPsych Bull* 39(1) (Feb. 2015) 1–5. https://www.ncbi.nlm.nih.gov/pmc/articles/PMC4495825/

Chaim Tyrer of Tchernovitz. *Be'er Mayim Chayim.* Translated in *Eternal Questions: Reflections, Conversations*

Chaim of Volozhin. *Nefesh HaChaim.*

Cordovero, Moshe, *Tomer Devorah.*

Dan, Joseph, *The Teachings of the Hasidim.* Millburn, NJ: Behrman House, 1983,

"Data and Statistics on Children's Mental Health." https://www.cdc.gov/childrensmentalhealth/data.html.

De Vidas, Eliyahu. *Reshit Chokhmah.*

Dessler, Eliyahu Eliezer. *Michtav Me'Eliyahu* volume 5.

Deutsch, Lindsay. "13 of Maya Angelou's Best Quotes." https://www.usatoday.com/story/news/nation-now/2014/05/28/maya-angelou-quotes/9663257/.

Devarim Rabbah.

Dickinson, Emily. "'Hope' is the Thing with Feathers."

Diskin, Yehoshua Leib. *Teshuvot Maharil, Vol. I.*

Dolan, Eric W. "New psychology research finds that poor people are perceived as being less susceptible to pain." https://www.psypost.org/2021/09/new-psychology-research-finds-that-poor-people-are-perceived-as-being-less-susceptible-to-pain-61883.

Dvinsk, Meir Simha HaKohen. *Meschech Hochmah.*

Eisenstadt, Avraham Tzvi Hirsch. *Pitchei Teshuvah.*

Eliyahu of Vilna. *Aggadot of Chazal.*

Emerson, Ralph Waldo. *Essays.* London: Robson, Levey, and Franklyn, 1841.

Epstein, Yechiel Michel. *Aruch HaShulchan.*

Falk, Jacob Joshua. *Penei Yehoshua.*

Feigelson, Josh. *Eternal Questions: Reflections, Conversations, and Jewish Mindfulness Practices for the Weekly Torah Portion.*

Be'er Mayim Chayim 18:17:1. Translated in *Eternal Questions: Reflections, Conversations, and Jewish Mindfulness Practices for the Weekly Torah Portion*, Rabbi Josh Feigelson, p. 21.

Feinstein, Moshe. *Iggrot Moshe.*

——— *Orach Chayim.*

Frank, Anne. *The Diary of a Young Girl.*

Frankel, Viktor E. *Man's Search for Meaning.*

Franklin, Benjamin. *Poor Richard's Almanac.*

Freire, Paulo. *Pedagogy of the Oppressed.* New York: Herder and Herder, 1970.

Friedman, Hershey H. "*Placing a Stumbling Block Before the Blind Person: An In-Depth Analysis.*" http://www.jlaw.com/Articles/placingstumbling.html

Gallant, Batya. *Stages of Spiritual Growth.*

Gawande, Atul. "Hellhole." https://www.newyorker.com/magazine/2009/03/30/hellhole.

Gelles, David. "Mindfulness for Children." https://www.nytimes.com/guides/well/mindfulness-for-children

Gerondi, Yonah. *Rabbeinu Yonah on Pirkei Avot.*

——— *Sha'arei Teshuvah.*

Goldman, Brian. *A Question of Kindness.* Boston: Shambhala, 2014.

Greenberg, Irving. *The Jewish Way: Living the Holidays.* New York: Touchstone: 1993.

——— *Sage Advice.*

Gurevitz, David. "The Meaning of Justice in the Age of Frivolity"

HaLevi, Yehudah. *The Kuzari.*

Heifetz, Ronald, et al., "Leadership in a (Permanent) Crisis," *Harvard Business Review,* (2020) hbr.org/2009/07/leadership-in-a-permanent-crisis.

Heschel, Abraham Joshua. *The Insecurity of Freedom: Essays on Human Existence.*

——— *Man Is Not Alone.*

——— *Man's Quest for God.*

——— *Moral Grandeur and Spiritual Audacity.* New York: Farrar, Straus & Giroux, 1996.

——— *A Passion for Truth.* New York: Farrar, Straus and Giroux, 1983.

——— *The Prophets.*

——— *Who Is Man?* Stanford, CA: Stanford University Press, 1965.

Hilsenrath, Yakov Chaim. *Torah Ethics of Interpersonal Relationships.*

Hirsch, Samson Raphael. *Horeb.*

Horowitz, Yeshayahu. *Shelah HaKadosh.*

Ibn Ezra, Abraham. *Ibn Ezra on Deuteronomy.*

Ibn Pekuda, Bahya. *Hovot HaLevavot (Duties of the Heart).*

Isserles, Moses. *Shulchan Arukh,* Yoreh De'ah.

Isserlin, Yisrael. *Terumat Hadeshen.*

Jaffe, David. *Changing the World from the Inside Out.* Boulder, CO: Trumpeter, 2016.

Jerusalem Talmud.

"Jewish Funeral Cost." https://personalfinance.costhelper.com/jewish-funerals.html.

Jobs, Steve. "Stanford University Commencement."

Kagan, Israel Meir. *Ahavat Chesed.*

Kasher, Menahem. *Torah Shelemah.*

Karelitz, Avrohom Yeshaya. *Emunah U'Bitachon.*

Karo, Joseph. *Orach Chaim.*

——— *Shulchan Aruch.*

Keats, John. "Ode on a Grecian Urn."

Kohelet Rabbah.

Kook, Avraham Yitzchak HaKohen. *Iggerot HaRe'aya.*

——— *The Lights of Faith.*

——— *Midot HaRe'iya.*

——— *The Moral Letters.*

——— *Olat Re'ayah, volume 1.*

——— *Orot HaKodesh.* Another instance spelled differently. Also says: "Also see his *Midot Harayah* on Love, Section 11, p. 27"

——— *Orot HaKodesh volume 3.*

——— *Orot HaTorah.*

——— *Shemoneh Kevatzim.*

——— *A Vision of Vegetarianism and Peace.*

Kroenke, Candyce H., Kubzansky, Laura D., Schernhammer, Eva S., Holmes, Michelle D., Kawachi, Ichiro. "Social networks, social support, and survival after breast cancer diagnosis." J Clin Oncol. 1;24(7) (2006) 1105–11. https://pubmed.ncbi. nlm.nih.gov/16505430/#full-view-affiliation-1

Kronglass, Dovid. *Sichot Chochmah U'Mussar, Vo1 I.*

Kushner, Harold. *Conquering Fear.* New York: Knopf Doubleday, 2010.

——— *Who Needs God.* New York: Fireside, 2002.

Lamm, Maurice, *The Jewish Way in Death and Mourning*. Jonathan David Publishers, 2000.

Lamm, Norman, *Seventy Faces: Articles of Faith, Vol. 2*. Hoboken, NJ: Ktav, 2002

Lefin of Satanov, Menachem Mendel. *Cheshbon Ha-Nefesh*.

Levi Yitzchak of Berditchev. *Kedushat Levi*.

Levinas, Emmanuel. *Beyond the Verse: Talmudic Readings and Lectures*.

Levovitz, Yerucham. *Da'at Torah*.

Lewis, C.S. *The Four Loves*. New York: Harcourt Brace & Company, 1960.

Lichtenstein, Aharon. "Alei Etzion 16: Kofin Al Middat Sedom: Compulsory Altruism?" https://www.etzion.org.il/en/philosophy/great-thinkers/harav-aharon-lichtenstein/alei-etzion-16-kofin-al-middat-sedom-compulsory.

———— *By His Light: Character and Values in the Service of God*. Jersey City, NJ: Ktav, 2003.

Liebermann, Yehoshua. "Responsibility of the Firm to the Environment." *The Orthodox Forum: Jewish Business Ethics*. (1999)

Lincoln, Abraham. "Second Inaugural."

"Loneliness in America" https://newsroom.thecignagroup.com/loneliness-in-america#:~:text=A%20Post%2DPandemic%20Look%20at,58%25)%20are%20considered%20lonely.

Luzzatto, Moshe Chaim. *Mesilat Yesharim*.

Maimonides, Moses. *Guide for the Perplexed*.

———— *Guide for the Perplexed, Vol. III*.

———— *The Guide of the Perplexed*.

———— *Mishneh Torah*.

———— *Rambam on Mishnah*.

———— *Rambam on Pirkei Avot*.

———— *Sefer Hamitzvot*.

Maltz, Judy. "The Israeli Chief Rabbinate's Blacklist: A Guide for the Perplexed." http://www.haaretz.com/jewish/news/.premium-1.800609.

These words are an excerpt from Rabbi Matanky's eulogy for Rav Gedalia Dov Schwartz o.b.m., the esteemed *Av Beit Din* (Head of the Rabbinical Court) of both the Chicago Rabbinical Council and the Rabbinical Council of America, recorded in the online forum *Lehrhaus*.

Mekhilta d'Rabbi Yishmael.

Midrash Rabbah.

Midrash Sifra.

Midrash Sifri.

Midrash Tanchuma.

Midrash Tanhuma Yashan.

Miller, Greg. "Why Loneliness Is Hazardous to Your Health." *Science* 14, vol. 333 no. 6014 (2011) 138–40.

Mishnah.

Mittleman, Alan. *Human Nature & Jewish Thought, Judaism's Case for Why Persons Matter*.

Morinis, Alan, *Every Day, Holy Day*.

———— *With Heart in Mind*. Boston: Shambhala, 2014.

Nachman of Bratslav. *Hayei Moharan*.

Nachman of Breslov and Nosson of Breslov. *Siach Sarfei Kodesh*.

Neiman, Susan. *Moral Clarity*.

Neff, Kristen, Christopher Germer. *The Mindful Self Compassion Workbook, Self-Compassion and Anger in Relationships*. New York: Guilford, 2018.

Niebuhr, Reinhold. "Serenity Prayer."

Obama, Barack. *A Promised Land*. New York: Crown, 2020.

Onkelos Genesis.

Onkelos Leviticus.

Orchot Tzadikim.

Orlick, 1998

Owens, Lama Rod. *The Path of Liberation through Anger*. Berkeley, CA: North Atlantic, 2020.

Palmer, Parker J. *The Courage to Teach: Exploring the Inner Landscape of a Teacher's Life*. San Francisco: Jossey-Bass, 2017.

"Participating in Activities You Enjoy As You Age." https://www.nia.nih.gov/health/participating-activities-you-enjoy-you-age.

Pesikta d'Rav Kahana.

"Photo: Gravestone of the Maharal." https://www.tripadvisor.com/LocationPhotoDirectLink-g274707-d275221-i59955931-Stary_zidovsky_Hrbitov-Prague_Bohemia.html.

Pirkei Avot.

Pirkei D'Rebbe Eliezer.

Poe, Edgar Allan. *Complete Tales and Poems*.

Polsky, David. His commentary on Parshat Vayera.

—— "Reflections on the Amidah." *Worship of the Heart*, edited by Shalom Carmy, pg. Jersey City: Ktav, 2003.

Reiss, Yona. "SHALOM BAYIT: THE PARADIGM OF THE PEACEFUL JEWISH MARRIAGE."

Rosenberg, Shimon Gershon. *Faith Shattered and Restored: Judaism in the Postmodern Age*.

Ryan, M.J. *Random Acts of Kindness Then & Now*.

Saadia Gaon, *Sefer HaMizvot of Rav Saadia Gaon*.

Sacks, Jonathan. *Celebrating Life.*.

—— *The Chief Rabbi's Haggadah*.

—— *The Dignity of Difference: How to Avoid the Clash of Civilizations*.

—— *The Power of Ideas*.

—— *Morality: Restoring the Common Good in Divided Times*. 2021.

—— *To Heal a Fractured World: The Ethics of Responsibility*. New York: Schocken, 2007.

—— *Tradition in an Untraditional Age*.

Salanter, Yisrael. *Ohr Yisrael*.

—— *Tenuat HaMussar, vol.1*.

Schimmel, Sol. *The Seven Deadly Sins: Jewish, Christian, and Classical Reflections on Human Nature*. New York: Free Press, 1992.

Schulweis, Harold M., *In God's Mirror: Reflections and Essays*. Hoboken, NJ: Ktav, 2003.

Schwartz, Dov. *From Phenomenology to Existentialism: The Philosophy of Rabbi Joseph B. Soloveitchik, Volume 2* Boston: Brill, 2013.

Sefer HaChinuch.

Shemot Rabbah.

Shinohara, Ryuu. *The Magic of Manifesting.*
Shmuel Eliezer Edels. *Chiddushei Aggadot.*
Shmulevitz, Chaim. *Selections from Sichot Mussar.*
Shneur Zalman of Liadi. *Tanya.*
Silverstein, David. *Jewish Law as a Journey: Finding Meaning in Daily Jewish Practice.*
Soloveichik, Ahron. *Od Yosef Yisrael Beni Hai.*
Soloveitchik, Joseph. *The Emergence of Ethical Man.*
——— *Family Redeemed.*
——— *Halakhic Man.*
——— *Out of the Whirlwind: A Theory of Emotions.*
Sperber, Daniel. *Minhagei Yisrael.*
St. John, Robert, *Ben-Gurion: Builder of Israel.*
Sullivan, Walter. "The Einstein Papers. A Man of Many Parts." https://www.nytimes.
    com/1972/03/29/archives/the-einstein-papers-a-man-of-many-parts-the-
    einstein-papers-man-of.html.
Tabory, Binyamin. *The Weekly Mitzvah.*
Tamari, Meir. "Spiritual & Ethical Issues in the Stories of Sh'mot." https://www.ouisrael.
    org/tidbits/
Telushkin, Joseph. *A Code of Jewish Ethics, Volume 2: Love Your Neighbor as Yourself.*
    (New York: Random House, 2009.
——— *You Shall Be Holy.*
Tierney, John. "A Serving of Gratitude May Save the Day." https://www.nytimes.
    com/2011/11/22/science/a-serving-of-gratitude-brings-healthy-dividends.html.
"A Tip to Overcoming Anxiety by Rabbi Dr. Abraham J. Twerski." https://jewishmom.
    com/2013/03/10/a-tip-to-overcoming-anxiety-by-rabbi-dr-abraham-j-twerski/.
Tolle, Eckhart. *A New Earth: Awakening to Your Life's Purpose.* New York: Penguin,
    2006.
Tosafot.
Tractate Derekh Eretz Rabbah.
Tutu, Desmond. "Let South Africa Show the World How to Forgive." https://www.sol.
    com.au/kor/19_03.htm.
Tutu, Desmond, and Mpho Tutu. *The Book of Forgiving.*
Twerski, Abraham J. *Do unto Others.*
Tzu, Lao. *Tao Te Ching.*
Vayikra Rabba.
Vital, Chaim. *Shaarei Kedushah.*
Walzer, Michael. *Exodus and Revolution.*
——— *Politics and Passion: Toward a More Egalitarian Liberalism.* Yale University, 2004.
Wei, Marlynn. "More than just a game: Yoga for school-age children." https://
    www.health.harvard.edu/blog/more-than-just-a-game-yoga-for-school-age-
    children-201601299055
Wolbe, Shlomo. *Alei Shur.*
——— *Alei Shur, Vol. I.*
——— *Alei Shur, Vol. II.*
Wolfson, Ron. *Time to Mourn, A Time to Comfort: A Guide to Jewish Bereavement.*
Wolpe, David. *Making Loss Matter: Creating Meaning in Difficult Times.*

Wolpe, David. *Twelve Jewish Steps to Recovery (2nd Edition): A Personal Guide to Turning from Alcoholism and Other Addictions.* Woodstock, VT: Jewish Lights, 2015.

Wurzburger, Walter S. *Ethics of Responsibility: Pluralistic Approaches to Covenantal Ethics.* New York: Jewish Publication Society, 1994.

Yaakov Leiner of Izhbitz, *Beit Yaakov on Torah.*

Yang, Keming, and Christina Victor. "Age and Loneliness in 25 European Nations." *Ageing & Society* 31(8) (2011) 1368–1388. https://www.cambridge.org/core/journals/ageing-and-society/article/abs/age-and-loneliness-in-25-european-nations/CB2D91D8793AA3522286EAD7203FA492.

Yitzchak of Korbeil. *Sefer Mitzvot Katan.*

Yitzchaki, Shlomo. *Rashi on Talmud.*

——— *Rashi on Tanakh.*

Rashi, ad loc.

Yuval, Moshe Mordechai. *Sefer Ruach Chayim.*

Zaitchik, Chaim Ephraim. *Sparks of Mussar: A Treasury of the Words and Deeds of the Mussar Greats.*

Zohar.